IMAGINING AFTER CAPITALISM

IMAGINING AFTER CAPITALISM

Andy Hines

tp

Triarchy Press

Published in this First Edition in 2025 by:
Triarchy Press
Axminster, England

info@triarchypress.net
www.triarchypress.net

Copyright © Andy Hines 2025

The right of Andy Hines to be identified as the author of this work has been asserted by them in accordance with the Copyright, Designs and Patents Act, 1988.

No part of this publication may be reproduced, stored in a retrieval system or transmitted in any form or by any means including photocopying, electronic, mechanical, recording or otherwise, without the prior written permission of the publisher.

All rights reserved.

A catalogue record for this book is available from the British Library.

Cover design: Denise Worrell, using source image *concept-cryptographic-nft-on-a-hundred-dollar-bill-franklin-in-glasses* created by Gesrey.

Print ISBN: 978-1-917251-03-7
ePub ISBN: 978-1-917251-04-4

CONTENTS

FIGURES viii
TABLES ix
ACKNOWLEDGEMENTS xi

CHAPTER 1 - INTRODUCTION AND APPROACH 1
   1.1   Why After Capitalism? 2
      1.1.1   Theory of change 4
      1.1.2   Voice, tone and intended audience 6
   1.2   Focal issue 8
   1.3   Framework Foresight approach 11
      1.3.1   How the guiding images "fit" 18
   1.4   After Capitalism framework 18

PART I. THE RESEARCH **31**
CHAPTER 2 - SIGNALS AND DRIVERS 33
   2.1   Framing: Three horizons and the domain map...................... 33
   2.2   Scanning and researching 38
   2.3   Drivers 39
      2.3.1   Shifting values 41
      2.3.2   Technology acceleration 49
      2.3.3   Inequality 53
      2.3.4   Automation 59
      2.3.5   Stagnation 62
      2.3.6   Climate and carrying capacity 65
      2.3.7   Ineffective left 68

CHAPTER 3 - THE BASELINE 73
   3.1   Context 74
   3.2   Driver outcomes 76
   3.3   Key assumptions guiding *Neoliberal Capitalism* 78
   3.4   Other factors disintegrating the Baseline 81
      3.4.1   Tribalism 81
      3.4.2   Disaffected youth 83
      3.4.3   The dispossessed 83
      3.4.4   Neofeudalism 85

3.4.5	Emergence of myriad varieties of capitalism	85
3.4.6	Compilations	95
3.5	Baseline scenario	96

CHAPTER 4 - TRANSITIONS 99

4.1	Collapse scenarios	100
4.1.1	Driver outcomes	100
4.1.2	Overshoot	102
4.1.3	Class War	103
4.1.4	Rogue AI	103
4.2	New Equilibrium Scenarios	104
4.2.1	Driver Outcomes	105
4.2.2	New Sources of Value	107
4.2.3	Collaborative Sharing Platforms	111
4.2.4	Sustainability transition	119

PART II. THE GUIDING IMAGES 123
CHAPTER 5 - CIRCULAR COMMONS 130

5.1.1	Driver outcomes	135
5.1.2	Challenges and responses	137
5.1.3	Purposes	151
5.1.4	Principles	155
5.1.5	Tools	161
5.1.6	Personal	165
5.1.7	Leadership	166
5.1.8	Pathway	167
5.1.9	Templates	175

CHAPTER 6 - NON-WORKERS' PARADISE 193

6.1.1	Driver outcomes	198
6.1.2	Challenges and responses	199
6.1.3	Purposes	208
6.1.4	Principles	210
6.1.5	Tools	214
6.1.6	Personal	218
6.1.7	Leadership	218
6.1.8	Pathway	220
6.1.9	Templates	225

CHAPTER 7 - TECH-LED ABUNDANCE	240
7.1.1 Driver outcomes	244
7.1.2 Challenges and responses	246
7.1.3 Purposes	250
7.1.4 Principles	253
7.1.5 Tools	255
7.1.6 Personal	257
7.1.7 Leadership	257
7.1.8 Pathway	259
7.1.9 Templates	262
7.2 Comparing the images	268
CHAPTER 8 - IMPLICATIONS	271
8.1 Past: As prologue?	272
8.2 Present: Comparing drivers across the scenarios	274
8.3 Future: Utopia not impossible	277
8.4 The Global Question	278
8.5 Pathways to the guiding images	281
8.5.1 Reform delays the inevitable	282
8.5.2 What might evolution look like	283
8.5.3 Revolution	285
8.5.4 Ways to intervene in a system	287
CHAPTER 9 - CONCLUSION: TEN SHIFTS	290
9.2 In closing	302
GLOSSARY	304
REFERENCES	311

FIGURES

Fig. 1.1 The Three Horizons framework 12
Fig. 1.2 Houston Archetype Technique 16
Fig. 1.3 AC Definitions 17
Fig. 1.4 *After Capitalism* scenarios 28
Fig. 2.1 *After Capitalism* domain map 35
Fig. 2.2 Three horizons of *After Capitalism* 36
Fig. 2.3 Diigo scanning library example 38
Fig. 2.4 Four values types 41
Fig. 2.5 From apartness to integrated 47
Fig. 2.6 Three levels of AI 51
Fig. 2.7 Three classes 54
Fig. 2.8 Automation Pathways 59
Fig. 2.9 Stagnation's Vicious Circle 62
Fig. 2.9 Earth Overshoot Day 66
Fig. 3.1 Surplus populations 85
Fig. 4.1 New Equilibrium futures 105
Fig. 4.2 *Collaborative Sharing Platform* concepts 114
Fig. 0.1 The *After Capitalism* guiding images 127
Fig. 5.1 Climate and carrying capacity challenges 137
Fig. 5.2 Rise of the FIRE economy 144
Fig. 5.3 Alternatives to growth 147
Fig. 6.1 Post-work 200
Fig. 6.2 Key roles of jobs 203
Fig. 7.1 *Tech-Led Abundance* concepts 245
Fig. 8.1 Key tests for the guiding images 277
Fig. 8.2 *After Capitalism* headlines 285
Fig. 9.1 The values split 292
Fig. 9.2 The growth story 296

TABLES

Table 1.1 Framework Foresight (FF) method 11
Table 1.2 Image analysis template 14
Table 1.3 Describing the archetypes 15
Table 1.4 After Capitalism concepts 20
Table 2.1 Seven drivers 39
Table 2.2 Support for capitalism by age group 43
Table 3.1 Driver outcomes in Baseline 76
Table 3.2 Varieties of capitalism 87
Table 3.3 Factors disintegrating capitalism 95
Table 3.4 Baseline scenario summary 97
Table 4.1 Driver outcomes in Collapse 101
Table 4.2 Driver outcomes in New Equilibrium 105
Table 0.1 Eight ways that *After Capitalism* meets Polak's image criteria ... 124
Table 0.2 Image analysis template updated 129
Table 5.1 Driver outcomes in *Circular Commons* 136
Table 6.1 Driver outcomes in *Non-Workers' Paradise* 198
Table 7.1 Driver outcomes in *Tech-Led Abundance* 244
Table 7.2 Comparing the images 268
Table 8.1 Views of the future from the past 273
Table 8.2 Comparing drivers across selected scenarios 275
Table 8.3 Meadows' systems intervention for *After Capitalism* 288

ACKNOWLEDGEMENTS

There are plenty of thanks required when a project stretches out almost a decade. Let's begin at the beginning.

Professor Terrence O'Donnell (deceased) at Salem State College for getting me interested in the future and leading to Frederick Polak's (1973) *The Image of the Future.*

Then grad student Christopher Manfredi who sparked the After Capitalism conversation in Spring 2012 that culminated in it as the topic of our Spring Gathering that year.

Former students Tim Morgan, Collin Sledge, Daniel Riveong, and Maria Romero for their help in scanning. Tim also routinely brought great comments to blog posts on the topic.

Wendy Schultz for her excellent work on the topic of Images of the Future, including developing and teaching a summer elective on the topic for the University of Houston Foresight program.

Alum Gary Hamel for review and editing the many blog posts.

Alum Mina McBride for wise counsel on all aspects of the book project.

Vincent Hines for bringing a valuable perspective and the energy and enthusiasm in an amazing summer push to getting the book over the finish line.

The amazing alum Denise Worrell for designing the better-looking graphics in the book.

Last but not least, the many students who've taken the Houston Foresight journey, and have either patiently endured and/or participated in the many class discussions on the After Capitalism topic. It's in your hands now to help make it happen!

Chapter 1 – INTRODUCTION AND APPROACH

We need a new lodestar, a new map of the world. In our terms, a guiding image of the future. — Rutger Bregman

You may well be among the many believing that it is easier to imagine the end of the world than the end of capitalism (ironically, those two concepts may indeed be related). I once thought so too. I invite you to accompany me on a journey to possibilities beyond today's dominant capitalist system. At the finish you may come to believe that a better approach is indeed possible. Perhaps then you will join me in the mission of spreading this news of hope for a better tomorrow. In short:

- The good news is that there are indeed viable guiding images for life after capitalism.
- The bad news is that it is going to be a long, tough ride for at least the next several years, if not longer, and a "good" future is by no means guaranteed.
- The ugly news is that we have no choice but to develop alternatives, because capitalism is in trouble.

This work is US-focused, given the country's position as an exemplar of neoliberal capitalism, and the primary focus on one country enables the telling of a more cohesive story. It is noteworthy that despite this exemplar status, the Heritage Foundation ranks it as only the 25th "most capitalist" country, using degrees of economic freedom as the key criteria. Singapore, Switzerland, and Ireland top the list (Heritage Foundation, 2023). International examples are brought in throughout the text to reinforce the point that *After Capitalism* is indeed a global question, not just a US one. For example, the seven key drivers of change in Section 2.3 are happening across the globe. While they are primarily explained from the US perspective, global examples are included to demonstrate their reach.

This chapter begins with a note on the style and then describes the focal issue. Next, the method is explained, and the chapter concludes with a discussion of the *After Capitalism* framework.

1.1 Why *After Capitalism*?

The topic sprang from the minds of my students in the University of Houston Foresight program (Hines 2014) back in 2012. The leading advocate was Graduate Assistant Christopher Manfredi, who brought tremendous energy and enthusiasm to it, which sparked many rich classroom discussions. We devoted our annual Spring Gathering that year to "After Capitalism." We planned to spend the morning laying out the problem and the afternoon generating solutions. The day was quite fruitful, but we found that far more time was spent on the problems than the solutions.

My initial research found that there indeed were lots of ideas but few comprehensive works on the future of the next economy. There were many calls to reform the existing system but few advocating entirely new approaches. The new ideas were fragmented and preliminary — a case of what futurists call weak signals.

Further scanning led me to seriously question the future of capitalism. I started with several books touching on the future after capitalism, and five years later, in 2017, I set up a scanning library to identify and capture signals of change more rigorously. The scanning revealed many problems with capitalism that brought to mind Jim Collins's (2001) concept that one must "confront the brutal facts" — in this case the possibility of capitalism's demise — so that we "don't ever lose faith in our search for something better." I was not ideologically opposed to capitalism, but I started to believe that perhaps its time was up. Over its course, capitalism had stimulated economic growth, produced wealth, and raised overall standards of living (not for all, of course]. But now we are dealing with all the consequences of that growth, from inequality to climate change to social and political instability. Put simply, capitalism is not a good fit for the emerging future. Jim Dator (2017) puts it bluntly: "If we don't use the unfolding collapse of contemporary social and environmental systems as an opportunity for imagining and creating viable social and environmental systems in their stead, others will use the collapse to create worlds more to their liking than to ours. For us to grasp this thin thread of possibility requires a great deal of wisdom, insight, creativity and innovation, and a kind of entrepreneurship of which we all should be a part."

Once we accept this "brutal fact" of the possibility of capitalism's demise, we need alternatives. Kate Raworth (2017, 20), who developed the influential doughnut economy concept, was influenced by cognitive linguist

George Lakoff's assertion that it is absolutely essential to have a compelling alternative frame if the old one is ever to be debunked. Simply rebutting the dominant frame will, ironically, only serve to reinforce it. Pointing out the flaws of the existing system without an alternative can be counterproductive. The challenge was the relative scarcity of alternatives, which reminded me of Polak's (1973) *Image of the Future* that lamented the absence of positive guiding images of the future in contemporary society. Part 2 of this work, The Guiding Images, will explain the concept in depth. The relevant point here is that he found that the central feature of successful civilizations of the past was that they were guided by a common positive image of their future.

I revisited Polak's work and started looking for guiding images. I did find several pieces emphasizing the importance of guiding images:

What Guiding Images Do
Guiding images tie the future to the present. They provide a stimulus for change and serve as a guide for decisions and actions to achieve that change.

- Futurist Patrick Van der Duin (2009) drew on the work of cultural historian William Irwin Thompson to promote the idea that images ***emerge organically*** at an unconscious mythological level. This also connects to the myth-metaphor level of the popular Causal Layered Analysis tool developed by futurist Sohail Inayatullah that outlines the importance of the underlying stories we live by (1998).
- Medina Vasquez (2003) notes that the ***future and the present are tied*** by images, which have an anticipatory and strategic function.
- Masini and Van Steenbergen (1983) suggest images of the future are the ***stimulus to change*** the present.
- Van der Duin (2009) cautions, however, that there must be a ***conscious will*** for an image to actualize.
- Masini (1993) emphasizes the capacity of images to build the future or serve as **guides for planning decisions** (Shipley, 2002).

But there was very little in the way of actual guiding images! This work steps into this void and identifies three potential guiding images of the future after capitalism. What I eventually found regarding guiding images is organized and synthesized as "AC Concepts." Table 1.4 outlines the 52 AC

Concepts included in this book. While much more will be said about the three guiding images, it is useful to introduce them at a high-level up front:

- **Circular Commons.** Expands the concept of sustainability to embrace circular principles as part of a social, political, and economic commons.
- **Non-Workers' Paradise.** A play on the socialist idea of the workers' paradise, but in the *After Capitalism* world we are not working in paid jobs as a means of sustenance.
- **Tech-Led Abundance.** Technological progress drives and leads to abundant wealth that fixes the core distribution problem of capitalism.

1.1.1 Theory of change

This is a book about change. So, a word is in order about the underpinning theory of change here (Peck 2009). In the Houston Foresight program that I lead there is an entire class on social change that explores a dozen theories of social change (Bishop and Hines 2012), which is also referred to as macro-history (Inayatullah and Galtung 1997). At the root of the theories is how one views the direction of change: random, cyclical, or developmental:

- **Random**: there is no overall direction to change.
- **Cyclical**: change in a recurring pattern — what goes around comes around.
- **Developmental**: change in a consistent direction over time; one variation, Progress, assumes that the direction is a positive one; Development is neutral on whether the change is good or bad.

This work assumes "Developmental" with its consistent direction of change over time, with caveats.

First, it explicitly avoids the notion that progress is inevitable. While the guiding images are offered as positive and could be viewed as Progress, the possibility of a Collapse future is also noted and briefly described. In fact there is a proliferation of collapse or even "end of times" works: from Pogany's (2015) "Dark" period to the Stockholm Resilience Center's Hothouse Earth future (Steffen et al, 2018) to Ziehan's (2022) *The End of the World is Just Beginning*, and one might put Long-Termism in here as well (MacAskill, 2022), and so on. These dystopic images fit with our Collapse archetype described in Chapter 4.

Second, however, it allows for some cyclicality — there can be steps backward, sideways, and forward, and iterations within the overall consistent direction. Current research on the Houston Archetype Technique (see Table 1.1), which is part of the method for this work, suggests the possibility of a New Equilibrium Loop, that is, change follows a pattern of several challenge-and-response loops, within a larger pattern of a developmental direction. Similarly, the Three Horizons framework (see Table 1.1), which is central to this work, has a cyclical aspect in that the three horizons are a cycle that repeats over time — the Horizon 3 Transformation future eventually becomes the Horizon 1 Baseline or current system. The Developmental interpretation of the Three Horizons cyclicality is that this new Horizon 1 Baseline reflects development — it is not going backward to a previous state but represents a new state with greater complexity and choice. The overall orientation is still development — toward greater complexity with more options and choices — albeit with cyclical characteristics.

The third caveat recognizes that the developmental model may be guilty of over-simplification. The random concepts fit here. Futurist Zia Sardar's (2010) post-normal times questions any model hinting at linearity — as developmental models do to some extent. He emphasizes interconnections amongst complexity, chaos, and contradictions. His view suggests developmental models would fit in a normal context that no longer exists. But post-normal and related ideas are also assumptions that have yet to be proven. Development theory would certainly agree that today's context could be termed post-normal. It would also agree that complexity, chaos, and contradictions are significant contextual factors, but nonetheless takes the view that a development pattern can be discerned and that it provides a useful framework for exploring the long-term future.

This work re-asserts the utility of big-picture, long-term thinking supported by developmental theory, which has fallen out of favor. The disfavor can be traced back to Lyotard's (1979; 1984) influential work on the postmodern turn, which favors local, contextual, and situation-specific explanations over broad, global, and more generalized ones such as development theory. This postmodern turn, which is particularly prevalent in academia, questions the very idea of grand or meta-narratives. It rejects the whole notion of guiding images of the future, with the criticism that they are hegemonizing or colonizing because they do not specifically address local differences. This work acknowledges the importance of the local, contextual, and situation-specific — indeed the resulting images focus attention on this context — but does not agree that this means we cannot also usefully identify a larger concept of global, big-picture narratives/guiding images. It sees the local and global as complementary.

It is not required that you adopt a development theory of social change, but that you can at least see it as a possibility. That is one of the greatest assets of a futurist — the ability to embrace and understand an alternative view or alternative future, even when you may not believe it. Futurists embrace the idea that our view of what is happening or should be happening may be wrong, and therefore it is important to search for and understand alternatives. So, you don't need to believe in development theory, but see it as a plausible explanation for how the future unfolds.

1.1.2 Voice, tone and intended audience

Most buyers of this book will be supporters of the idea of *After Capitalism*. Nonetheless it's written in a way that invites skeptics to join the inquiry. The arguments rely on data and logic and are intended to make a reasonable case to anyone — not just supporters. I do ask supporters to pass it on to the skeptics they know and perhaps we can expand the range of people thinking about *After Capitalism*.

While it is US-centric, given the US position at the center of neoliberal capitalisms, it is hoped that sufficient examples are provided for the non-US reader to be persuaded that it is indeed a global phenomenon. Interestingly, half the authors of the 52 AC Concepts are based outside the USA.

The hope is that these images will have a wide enough popular appeal to function as North Star guides. Most readers will likely prefer one of the three guiding images ultimately developed; some might prefer a mix. For skeptics, maybe you can find one that is at least palatable. I would be satisfied if you at least could come to terms with the potential end of capitalism and accept that this would not be the end of the world.

This book will spend time chronicling the demise of capitalism to persuade readers of the need for new guiding images. There is a strong foundational belief that capitalism is inevitable. The case against it needs to be strong. Thus, there are lots of citations first because it is primarily a work of synthesis and second to demonstrate that "I am not making this up" [referring to an old favorite humorist, Dave Barry]. Some of the ideas may seem far-fetched. But they are grounded in solid research from multiple sources.

In sum, there are likely three kinds of readers and appeals:

- <u>Supporters</u>: already in the alternatives camp and looking for ammunition.

- <u>Skeptics</u>: have some doubts and gathering information.

- <u>Opponents</u>: most likely won't read the book; if they do, it is to refute the arguments.

So, you're probably a supporter or maybe a skeptic. I am not going to bother trying to persuade the opponents. Neither should you. Rather than waste time there, let's focus on strengthening the case for supporters and bringing more skeptics into our camp.

Given this strategy of bringing more supporters into the fold, let's not demonize capitalism, which would likely turn off those who might be on the fence or at least willing to listen. We can take the position introduced in the previous section that capitalism was arguably an effective system for economic development that fit the context of the industrial revolution era by promoting economic growth. It did its job, so-to-speak, but it simply doesn't fit well with today's emerging context. We can acknowledge that our more radical colleagues might favor a more confrontational approach due to the seriousness of the situation. It's a good thing to have a variety of approaches. Nonetheless the approach here is "you can catch more flies with honey than with vinegar."

The guiding images of the *After Capitalism* future can be used in your work and shared with your colleagues and clients. So this book is written in a way that you in turn would feel comfortable handing it to your colleagues, clients, and friends. It is hoped that this work will also appeal to those interested in the future who do not have a background in foresight, as well as those curious about how a futurist sees this future. Other reasons for reading this work include:

- You might simply be searching for ideas about how to make a better future.
- You might be among the growing ranks of those disenchanted with capitalism and looking for something else.
- You might entertain some ideas about sustainability; the commons; a post-work future; a more inclusive, equitable, and co-created future; an abundance future led by spectacular advances in technology… and be curious to see how they might come together in a systematic way to create a better future.

The intent is to share just enough about the methodology to make a strong case for the guiding images by showing that they are derived from a rigorous futurist approach. Another means of bolstering the credibility of the resulting images is by providing literally hundreds of citations — these ideas are not merely wishful thinking! It will not include the light breezy anecdotal stories typical of business bestsellers, but sprinkle in a few geeky methodological points, i.e., the difference between images, visions, and utopias. I want readers to understand the rationale of these guiding images and come away with hope for a better future, persuaded of the possibilities for a new system beyond capitalism that isn't simply a recycling of the old socialist or communist programs. I hope the guiding images are compelling enough to spark interest and ultimately galvanize action.

This is a book about what, not how. What could the future be like? It is my hope that crafting plausible positive guiding images will spur interest in how to get there. The how-to is a separate book that really is not worth writing unless there is already an established destination worthy for us to consider. If you are deciding where to go on vacation, it doesn't make sense to plan the itinerary until you know where you are going. A trip to Miami will have a much different itinerary than one to Paris, Dubai, or the Taj Mahal. So, let's decide where we want to go first!

Let's make a deal right here that the spirit of this journey is one of exploring alternatives — rather than producing the right answer. Admittedly, we are taking a position that capitalism is not the right answer. But we want to persuade those still tied to it and suggest why it's time to change, in the spirit of "come with us" rather than "we're right and you're wrong."

These guiding images are offered up as options or choices. I invite others to create additional images. My purpose is to contribute to the possibility space rather than dictate the menu that one must choose from.

1.2 Focal issue

Framework Foresight begins an exploration of the future by identifying a key framing issue or question to guide the project (Hines et al., 2017).

> What are potentially compelling guiding images of the next system after capitalism?

The use of the term capitalism covers more than just the economy. Capitalism is broadly defined here as encompassing the supporting STEEP+ context: social/ cultural, technological, economic, environmental, and political/ideological — and sub-systems. Several of our AC Concept authors make this point:

- Mason (2015) observes that capitalism entails the whole system needed to make society function with an emphasis on markets and private ownership.
- Harari (2017a) notes that the mantra of economic growth underlying capitalism has moved into the realm of making ethical judgments with almost religious conviction.
- Srinivasan (2017) suggests it's useful to think of capitalism as an operating system.

> **STEEP**
>
> The acronym STEEP (social, technological, economic, environmental, and political) is commonly used by futurists as a set of categories to account for the broad global context external to the specific domain being explored. The + is used to indicate additional categories beyond the five principal ones. In the Framework Foresight method used here, STEEP categories account for the broad context and a domain map of categories is created to explore the domain – in this case, *After Capitalism*.

This book opened with people's belief in the inevitability of capitalism. How to change that is a central challenge that needs to be addressed in looking for alternatives. It is not going to be easy! We will talk a fair bit about the importance of values — as they are relevant in this context. A central feature of the "capitalism is inevitable" argument is that it taps into the competitive instinct and relies on the "humans are wired to compete" (Diamandis, 2012) or "survival of the fittest" assumptions.

Not everyone believes this of course, but it is a central argument supporting capitalism, since it is the system that may appear to offer the best fit with human nature. Other books and authors reviewed for this work, such as Bollier (2014), discuss the potential for cooperation, and raise questions about the inevitability of selfish humans maximizing their prospects at the expense of others. Eisler and Fry (2019) make a strong case that debunks the popular idea that people are hard-wired for domination, selfishness, or greed. They point out historical precedents for partnership approaches that emphasize empathy, equity, and caring. They argue that the dominator approach has simply become entrenched and reinforced in familial, educational, religious, political, and economic structures. In short, it can be "unentrenched" should we make that choice.

My challenge to the belief that we are "wired to compete" is that it assumes a static view of human values. Supporters of capitalism and competition are describing the modern values paradigm and assuming that this is the end of the story. Modern values, described in more detail in Section 2.3.1, emphasize competition, achievement, and victory — a perfect fit for capitalism. A pernicious aspect of modern values focused on individual achievement is that capitalism exploits this in a hyper-personalized marketing approach that dramatically favors the individual over the group. However, values are shifting away from modern, and the fit will become less perfect. The developmental view of social change suggests that this high-competition phase of modern values is just that — a stage. It is not inevitable, hard-wired, or human nature. Indeed, the transition to postmodern values brings forth a different idea that emphasizes the common good over the individual one.

> Valuing individual success over the common good is not human nature, but a stage of development.

It should be noted that there are far more concepts that seek to fix capitalism than ones that seek to replace it. We will keep the focus on what's to come after capitalism — the reform concepts will only be covered to the extent that they aid understanding of the transition to *After Capitalism*. It's not an on-off switch from the old to the new, but more like a morphing over time. Thus, some coverage of the potential transition is helpful.

Ultimately, whether one of these guiding images or a combination of them is pursued is a choice. Futurist Richard Lum (2014, 1) observed that:

> *A review of current global trends such as population growth, continuing industrialization, rising energy demand, massive urbanization, and long-term climate change shows that humanity is entering uncharted territory with respect to the material and organizational challenges it will face in the coming decades. Yet, despite these considerable challenges, a review of humanity's history and an exploration of the presently dim outlines of the future both strongly suggest that humanity can and is developing the insights and tools to dramatically raise the material security and affluence for all if it chooses to do so. Thus, the future is very much a matter of vision and of choice.*

It won't be easy. Futurist Riel Miller (2006) suggested that strategic choice as part of a transformation will confront opposition and ignorance. One might add fear of the future. A personal observation from working with many different individuals and organizations over the last thirty years is that the last five or so years have been characterized by a relatively high degree of fear, uncertainty, and pessimism regarding the future. Lepore (2017) talks about the mostly dystopic view of the future, one of submission, helplessness and hopelessness; of an untrusting, lonely, and sullen twenty-first century. Opposition, ignorance, fear, and pessimism are hardly ideal conditions for transformative change!

1.3   Framework Foresight approach

The book is structured using the University of Houston's Framework Foresight method (Hines & Bishop, 2013; Hines, 2020).

Table 1.1 Framework Foresight (FF) method

ACTIVITY	DESCRIPTION	DELIVERABLE
Framing	Scoping the project, defining the focal question, and mapping the domain	Domain description & domain map
Scanning & Researching	Finding, collecting, and analyzing signals of change	Scanning library
	Review relevant books/works using a common image analysis template	Image analysis templates
	Information synthesized into a set of key drivers	Drivers
Futuring	Houston Archetype Technique identifies a baseline and alternative futures using archetypes (Baseline, Collapse, New Equilibrium, and Transformation)	Archetype futures aligned on Three Horizons framework: in this case the scenarios are structured as "guiding images" (see Table 1.2)
Visioning (Implications Analysis)	Identifying important and provocative implications of scenarios	Light implications analysis as the "how to" is beyond scope of this work
Designing & Adapting (Conclusion)	Identifying options for action and implementing a strategic approach and ongoing monitoring	Concludes with top ten shifts to summarize key insights

Imagining After Capitalism | 11

Table 1.1 notes that an important modification was a light treatment of the implications step. Since the key purpose is to identify the guiding images themselves, the implications (visioning), plans (designing), and actions (adapting) are lightly discussed. The emphasis is on the first three steps that create the guiding images. Practically speaking, if the guiding images prove useful, then detailed follow-on work on the three "how to" steps will be worth the effort.

First things first. Table 1.1 lists Framework Foresight's six steps, briefly describes them, and highlights key deliverables for this exploration.

Framing. The method begins by identifying the domain or topic to be explored: in this case, the future after capitalism. The framing of capitalism as more than just economic was described above in the "Focal Issue" section. Next is timeframe, which was organized using the Three Horizons framework (Curry and Hodgson, 2008; Sharpe, 2013).

- <u>Horizon One (H1)</u> is typically the baseline future of continuity, which is most often set as the next 3-5 years, but can last longer.
- <u>Horizon Two (H2)</u> is the transition zone of disruptions to the Baseline. It is typically set ten years out, but the H2 transition can be shorter or more often longer.
- <u>Horizon Three (H3)</u> is anything beyond H2; it is the realm of the next new system.

Figure 1.1 The Three Horizons framework

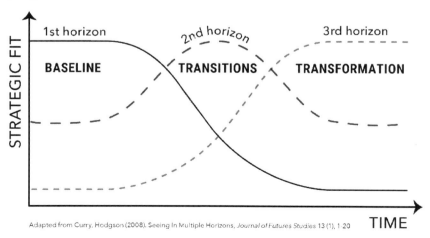

Adapted from Curry, Hodgson (2008). Seeing In Multiple Horizons, *Journal of Futures Studies* 13 (1), 1-20

It is important to note that all three horizons exist to a degree in the present: H1 is most prominent, then H2, and H3 is the weakest. Over time, the relative strengths shift, with H1 weakening as H2 and H3 gain strength.

The timeframe was set as 2040-2050. While most of my project experience helps clients understand the transitions ahead in H2, a project timeline is occasionally set to focus on describing the new system of H3. For instance, our Houston Foresight Program did a project on the *Future of Work* to 2050 for NASA's Langley Research Center (Hines 2017b). This project looked out to 2050 because the client wanted to be sure to stretch the organization to think well beyond the Baseline. That work, other client work over the years, and the research for this book persuaded me to set the H3 transformation at 20-30 years from now (2040-2050).

A visual domain map organizes the categories and sub-categories to guide the exploration of the domain (see Figure 2.1 in the next chapter).

Scanning and researching. Scanning is the search for signals of change. The search is guided by the domain map. The categories and sub-categories provide a keyword system that helps to organize the search for individual scan hits — a blog post, online article, journal, or video. The scan hits are collected in a cloud-based library. The Houston Foresight program has been using Diigo for this over the last several years and this project did as well.

Another significant input was the review of dozens of works — mostly books and some reports — touching on aspects of *After Capitalism*. The 52 works selected for review are referred to as "AC Concepts" with AC short for *After Capitalism*. Of these, 28 were analyzed using the image analysis template below.

This template was crafted specifically for this book. It was significantly influenced by the ideas and materials from a summer class offered by Houston Foresight in 2016 called "Images of the Future" taught by Dr. Wendy Schultz. Schultz (2016) did a tremendous job in developing this class and presented several analytic frameworks for understanding and evaluating images. The template is shown in Table 1.2 and is described in detail in Part 2 where the H3 guiding images are outlined.

The research is synthesized into a set of drivers, which are defined as thematic clusters of related scan hits and research inputs that are key influencers of change in the domain. Drivers are the bridge between the scanning and research and the scenarios/images. A dozen or so drivers are crafted in a typical foresight project. For this project we kept it simple with seven. The drivers are subsequently used as the key building blocks of the scenarios.

Table 1.2 Image analysis template

CATEGORY	DESCRIPTION
Author	Who proposed it and why (purpose)
Time horizon	Stated, implied, or unclear
Scope	Global/regional/national or affluent/emerging/poor
Key drivers	<u>Bold relevant ones</u>: Shifting values, Technology acceleration, Inequality, Automation, Stagnation, Climate and carrying capacity, Ineffective Left
Key ideas	The most important ideas put forth by the concept
Ideal or guiding values	Something akin to an organizing principle/motivation, i.e., create a more just or fair society
Emotional, aesthetic, and spiritual aspects	Is it appealing or compelling?
Personal	How are individuals affected by this future? Who's bearing the most costs, who's accruing the benefits?
Pathway or plan	Rough sense of steps for achieving

Futuring. Several years ago, the Houston Foresight Program adopted a modified version of Dator's (2009) four futures archetype approach (Hines, 2020) that we now refer to as the Houston Archetype Technique (the HAT). The principal tweak to his approach was to genericize his archetype scenarios of the future of the world by extracting their underlying patterns of change. Archetype is a fancy word for "typical pattern of change." This way, we can explore any domain by applying the archetypes.

It starts with the Baseline, which captures how the domain currently operates and extrapolates it into the future without any major surprises. So, how does the future look if what is happening today continues without any shifts? Many times, our students will say, "wait, we know there will be shifts!" Indeed, we agree, but with this technique, the shifts indicate a move to another of the archetypes. So, no shifts in the baseline. We have found it useful to start with the Baseline, as it is what most people believe the future will be like — today, only more so. Starting with the familiar future in essence gives us permission to explore alternative outcomes.

The HAT technique (Figure 1.2) takes the set of drivers and projects their outcomes in each of the four archetypes. The *After Capitalism* drivers will be described in Chapter Two. This provides a set of building blocks or plot elements upon which the scenarios/guiding images can be constructed.

| Table 1.3 Describing the archetypes

ARCHETYPE	DATOR'S ARCHETYPES	PATTERN OF CHANGE	AFTER CAPITALISM
Baseline	Continued Growth	The present trends and forces within the domain continue without any major disruptions or surprises. The domain continues along its current trajectory.	+ Neoliberal Capitalism
Collapse	Collapse	The domain "breaks" or falls into a state of dysfunction. The established way of doing things no longer works, and there is a decline in the "health" of the domain.	+ Ecosystem collapse + Bad AI + Class war
New Equilibrium		The domain is confronted with a major challenge to how it has been operating and is forced to adapt and compromise in order to "save itself" and keep the basic structure of the domain intact.	+ Sustainability Transition + Collaborative Sharing Platforms + New Sources of Value
Transformation	Discipline & Tech Transformation	Entails fundamental change to the domain. The rules of the game are "scrapped" and new ways of doing things emerge.	+ Circular Commons + Non-Workers' Paradise + Tech-Led Abundance

Imagining After Capitalism | 15

This is a simple and straightforward approach that has achieved good results from both students and clients.

| **Figure 1.2** Houston Archetype Technique

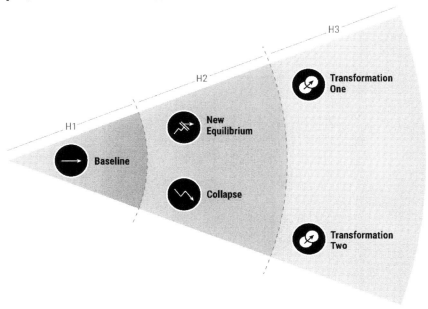

Table 1.3 explains the patterns for each archetype and includes the *After Capitalism* concepts fitting the archetypes, noting the original conception of futurist Jim Dator. Interestingly and perhaps not surprisingly, the guiding images developed in this work resembled the original archetypes proposed and developed by Dator (2009b). Dator (2014, 497) reviewed the "billions" of "images of the futures" that can be found and sorted them into four generic alternative futures: *grow, collapse, discipline* or *transformation* were empirically derived observations of images that he saw in the real world.

The HAT maps these archetype scenarios onto the Three Horizons framework. The HAT assumes that the domain begins in the Baseline in H1, moves through H2 either via Collapse or New Equilibrium, and finally reaches Transformation in H3. The logic of the development of the domain using Three Horizons is as follows:

- The H1 Baseline eventually begins to decline
- The domain moves into H2, either via Collapse or New Equilibrium
- When the H2 transition is complete, the domain then moves into H3 Transformation and is renewed (new system with new rules).

Visioning (Implications analysis) is about connecting the scenarios to the client. Put simply, what are the short-, medium-, and long-term consequences and what can be done about them, starting now? The Houston Foresight program has used Futures Wheels (Gordon and Glenn, 2009) and Joel Barker's Implications Wheel among the various tools for generating implications.

For this work, the focus on implications is exploring the plausibility of the changes in the previous chapter by looking at history, the drivers in the present, and the role of images or utopias in the future. A significant issue — how global does *After Capitalism* have to be? — is also discussed.

Designing and Adapting (Conclusions). Designing and Adapting is about taking action based on the implications. It involves designing a proactive approach to the future and identifying actions to take in the short-, medium- and long-term. This work is focused on identifying the guiding images and leaves details of how to implement for follow-up work. The last chapter draws out 10 key lessons from the from the *After Capitalism* research.

| **Figure 1.3** AC Definitions

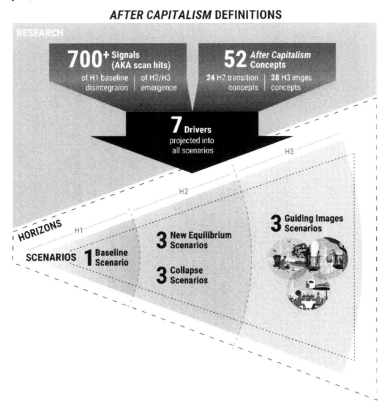

1.3.1 How the guiding images "fit"

This book differs from my typical work as a futurist in that it is focused on developing preferred scenarios (aka preferred futures), which are called "guiding images." Figure 1.3 shows how guiding images fit with the Three Horizons timing and how they connect to other scenarios and the research. There are three guiding images that suggest what an H3 transformation might look like. Each gets a separate chapter. There are also briefer treatments of six scenarios that describe potential H2 transition futures that bridge H1 to H3. H1 is described by one baseline scenario — only one is needed as it is describing the current system extrapolated forward. The three guiding images, the focus of the work, are contextualized by identifying scenarios in H1 and H2 that give a sense of the path to reaching them, and all scenarios are based on a common research foundation.

1.4 *After Capitalism* framework

The exploration started by looking for concepts about a new economy, next economy, post-, or *After Capitalism*. The initial collection of AC Concepts was quite loose. If the AC Concept spoke to a future economic approach, model, or system — even it did not really get very far into the future or it was not very comprehensive — it was captured (Hines, 2016).

I had been loosely doing scanning in addition to reading some books, and had collected a bunch of interesting ideas, When I hit three dozen AC Concepts, it was time to start thinking about organizing schemes. I started with our Framework Foresight method, and it led to two immediate useful activities:

- First was the creation of the ***domain map*** and the tagging/retagging of the scanning library. A domain map is a simple but useful tool for considering organizing schemes for a domain.
- Second was the introduction of the ***Three Horizons framework***. In order to sort AC Concepts by time horizon, it was necessary to develop a sharper sense or definition of what was the baseline or current system (H1), what a new system with new rules might look like (H3) and, and the transition concepts (H2).

These two activities were related. The domain map was organized using the Three Horizons model. The signals branch is H1; the transitions branch is H2, and the images branch is H3. This really helped! It forced me to think hard about each concept and where it fit. Table 1.4 shows each of the 52 AC concepts sorted by time horizon. Below that, Figure 1.4 visually represents how the resulting scenarios are organized along the three horizons.

No categorizing scheme is perfect. Some of the works reviewed did fit squarely into one of the three horizons and a category within them. Others were more challenging, as they had pieces fitting in several categories. A good example is Rifkin's (2014) *The Zero Marginal Cost Society: The Internet of Things, the Collaborative Commons, and the Eclipse of Capitalism.* Looking at his title, the Internet of Things fits as an H1 signal (it's already here); the collaborative piece fits in H2 transitions, and the commons fits in H3 Images. Digging into the book, a central idea was "the economy of abundance," thus it grouped with the concepts comprising the H3 *Tech-Led Abundance* image.

The works are listed by distance from the present, that is the H3 Transformational guiding images are first, followed by the H2 New Equilibrium images. Note that individual Collapse and Baseline concepts are not listed here since they are outside the key focus of positive guiding images.

AC Concepts needed to be future-focused

This work used "future-focused images" as the key sorting criteria. That is, did the work have a discernable future-focused image or could one plausibly be imagined from it? For example, some concepts seemed promising but ended up not being included:

Futurist Edie Weiner suggested that a transition past the post-industrial era has already taken place to what she calls the emotile economy, and that a new transition to the "metaspace economy" was underway (The Future Hunters, 2015). But when one digs into the metaspace economy concept, it provides a framework of where to look for changes ahead but does not project a specific direction or outcome – thus it was not included.

On Earth Day 2019, the UN New Economic Paradigm called for a swift and bold shift in their approach to sustainable economic and human development by transitioning from capitalism to 'happytalism' (UNIDO Happiness, 2019). It's an interesting and clever concept, but it lacked a description of the image of the future, so it was not included.

Table 1.4 *After Capitalism* concepts

#	CONCEPT	SOURCE*	BRIEF DESCRIPTION
**TRANSFORMATIONAL CONCEPTS**
<u>Circular Commons</u>
1	Betterness	Umair Haque (2011)	Adopt a positive paradigm that enables human potential by challenging business to do better by focusing beyond the bottom line to considering real human welfare.
2	Circular	MacArthur Foundation (2013)	Today's goods are tomorrow's resources, which forms a virtuous cycle of durables designed for re-use, and consumables made of compostable materials that can be returned to the earth.
3	Commons 1	David Bollier (2014)	Adopt a common approach in which the many manage resources that could in turn be a vehicle for political emancipation and societal transformation.
4	Commons 2	Massimo de Angelis (2017)	A highly local model in which people self-organize socially and politically within communities to pool and govern resources in common.
5	Degrowth	Giorgos Kallis et al. (2015)	Seeks to eliminate economic growth as a social objective and favors grassroots practices such as eco-communities, co-ops, local currencies, barter, commons, etc.
6	Doughnut	Kate Raworth (2017)	Suggests a social foundation of well-being that no one should fall below and an ecological ceiling of planetary pressure that should not be exceeded.

#	CONCEPT	SOURCE*	BRIEF DESCRIPTION
7	Eco	Otto Scharmer (2013)	Advocates a switch from current ego-centric approaches leading toward planetary disaster to eco-centric ones that emphasize the well-being of the whole.
8	Local	BALLE (n.d.)	*Business Alliance for Local Living Economies* promotes a global system of human-scale, interconnected local living economies.
9	Post-Growth	Tim Jackson (2015)	Emphasizes strengthening ecologically and socially sustainable practices given the physical limits of the earth.
10	Sacred/Gift	Charles Eisenstein (2011)	Suggests shrinking the formal economy and shifting money away from being a store of value to primarily a medium of exchange, including the adoption of negative interest to discourage rentier approaches.
11	Steady-State	Herman Daly (2010)	An economy characterized by relatively stable size that leaves room for nature and provides high levels of human wellbeing.
12	Sufficiency	Sam Alexander (2012)	A degrowth approach that aims for a world in which everyone's basic needs are modestly but sufficiently met, in an ecologically sustainable, highly localized, and socially equitable manner.
13	Wellbeing	Lorenzo Fioramonti (2016)	Argues for shifting away from GDP as a performance assessment tool to more holistic measures.

#	CONCEPT	SOURCE*	BRIEF DESCRIPTION
Non-Workers' Paradise			
14	Alter-Worlds	Ian Shaw and Marv Waterstone (2020)	Looks to leverage movements springing up outside or on the margins of the system such as temporary and permanent autonomous zones, workers' councils, etc., that offer potential for a post-capitalist politics.
15	Communism	Peter Frase (2017)	A vision of communism illustrated by four scenarios based on uncertainties of scarcity/abundance and inequality, with automation as a prerequisite.
16	Economic Democracy	David Schweickart (2011)	A socialist approach with market and democratic features centered on three key concepts: worker self-management, a market for enterprises, and social control of investment.
17	FALC Fully Automated Luxury Communism	Aaron Bastani (2019)	Advocates a shift towards worker-owned production, a state-financed transition to renewable energy and universal services that is aided by technological progress and placed beyond commodity exchange and profit.
18	Pluralist Commonwealth	Gar Alperovitz (2013)	Advocates an evolutionary reconstruction path based on democratization of wealth, community as a guiding theme, decentralization and substantial democratic planning to achieve economic, democracy-building and ecological goals.
19	Post-capitalism	Paul Mason (2015) Srnicek & Williams (2016)	Makes the case for *Neoliberal Capitalism* declining and the need to design a transition and create a "new hegemony" vision of an abundance future.

#	CONCEPT	SOURCE*	BRIEF DESCRIPTION
20	Precariat*	Guy Standing (2014)	Describes a "new proletariat" social class as a key element driving change to the future.
21	Solidarity*	Lol & Jimenez (Solidarity Economy Initiative) (2017)	Social justice movement among lower-income people of color seeking to go beyond socialism and communism by shifting consciousness, building political power, and creating economic alternatives.
22	Utopia (for Realists)	Rutger Bregman (2017)	Suggests that reduction of work is a political ideal; makes the case for universal basic income and the need for a massive redistribution of wealth.
		Tech-Led Abundance	
23	Abundance	Peter Diamandis (2012)	Technological progress is such that within a generation, goods and services once reserved for the wealthy few will be available to any and all who need them.
24	Homo Deus	Yuval Harari (2017)	Biology and robotics are enabling the upgrading of humans into new species via any of three paths: biological engineering, cyborg engineering, and the engineering of non-organic beings.
25	Singularity	Ray Kurzweil (2005)	Exponential technological change leads to machine intelligence surpassing humans and eventually no clear distinction between humans and machines.
26	Super-intelligence	Nick Bostrom (2014)	Explores paths to beyond-human superintelligence, the strategic choices available to it, and what can be done to shape the initial conditions.

#	CONCEPT	SOURCE*	BRIEF DESCRIPTION
27	Transhumanism	Max More (2013)	An intellectual and cultural movement seeking to improve the human condition through technology development, including eliminating aging and enhancing human intellectual, physical, and psychological capacities.
28	Zero Marginal Cost	Jeremy Rifkin (2014)	Massive economies of scale provided by digitization push the cost of reproducing information to zero, thus enabling abundance.

NEW EQUILIBRIUM TRANSITIONS
Sustainability Transition Concepts

#	CONCEPT	SOURCE*	BRIEF DESCRIPTION
29	Conscious	John Mackey (2013)	Reinvigorate capitalism by doing business guided by principles of higher purpose, stakeholder orientation, and conscious leadership and culture.
30	Green	UNDESA (2013)	Shaping and focusing policies, investments and spending towards green sectors, e.g. renewable energy, waste management, green building, sustainable agriculture, etc.
31	Regenerative	John Fullerton (2015)	Converted Wall Streeter's concept for reforming capitalism with sustainability as the core idea for economic-system design with eight core principles.
32	Satoyama	Kosuke Motani (2017)	Japanese concept of socio-ecological production landscapes promoting local circulation of resources, money, and goodwill within a community through barter and self-sufficiency.
33	Sustainable	Bruntland Commission (1987)	Meeting the needs of the present without compromising the ability of future generations to meet their own needs; 17 goals and 169 targets for people, planet, and prosperity.

#	CONCEPT	SOURCE*	BRIEF DESCRIPTION
Collaborative Sharing Platform Concepts			
34	Collaborative	Rachel Botsman & Roo Rogers (2010) Owyang (2015)	Using technology to enable networking and greater sharing of resources and information among communities, including sharing, bartering, lending, trading, renting, gifting and swapping.
35	Fourth industrial revolution	Klaus Schwab (2016)	Maps out a digital revolution characterized by a fusion of technologies that is blurring the lines between the physical, digital, and biological spheres driving exponential change.
36	Gig	Gerald Friedman (2014)	Characterized by flexible employment (e.g., contingents, temps, contractors) for workers employed on particular tasks for a defined time who then move on to the next.
37	Hybrid	Lawrence Lessig (2008)	Builds upon both the sharing and commercial economies, in which commercial leverages sharing, and sharing leverages the commercial.
38	P2P	Navi Radjou & Jaideep Prabhu (2015)	A bottom-up approach to value creation enabled by peer-to-peer networks and do-it-yourself platforms.
39	Platform	Marshall Van Alstyne et al. (2016)	Platform businesses bring together producers and consumers in high-value exchanges to grow via network effects.
40	Second	Brian Arthur (2011)	Describes the backbone technological infrastructure enabling digitization that in turn is creating a "... vast, automatic, and invisible economy."

#	CONCEPT	SOURCE*	BRIEF DESCRIPTION
41	Second Machine Age	Brynjolfsson & Macafee (2016)	Observes that the economy is at the inflection point of a shift as profound as the Industrial Revolution driven by new technologies that are exponential, digital, and combinatorial.
42	Sharing	Arun Sundararajan (2016)	Characterized by recirculation of goods, increased utilization of durable assets, exchange of services, and sharing of productive assets.
	**Sources of New Value**		
43	Algorithm/ Data	Viktor Mayer-Schonberger & Thomas Ramge (2018)	Algorithms and big data will enable markets to function much better, eclipsing the role of firms and even the roles of price and money in decision-making.
44	Artisan	Lawrence Katz (2014)	People use their own personal style and abilities to complement Information and Communications Technologies ICT technology and provide better experiences.
45	Attention	Tom Davenport & John Beck (2000)	Value is earned by getting attention – the scarcest resource in an information-rich world.
46	Experience	Joe Pine (1999)	Shift in emphasis from goods to services to experiences in which the design of even routine interactions ought to be special.

#	CONCEPT	SOURCE*	BRIEF DESCRIPTION
47	Intangible	Jonathan Haskel & Stian Westlake (2017)	An intangibles-focused economy (1) creates scale (scaling via IP, supply chains, branding, software, etc.); creates spillover (easy for a firm to copy ideas from another firm); has high sunk cost (which makes banks less likely to invest, thus requiring VC), and creates incentives for synergies (reason why cities and culture of openness are important).
48	Leisure	Graham Molitor (1999)	Hospitality, recreation, and entertainment – leisure-oriented businesses – will be accounting for the majority of the economy.
49	Network	Network Capitalism (2018)	Suggests reinventing capitalism by creating high-value networks and mutually beneficial partnerships to make money and create a better world.
50	Philanthro-capitalism	Matthew Bishop (2018)	Philanthrocapitalists see a world of big problems that they, and perhaps only they, can and must put right.
51	Purpose	Aaron Hurst (2016)	Reorienting economic activity by connecting people to their purpose, i.e., through serving needs greater than their own and building community.
52	Relationship	Jerry Michalski (n.d.)	Distinguishes between anonymous and commoditized transactions and value-added relationships as source of greater value.

*Source is [generally] how I heard first heard about the concept and/or later determined a more representative work – not always (but mostly) the originator of the concept.

The *After Capitalism* scenarios are below. Figure 1.4 shows how the Houston Archetype Technique maps the *After Capitalism* scenarios across the Three Horizons framework. The Baseline, Neoliberal Capitalism, is described in Chapter Three, the Collapse and New Equilibrium scenarios in Chapter Four, and the key focus of the work, the transformational guiding images of H3, are described in Chapters 5, 6, and 7.

Figure 1.4 *After Capitalism* futures

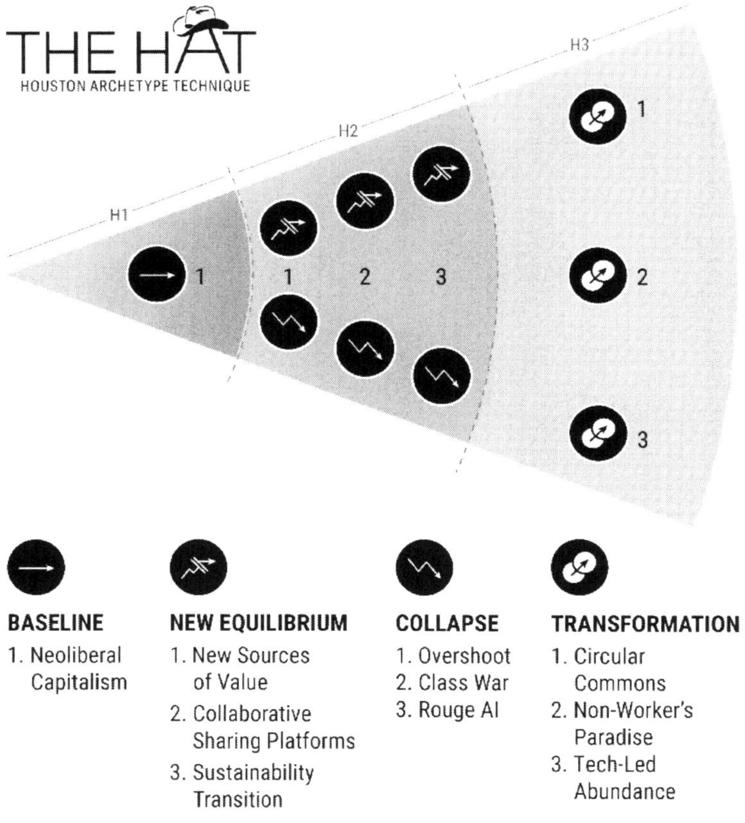

THE HAT
HOUSTON ARCHETYPE TECHNIQUE

BASELINE
1. Neoliberal Capitalism

NEW EQUILIBRIUM
1. New Sources of Value
2. Collaborative Sharing Platforms
3. Sustainability Transition

COLLAPSE
1. Overshoot
2. Class War
3. Rouge AI

TRANSFORMATION
1. Circular Commons
2. Non-Worker's Paradise
3. Tech-Led Abundance

The book is organized into nine chapters:

Chapter 1 introduces the book with its theory of change, why it was written, and the approach, and framework.

Part 1 describes the research approach and sets the stage for the H3 Transformation guiding images by exploring changes and potential scenarios along the pathway:

Chapter 2 covers the signals of change, which are synthesized as the seven key drivers of change.

Chapter 3 covers the H1 baseline scenario of Neoliberal Capitalism and its demise.

Chapter 4 covers the H2 transition by briefly describing the Collapse scenarios (Overshoot, Class War, and Rogue AI) and the New Equilibrium scenarios (New Sources of Value, Collaborative Sharing Platforms, and Sustainability Transition).

Part 2 covers the H3 Transformation guiding images:

Chapter 5 describes the environmentally driven *Circular Commons*.

Chapter 6 describes the socially and politically driven *Non-Workers' Paradise*.

Chapter 7 describes the technologically driven *Tech-Led Abundance*.

Chapter 8 covers the implications of the work.

Chapter 9 concludes the work by outlining 10 shifts that are needed.

PART I. THE RESEARCH

Chapter 2 – SIGNALS AND DRIVERS

We're in a science fiction novel, as a culture. Science fiction is the realism of our time, as I've been saying over and over again. It's the best way to describe the world that we're in.
— Kim Stanley Robinson (O'Keefe, 2020)

2.1   Framing: Three horizons and the domain map

The Framework Foresight method begins by scoping the project, which includes setting the timeframe and developing a domain map. The domain map, which will be explained further below, is a visual representation of the boundaries and key categories and sub-categories to be explored in the scanning and research phase. It is an outline of the domain in visual format (Hines & Bishop, 2013). The timeframe is organized around the Three Horizons framework introduced in Section 1.3. It is worth mentioning here the enormous contribution of Three Horizons, as it makes numerous appearances in this work. It proved to be a perfect framework for organizing the pathway and sense of the timing of the journey to the guiding images. My initial exposure to the framework was from Curry and Hodgson's (2000) "Seeing in Multiple Horizons" piece, and my understanding of it was further solidified by their colleague Bill Sharpe's (2013) *Three Horizons: The Patterning of Hope*. The framework has been instrumental in my practice, and we make great use of it in our teaching at the University of Houston Foresight program.

An interesting development for this project was organizing the domain map using the three horizons as key categories. The three horizons as defined for *After Capitalism* are:

- H1: The current Neoliberal Capitalist system, which is gradually losing "fit" over time. The signals of change here focused on the decline of this existing system. Just the basics of the baseline story were outlined, since the current Neoliberal Capitalist system is well understood.
- H2: The intermediate transition space bridges the old (H1) and the new (H3). It is typically unstable and characterized by competition between alternative paths to the future. Various paths or transition AC Concepts were identified using the rule of thumb that they would have one foot in H1 and one in H3 — a mix of old and new. Uber is a

good example. It has elements of a newer sharing economy, but probing a little deeper, it can be seen as just another exploitative approach in which the capitalists — owners and shareholders — get wealthy at the expense of the workers/drivers.

- <u>H3:</u> The transformation space that emerges and displaces the old H1 system; ideas or arguments about H3 are typically marginalized in the present. The H3 AC Concepts are of greatest interest to us. They sort into three categories:
    - The environmentally driven ones are synthesized as *Circular Commons*.
    - The politically driven ones are synthesized as *Non-Workers' Paradise*.
    - The technologically driven ones are synthesized as *Tech-Led Abundance*.

It quickly became apparent that works talking about the new or next economy were very often H2 transition AC Concepts that were variations on capitalism. It was harder to find AC Concepts that truly stretched into H3 and talked about a new way of doing things.

There is no strict timeframe for each horizon. It depends on the topic. Some topics change quickly (mobile communications) and some slowly (forestry). As a convention, one assumes the domain is in H1, but it is fair to question "where" in H1. Is it at the beginning, or is it on the cusp of an H2 transition? For our purposes here, it is assumed that the current capitalist system has perhaps another decade of preeminence. But it could be that the decline is faster or the current system lasts longer. Futurists continually monitor the environment and look for signs that the timing is either happening faster or slower.

The H2 transition AC Concepts give us a picture of what that shift might look like. They are already appearing to some extent today, and some will become more prevalent over time. If we allow a decade or two for the H2 transition, on top of the 10 years for the decline of H1, this suggests an H3 system is 20 or 30 years away. It is important to keep in mind that these are rough ballpark estimates. We have learned that trying to precisely predict the timing of the future is nearly impossible in the uncertain, complex, and volatile context in which we are living; thus we monitor.

The domain map shown in Figure 2.1 was created using the free cloud-based tool Coggle which the Houston Foresight program has used successfully for several years. For scanning, the domain map provides a visual guide to categories to consider when searching for signals of change. The categories are also used as tags to organize the scan hits. There are currently over 700 scan hits in the *After Capitalism* scanning library in Diigo.

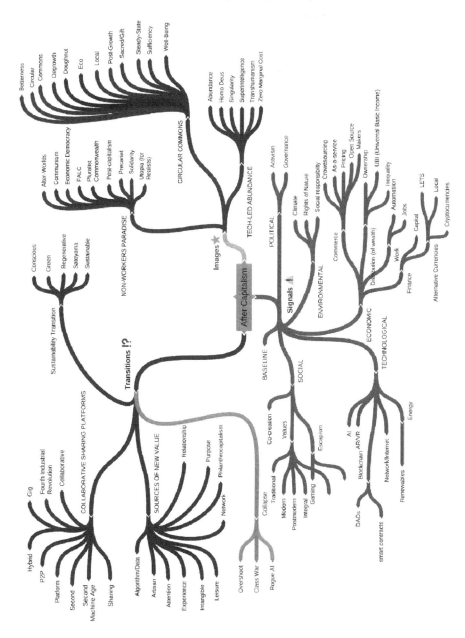

Figure 2.1 *After Capitalism* domain map

Imagining After Capitalism | 35

This map has gone through multiple iterations. Shown here is the cleaned-up version resulting from what was learned during scanning and research.

- The H1 branch, *Signals*, organized the search for general signals of change using the classic STEEP categories (social, technological, economic, environmental, and political).

- The H2 branch, *Transitions*, organized the search for AC Concepts relating to the H2 transition scenarios. It had three major branches: one for AC Concepts that identify sources of new value within the current system, and two that have elements of old and new: *Collaborative Sharing Platforms* and *Sustainability Transition*. A fourth branch covered the potential pathway of Collapse.

- The H3 branch, *Images*, organized the search for guiding images of the next system.

Figure 2.2 overlays the three main domain map categories on the basic Three Horizons framework. The X-axis is time. The solid-line curve shows how the signals give way to the transition concepts that eventually give way to the transformation images. The Y-axis is strategic fit, or how well the signals, concepts or images fit strategically, that is, describe what is actually happening. In the signals stage, the fit is weak as the change is still very new; as the signals coalesce into transition concepts, their strategic fit increases, and finally as the images come into being, they strategic fit is quite strong.

| **Figure 2.2** Three horizons of *After Capitalism*

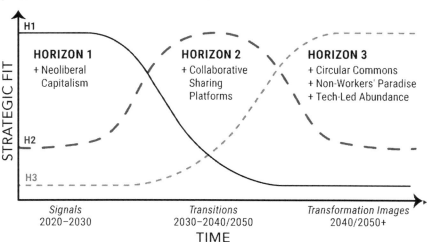

36 | Chapter 2: Signals and Drivers

- In the H1 timeframe of the next 10 years, the *Neoliberal Capitalism* scenario has the highest degree of strategic fit in the present but is in significant decay by 2030 and fades away by 2040/2050.

- In H2 timeframe of 10-20 years from now, the *Collaborative Sharing Platforms* scenario (used as an example, as there are six H2 transition scenarios), has the strongest fit in 2030; and it too fades in the 2040/2050 timeframe.

- In the H3 timeframe of 20-30 years from now, the three Transformation guiding images have a low degree of fit in the present, pick up steam in H2, and eventually one or some combination becomes the new system in the 2040/2050 timeframe.

The logic of scanning using the Three Horizons model is that new ideas, or weak signals of change, start in the present as indicators of either the H2 transition or the H3 transformation. Some weak signals will eventually gather strength and become an emerging issue (or discontinuity/disruption) in H2. The emerging issue gains strength and becomes part of the H3 transformed system. The promise of scanning is that if you do your scanning homework over time, you will not be surprised by a change. The signs of *After Capitalism* are already emerging. We don't yet know precisely which changes will happen, or precisely when. But we will know the changes to be looking for and will not be "blindsided by change" … the frequent complaint of so many leaders and organizations. We will see it coming! Let's take a few examples from my own experience: (Hines, 2020b)

- Self-driving vehicles: I visited a major automobile manufacturer in the ***early 1990s*** to participate in a project on Intelligent Vehicle Highway Systems, aka self-driving cars.

- 3D printing: I wrote a report in the ***mid-1990s*** on the Future of Desktop Manufacturing, aka 3D printing

- AI/machine learning: I lost track of how many times we wrote about this in the ***1990s, 2000s, 2010s***, and more to come.

- Global pandemics: We wrote about global pandemics in our *2025* book published in ***1996***.

The common denominator is that if organizations were paying attention, they would have seen all four of the above when they were H3 weak signals at least ***thirty years ago***! Today's "surprises" come to most organizations' attention very late in their development – futurists see them earlier.

The point here is that *After Capitalism* should not come as a surprise. The signals of the current system decline are already here. The transition pathways are becoming clearer. What is missing is the focus of this book: to suggest what H3 might look like. The signals of the H3 images are already here as well! Readers of this book will not be blindsided by the demise of capitalism. In fact, you are far more likely to find yourself impatient. The curse of the futurist is "why is this change taking so long."

2.2   Scanning and researching

In Framework Foresight, once the domain is described and mapped, scanning begins. Scanning — more formally horizon scanning — is the process of identifying, collecting, and analyzing the signals of change in a domain. A scan hit may be an article, blog post, video, or any web-based format. The main attribute of any collection library is that it enables the key information to be entered quickly. Diigo, for instance, provides a handy icon on the bookmark bar, which pulls up a form that captures the link, allows one to enter in a paragraph or two descriptions of the hit, and has an entry for adding tags.

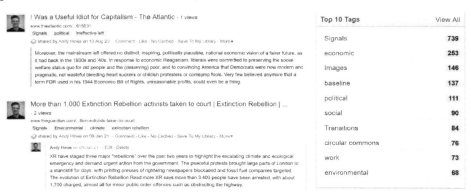

Figure 2.3 Diigo scanning library example

The domain map categories provide the first two tags and then a hit-specific keyword or two is added. This takes just a few minutes to enter and makes it very convenient to quickly pull up the categories or topics desired later on. It also includes a Top Ten tag counter, which provides a handy, at-a-glance means to see if the primary domain map categories are being adequately covered.

Where scanning looks for any signal of change, Framework Foresight also looks for specific types of futures-relevant information or inputs in four categories, which we call TIPPs (trends, issues, plans, and projections). As is typical in many, if not most, Framework Foresight projects, the method is customized to suit the project. In this case, the dozens of books reviewed were the primary type of specific information about the future. Non-book sources were also considered. Each of the works that were reviewed as primary *After Capitalism* sources is listed in Table 1.4. They were analyzed using the Image Analysis Template shown in Table 1.2.

Insights from book reviews were combined with analysis of the scan hits to craft the key drivers of change. In Framework Foresight, the drivers serve as the building blocks for the Baseline and alternative scenarios.

2.3 Drivers

| Table 2.1 Seven drivers

STEEP CATEGORY	DRIVER	DESCRIPTION
Social	Shifting values	Values are shifting from traditional (follow the rules) and modern (achieve) to postmodern (search for meaning) and integral (make a difference).
Technology	Technology acceleration	Technological capabilities continue to increase rapidly, often exponentially, in a wide range of sectors.
Economic	Inequality	Growing economic inequality is threatening the social order.
Economic (work)	Automation	Automation, driven by AI, is increasingly replacing jobs.
Economic	Stagnation	Economic growth is slowing in part due to inability to pay.
Environmental	Climate and carrying capacity	Climate change and humanity's growing ecological footprint are threatening the ecosystem.
Political	Ineffective Left	The far Left continues to be ineffective in catalyzing change.

Futurists typically use a version of STEEP categories to organize the research and drivers. The purpose is to ensure a balanced consideration of the domain, that is, avoiding either too much or too little focus on a particular category. This does not mean each category must be treated equally. Some categories will be more or less important in a particular domain.

Seven drivers emerged from the scanning and book research inputs as most important to the future of *After Capitalism*. They are listed and described in Table 2.1.

The seven drivers of change emerged as key themes from the research. A deliberate effort was made to identify a driver in each STEEP category to ensure a balanced approach to the topic, although in retrospect these drivers would probably have emerged naturally anyway. The drivers are a synthesis of the key changes in the domain that are used as the building blocks around which to build the scenarios.

The archetype technique used to create the scenarios begins by exploring potential outcomes for each driver individually. The scenarios emerge from their interactions. Two examples of how these interactions can be identified and described are:

- Dator (2014) identified an "Unholy Trinity" metaphor which suggests unfavorable drivers. He focuses on (1) the end of cheap energy, (2) challenges for economic growth, and (3) environmental decline, noting they are in fact aspects of one phenomenon — not separate entities. He later added (4) lack of governance, which expanded the concept to the "Unholy Trinity plus One" (Dator, 2009a).

- Eisenstein (2011) noted that the convergence of crises — in money, energy, education, health, water, soil, climate, politics, the environment, and more — can be thought of as a birth crisis of a new world emerging from the old. He asserts that the converging crises arise from a common root, the Separation, which describes humanity's split from nature (Eisenstein 2011).

It is important to note that while the drivers are significant factors in shaping the future, that does not exclude consideration of other factors. Nor are the seven chosen drivers the only ones. For instance, longevity was strongly considered for inclusion. There is a long-term trend toward increased life expectancy and the possibility of a technological breakthrough leading to a significant increase in life expectancy is reasonably high. If this were to occur, it would have an impact on the size of the population. Ultimately, I decided the likelihood of a significant impact of an extended human lifespan within the timeframe of *After Capitalism* — the next two or three decades — was too low. An important factor for sure, but ultimately it was decided that it was not on the same level of probability and importance as the seven that were chosen. This does not mean that it, or other factors, are not considered, but simply that the seven drivers are essential considerations.

The drivers are presented in order of their STEEP category, noted in Table 2.1 above.

2.3.1 Shifting values

Values are shifting from traditional (follow the rules) and modern (achieve) to postmodern (search for meaning) and integral (make a difference).

Figure 2.4 Four values types

Almost unnoticed, values are gradually shifting. This slow shift, however, is an important one that influences the paradigm of the system, cited by Meadows (1997) as the most powerful lever of system change. Despite this importance, values are mentioned rather cursorily, if at all, in most of the *After Capitalism* book concepts. Previous research suggests this might be an oversight. In *Consumershift* (2011), I drew heavily on two key sources of values data, the World Values Survey led by Ron Inglehart and colleagues, and Beck and Cowan's (1996) Spiral Dynamics. These works developed longitudinal data that project values shifts into the future. From this data, four value types were derived. The percentage of the population of that type

Imagining After Capitalism | 41

in the US is in parentheses (note: people can hold a mix of values from different types but typically have a primary orientation to a single type). Globally, several affluent countries, including Sweden, Finland, Norway, The Netherlands, Denmark, Iceland, New Zealand, Australia, and Canada, have lower percentages of traditional values and higher percentages of postmodern ones, with about a dozen other countries close as well, including Japan and Germany: (Hines, 2013; Inglehart, 2018)

- Traditional (20-25%): The focus is on following the rules and fulfilling one's predetermined role, with priorities such as respect for authority, religious faith, national pride, obedience, work ethic, large families with strong family ties, and a strict definition of good and evil. Traditional values are generally on the decline as economic development has stimulated a shift to modern and then postmodern and integral values.

- Modern (40%): The focus is on achievement, growth, and progress, with priorities such as high trust in science and technology as the engines of progress, faith in the state (bureaucratization), rejection of out-groups, an appreciation of hard work and money, and a determination to improve one's social and economic status. Rising levels of economic development that accompany modern values enable greater consumption and participation in consumer lifestyles. Modern values are slowing in affluent nations but rising in emerging economies.

- Postmodern (25-30%): The focus is on the search for meaning in one's life, with priorities such as self-expression, including an emphasis on individual responsibility as well as choice, imagination, tolerance, life balance and satisfaction, environmentalism, wellness, and leisure. This shift in priorities is enabled by higher degrees of economic security. This type emerged in the late 1960s/early 1970s and has been slowly growing since then to become an influential group shaping preferences in the affluent nations.

- Integral (2-5%): This emerging type is characterized by a practical and functional approach to drawing upon values that best fit the particular context. The first three value types derive from the World Values Survey, but this one is derived from Integral Theory and Spiral Dynamics. Integral values are increasing but start from a much smaller base.

The pattern, depicted in Figure 2.4, is a shift from left to right: from traditional to modern to postmodern to integral. Traditional values were once predominant, but eventually gave way to modern values, which are now the most prevalent type. But modern is giving way to postmodern, which will eventually give way to integral if the pattern holds.

Values and the young

Historically, values shifts skew slightly young. That is, younger age groups will have slightly higher percentages of newer values — in this case the emerging postmodern and integral values. The values shifts are often attributed to generational differences. While generations surely influence social change, I believe that the generational cohort effect is a secondary rather than primary influencer, with the values shifts being primary.

Studying generations has become a booming industry, though, and it has created the impression that most change is coming from the young. When a change is detected in the beliefs of younger people, it tends to induce a near panic reaction. For example, a now often cited, 2016 Harvard University survey that found that 51% of 18–29-year-olds in America no longer support capitalism. Only 42% percent said they back it, while just 19% were willing to call themselves "capitalists" (Blasi and Kruse 2018). This survey has been repeatedly referenced. A Gallup survey asking about positive views of capitalism confirmed the skew. In 2018, the percentages viewing capitalism positively were (Newport, 2018):

Table 2.2 Support for capitalism by age group

AGE GROUP	PERCENT VIEWING CAPITALISM POSITIVELY
18-29	45%
30-49	58%
50-64	60%
65+	60%

The declining support for capitalism among the youth is happening globally. For instance, in China, the "lying flat" phenomenon has emerged as a rejection of capitalism's hustle culture (Tong, 2022), while among youth in the UK, nearly 80% blame capitalism for the housing crisis and 67% want to live under a socialist economic system (Jones, 2022). The differences between age groups in Table 2.1 are not that great, and if it was just a generational difference, we'd expect to see more variation among the older groups, but it's practically the same. The values explanation says the young are more willing to take on new values and this explains the skew.

Modern values locking in capitalism

> The transition to postmodern and integral values suggests a more cooperative and communitarian worldview that is much more supportive of the common good, and is not naive, pie-in-the sky, or utopian – it's next!

Supporters of capitalism often argue that competitiveness is human nature. Diamandis (2012) celebrates competition and taps into it in quite useful ways with his XPRIZE competition, which has been sponsoring public competitions to encourage technological development to benefit humanity. But, as was argued in Section 1.2, that does not make it inevitable or all-encompassing.

Behavioral economist Sam Bowles (2016) explored the effects that market incentives have on behavior. He sought to challenge the idea that people are rational actors who pursue self-interest above all — a foundational view driving capitalism. He used Public Goods Games experiments that test whether citizens will contribute to a public good at some cost to themselves. In short, they will. He found that altruism, ethical commitments, aversion to inequity, and reciprocity, were guiding the behavior of many citizens/participants and that economic incentives were frequently counter-productive and crowded out socially useful impulses. A few years later, a study tested whether cooperative behavior rates varied across ten countries and found little difference (Frey, 2019).

Postmodern enoughness

British ecological economist Tim Jackson (2015) developed the concept of the "iron cage of consumerism" as a self-reinforcing loop between firms continuously producing novel products and the consumers who are continuously buying them. People work more so they can buy more. As they buy more, they need to work more, and on and on it goes. The postmoderns are breaking out of this cage — or at least trying. Enoughness, brought to my attention by Australian futurist Marcus Barber, is an update of the old voluntary simplicity idea. It is a reaction against materialism. More and more "consumers" — there is a growing distaste for that term — are deliberately consuming less. They find the notion of a consumer economy to be wrong-headed, seeing it as a confusion of means and ends.

Enoughness has a bit of an edge and anger to it. I often use the clip from the brilliant 1977 film "Network" in which the newscaster, live on the news, goes to the window and yells "we're mad as hell and we're not going to take it anymore." The Great Recession of 2008 forced people to confront their consumption patterns. It helped to raise awareness among people about accepting and even embracing a need for limits — "maybe growth can't continue forever?"

Going one step further, the enoughness folks are unhappy with the relationship between buyer and seller; they want to reconfigure or rebalance it. They don't want things they don't need and are asking hard questions about what they really do need. They don't want to deal with companies spinning and hard-selling them. They see a difference between transactions and relationships, and they want authentic connections and their viewpoints to be acknowledged. An example of this trend is the explosion of the "Buy Nothing" movement, which now spans 44 countries with over 5 million members. It is composed of networks of neighborhoods in which people do not buy things they need or throw out what they don't need, but instead share with each other free of cost. Bargaining and trading for goods is forbidden. Individuals help meet the needs of their neighbors solely for the reward of knowing they have helped another in their community (Sato, 2022). Participants still buy some things, such as food, but the goal is working towards making freely gifted goods and services central to their economic life. The data suggest that consuming or accumulating more goods and possessions does little to increase one's happiness. This knowledge has fueled a search for "what really matters" that is at the heart of postmodern values.

Participation and the Mean Green Meme

Integral theory (Wilber 2000) and the Spiral Dynamics (Beck and Cowan 1996) system it draws upon, refer to postmodern values as green (ironically a random color selection, not to depict environmentalism, although that is a feature of the postmoderns). Postmodern "greens," 25-30% of the US population (and similar percentages in other affluent countries, as noted in the introduction to Section 2.3.1 above), believe, as do all predecessor value types, that their values are the right ones, and if only everyone else would adopt them, everything would be fine. Integral values (yellow in the spiral system) are the first type to emerge that does not believe there is one right worldview — but they are only 2-5% of the population.

The healthy version of postmodern green values self-expression, community, participation, wellness, and sustainability among other things. But we are witnessing the unhealthy expression. Wilber (2003) explains how the Mean Greens take pluralistic relativism (everybody's view is equally true) to an extreme and suggest that no idea or belief is better than any other. Sprinkle in some narcissism and it gets twisted into "no one is going to tell me what to do," and "whatever I think is best." The relative applies to others rather than oneself. Rather than creating a community of togetherness, the world gets divided into good and bad, sensitive and insensitive, victims and victimizers. Some standard catch words of the green meme are pluralism, relativism, diversity, multiculturalism, deconstruction, anti-hierarchy, and so on. These are actually good things, but in the hands of the Mean Greens, they lead to outcomes such as the politically correct thought police. It leads to taking moral superiority stances on everything – everyone should drive an electric vehicle, not use plastic bags, wear face masks – or they are publicly shamed. While one might see these stances as good things, the dogmatism creates a divisive us-against-them atmosphere that makes discussion, compromise, and agreement difficult.

Emerging "second tier"

A particularly interesting idea from Spiral Dynamics is that of tiers. The traditional (Spiral blue), modern (Spiral orange), and postmodern (Spiral green) values are grouped as first tier. The defining characteristic of a first-tier value is that it believes that its worldview is the right one – as noted above. Integral (Spiral yellow) is the first type of a second-tier level, with the key characteristic being that its proponents do not believe there is one right set of values for every situation. The challenge or even peril of first-tier values, where people with different values dig in and refuse to compromise, is quite evident in the US and globally. A World Economic Forum piece observes that:

> "…political systems across the world are simultaneously experiencing deep disruption, with a startling escalation of polarization and tribalism … across nations as diverse as the US, France, Germany, the UK, Italy, Hungary, Austria, Sweden,

Poland, Brazil and the Philippines. In each of these countries we see similar patterns: public frustration with the status quo ... the division of groups into "us-vs-them", and political deadlock" (Dixon, 2019).

A key hope for the future is that integral values, currently the only second-tier type that is visible at 2-5% in affluent nations, will continue to grow and bring a more open and tolerant perspective.

Apartness

One of the key issues at the root of the need for guiding images is people's separation from nature. Humanity continues to put its needs front-and-center at the expense of everything else. Literally, people are "apart" from nature. The more we develop, the more apart we become – thus "apartness." The Ecosocialist AC Concept puts this apartness foremost, as its proponents believe capitalism must be dismantled in order to address the ecological crises. Redefining the relationship between human beings and the natural world is seen as essential (Knights, 2021). A step in that direction, for example, is re-examining the role of money. Nelson (2022) points out that capitalism relies on exchange value (pricing) rather than real value, which relates to actual human needs. It raises the diamond-water paradox – the contradiction that although water is more useful in terms of survival (real value), diamonds command a much higher price (exchange value) in the market. Similarly, Hermann (2021) talks about a use-value society, noting that participation in some form of democratic decision-making process would be essential for making it work.

| **Figure 2.5** From apartness to integrated

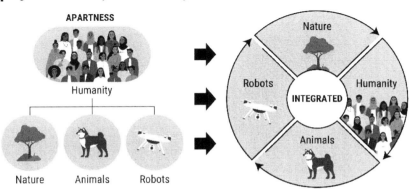

Modern values are at the heart of apartness, as they support reliance on science and technology as the fuel for economic growth, which in turn has contributed to the idea of mastering nature. They promote a view that nature's bounty should be extracted for the benefit of the economy. They no longer identify as part of nature, but rather as separate or superior.

This phenomenon has deep roots. The enclosure movement, initiated by the introduction of the English Game Laws of 1671, kicked-off the process of humanity's separation from nature. People who traditionally survived by living off the land were cut off from accessing it, unless they were one of the few who could afford to buy the land. Nature started to be seen as "natural capital" to be bought, privately owned, and managed for the benefit of the owners (Büscher and Fletcher, 2020).

Büscher and Fletcher (ibid.) of Wageningen University in The Netherlands suggest moving towards a new "convivial conservation" that operates under a degrowth framework. It promotes a more democratic form of resource management in which humans and nature work together. It recognizes autonomy of local communities to collectively pool resources to meet the needs of their own particular regions. Resources are redistributed equitably to remove the pervasive influence of large corporations through their efforts to privately own and manage nature in a top-down manner.

Implications of shifting values for After Capitalism

Neoliberal Capitalism is a perfect fit with modern values, and to a lesser extent with traditional ones. As these values decline, their replacements come with very different priorities. Globally, the shift to postmodern and integral values is underway and these are much less of a fit with capitalism. But currently these values have no alternative operating system to adhere to. So the goal of this work is to develop such alternatives in the form of guiding images. Postmodern values are driven by a search for meaning, for what's really important in life, such as sustainability, wellness, community, and participation. Integral values, estimated to be held by less than 5% of the population in affluent nations, could portend a much greater role for alternatives to capitalism. The H2 AC Concepts for reforming capitalism, such as Conscious Capitalism, are trying to accommodate these values shifts. But they do so within the capitalist frame, which may succeed for a while, but are ultimately unlikely to be able to solve capitalism's fundamental problems and make the transformative changes required for *After Capitalism*.

The challenge is the slow pace of change. Inglehart (2000) hypothesized that the post-World War II period, in which advanced industrial societies attained much higher real-income levels and welfare states emerged, would enable values shifts. He tested and found postmodern values in the 1970s in Great Britain, France, West Germany, Italy, the Netherlands, and Belgium. In the US, postmodern values emerged with the counterculture and Woodstock Generation of the 1960s and 1970s. Two generations later they are still only at around a quarter of the population — growing less than 1% a year. By our optimistic 2040 timeframe for *After Capitalism*, postmoderns and integrals should be at or over 40% of predominant values. While postmoderns are disinclined to capitalism, it may ultimately be the integrals who catalyze the transformation. Patten (2018) suggests how the integrals can develop a daily practice that is tied into a social activism to drive transformative change.

The ethos of integral values suggests an action orientation now. It is an open question whether this can scale up, or whether the transformation can happen before the myriad problems of today bring civilization to a "collapse" future (Hines, 2013).

2.3.2 Technology acceleration

Technological capabilities continue to increase rapidly, often exponentially, in a wide range of sectors.

Proponents of technology as the key driver of the future have a lot of ammunition. A cursory scan of potential technological breakthroughs can leave one's head spinning. Students of technology implementation understand, however, that translating technology breakthroughs into socially acceptable and commercially viable products or services is a tricky business. Many promising ideas never make it across the technology chasm from early adopters to the mainstream (Moore, 1991); or it takes much longer than initially thought (Hines, 2020a).

Kurzweil's (2005) Law of Accelerating Returns points out that technological change is exponential. Most people think of it as linear and thus underestimate the long-term gains in capabilities. Kurzweil sees its potential for not only solving many of the world's pressing problems, but enabling the uploading of human consciousness to computers, and all the way to reinventing the human species itself. He projects a point called the Singularity in which life is so radically altered that it is impossible to anticipate what lies beyond it. He and colleague Peter Diamandis (2009) founded the Singularity Institute to study this alternative future. Regardless of whether one believes in the Singularity outcome, accelerating technological capabilities are clearly with us. While they are perhaps the most recognizable proponents of accelerating technology, they are not alone. Brynjolfsson and McAfee (2016), in their very balanced exploration of the future impact of technology, cite the huge potential of exponential growth of most aspects of computing, the resulting extraordinarily large amounts of digitized information, and the possibilities for powerful recombinant innovation.

Now let's look at some of the prominent technological advances.

Digital transformation

When we apply the law of accelerating returns to a suite of digital transformation technologies — with AI, XR (extended reality), IoT (Internet of Things), big data, predictive analytics among the leading examples — extraordinary things happen. While the capabilities of the individual technologies are fascinating by themselves, they are increasingly being integrated. For instance, the IoT makes every device smart and connected to other devices and systems over the Internet which in turn creates immense amounts of big data that can be processed and analyzed using AI. Mayer-Schonberger and Ramge (2018) suggest that combining huge volumes of data with machine learning and algorithms will create more effective markets that identify the best possible transaction partners in the market for consumers. The application of big data gets even more interesting as predictive analytics capabilities come on board. Siegel (2013) summarizes predictive analytics as "technology that learns from experience (data) to predict future behavior of individuals in order to drive better decisions." In these cases, and perhaps as a rule, digital transformation has so far primarily been reinforcing capitalism.

But there are hints of its transformative capabilities. Many jobs and tasks are being automated by digital transformation technologies. Self-driving vehicles, for instance, are expected to replace truck drivers and other professional drivers. In other applications, digital transformation technologies complement and enhance what people can do. With extended reality tools, for instance, human capabilities are extended by assistance from augmented and virtual reality.

AI is perhaps the most influential of the suite of digital transformation technologies. Bostrom (2014) provides a handy guide for categorizing AI in three levels, shown in Figure 2.6.

There is wide disagreement among experts about if or when AI will surpass human intelligence. There does seem to be some expert consensus that it will take at least a few decades, but estimates range all the way out to 100 years. There is some disagreement on whether this will be for good, with a small group of luddites and digital utopians flanking a mainstream view of generally beneficial (Tegmark, 2018).

Emerging wave: bio/nano/robo & augmentation

ICT (Information and communication technologies) and bio/nano/robo can repair and eventually enhance human performance — for those who can afford it. While IT is at the center of Kurzweil's Singularity, he points out that it is intertwined with bio, nano, and robo technologies and leading to a future in which the distinction between humans and technology essentially disappears. Harari's (2017a) *Homo Deus* also projects the emergence of new species from these technologies.

| **Figure 2.6** Three levels of AI

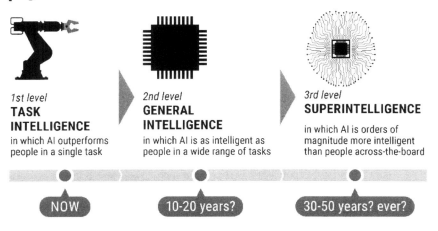

Even if we don't go as far as to become a new species, an increasing role for human augmentation seems very likely. It could take a variety of paths to dramatically increase human capabilities using biological and physical means such as advanced pharmaceuticals, CRISPR for genetic manipulation, smart prosthetics, implants, and wearables.

Other techs: Additive manufacturing, blockchain, energy, space, and transport

Whole books have been written on each of the "other techs," so the quick mention here relates to *After Capitalism*.

- Additive manufacturing: 3D, 4D, and nano-scale "bottom-up" manufacturing approaches enable decentralized on-demand fabrication. This ability to "go local" has interesting potential for decentralizing economic approaches.

- Blockchain: is a shared, distributed ledger that facilitates recording transactions and tracking assets in a network. Virtually anything of value can be tracked and traded on a blockchain network – this can reduce risk and cut costs. Blockchain-based smart contracts combined with AI and automated monitoring could be applied widely to sustainable resource management, reducing transportation congestion, or crime detection (Dao, 2017). The decentralizing potential is intriguing here as well.

- Renewable energy: Several of the AC Concepts talk about the great potential for a renewable energy revolution. Bastani (2019) for instance, notes that, in principle, solar is more than capable of meeting the world's expanding energy needs. He adds that it is unparalleled in the history of energy use to have a source continually get cheaper with double-digit percentage gains. This connects back to Kurzweil's point about accelerating returns and exponential growth, and Kurzweil indeed suggested in 2016 that solar would be the dominant energy source in a dozen years (Morris, 2016).

- Transportation: Advances point to increasing speed and (perhaps most impactful of all) pervasiveness of rapid delivery. Combined with advances in virtual technology, it enables a shifting sense of place. It raises intriguing questions, such as when should we get together in person and when is virtual okay? Should we go to the store, or have it delivered?

- Space: There could be a boost in economic production from space. Bastani (2019) suggests asteroid mining is poised to become the fastest-growing industry in history. He cites the example of the large asteroid 16 Psyche located in the belt between Mars and Jupiter. It is composed of iron, nickel and rarer metals such as copper, gold and platinum. Its iron content alone could be worth $10,000 quadrillion. He goes on to say that one estimate of the mineral wealth of NEAs (near Earth asteroids) if equally divided among every person on Earth, would add up to more than $100 billion each.

Implications of technology acceleration for *After Capitalism*

While technology acceleration is at the core of capitalism today, authors of several AC Concepts also see the potential of accelerating technology for creating a new economic order. Brynjolfsson and McAfee (2016) and Rifkin (2014) note that information is moving toward zero marginal cost of reproduction. Mason (2015) whose work makes an important contribution to the *Non-Workers' Paradise* image, observed that there is a growing body of evidence that the IT family of technologies, far from creating a new and stable form of capitalism, are dissolving it, corroding market mechanisms, eroding property rights and destroying the relationship between wages, work, and profit. He points out that:

- IT has reduced the need for work.
- Information goods are corroding the market's ability to form prices correctly.
- There has been a spontaneous rise in collaborative products that no longer respond to dictates of the market, e.g. Wikipedia.

A key question for *After Capitalism* is the motivation for applying accelerating technologies. In most cases they are reinforcing the capitalist regime and making entrepreneurs rich. But they may improve productivity so much that a capitalist system is no longer needed. Capitalism is based on the assumption of a scarcity of resources. Technology acceleration, however, could "solve" that scarcity issue and enable an abundance of resources that makes capitalism obsolete. For instance, Smart (2015) suggests that the rate of technological change has been accelerating throughout history and will continue to do so, thus putting us on the cusp of super-exponential acceleration of IT as well as nanotech. Indeed, several of the *Tech-Led Abundance* concepts rely on this driver of technology acceleration.

2.3.3 Inequality

Growing economic inequality is threatening the social order.

Inequality has been gaining more attention in recent years, but it has been worsening for decades. Ayres (2020) noted a shift to greater inequality starting in the 1970s. He observed that the more benign aspects of capitalism

– such as competition, a free market, and entrepreneurialism – retreated as financial speculation became more prominent. In the last 5-10 years, inequality has become a hot topic in the media. For instance, former Labor Secretary Robert Reich (2010) projected that the implications of failing to address inequality would result in political backlash against trade, immigration, foreign investment, high business, Wall Street, and government itself. Piketty's (2014) popular book *Capital* found that since the 1970s, income inequality has increased significantly in affluent countries.

A few years later the leader of the World Economic Forum, Klaus Schwab (2016) while promoting his Fourth Industrial Revolution concept, acknowledged that inequality represented his greatest societal concern. The concerns about inequality include government leaders as well. France's conservative finance minister Bruno Le Maire said capitalism could collapse if global inequality continues to rise. In a speech marking the start of France's presidency of the G7, he said the Group of Seven economic powers should consider setting a joint minimum corporation tax and tackle the power of giant multinational corporations (Thomas and Rivet, 2019). And even the capitalists themselves are worried. Salesforce's billionaire CEO Marc Benioff has criticized the "horrifying inequality" of America's economic system (Clifford 2019).

Structural aspects

Figure 2.7 Three classes

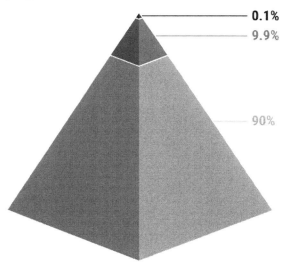

The basic problem is structural: capitalism produces inequality. Some factors in capitalism promote convergence of incomes, others promote divergence; on balance, divergence is the stronger force. Piketty (2014) makes perhaps the strongest case: the return on capital investments (which Piketty puts at an average of 5%) beats economic growth (a surrogate for income growth, which he puts at 1-2% on average). This creates an advantage for previously accumulated wealth that exacerbates inequality (Piketty, 2014). Put bluntly, capitalism has a systemic, built-in advantage that favors those who already have wealth. It's the "success to the successful" archetype, which systems thinker Daniel Kim (2018) describes as "an archetypal case of self-fulfilling prophecies. The outcome of a situation is highly dependent on the initial conditions." As will be described in Chapter 3 on the decay of the Baseline, capitalism has structural characteristics, such as promoting inequality, that are leading its demise.

A simple but enlightening breakdown of class structure in the US from Stewart (2018) is shown in Figure 12. It challenges the notion of a healthy middle class. He notes that while the top 1% is often the popular media target for having a disproportionate share of wealth, in reality it is even smaller than that – it is really the 0.1% who have been the big winners in the growing concentration of wealth over the past half century. This 0.1% holds roughly 22% of the wealth. The next group, the 9.9% holds almost 60% of the wealth; they have managed to hold on to their share of the economic pie over the last several decades. The 90% have the last 20% of the pie – roughly the same share as the top 0.1%. The shift over the last several decades has been more wealth going from the bottom 90% to the top 0.1%, with the share of the 9.9% holding steady (Stewart, 2018).

To put it a little more bluntly: "the result is growing polarization between an impoverished surplus population of losers; overworked middle-class families living an absurdly busy life and putting in ever more, and ever more intense, working hours in spite of unprecedented prosperity; and a small elite of winner-take-all super-rich whose greed knows no limits while their bonuses and dividends have long ceased to serve any useful function for society as a whole" (Streeck and Pilger, 2016, 334).

<u>Getting worse</u>

Economic inequality is largely driven by the unequal ownership of capital, which can be either privately or publicly held. Since 1980, large transfers of public to private wealth have occurred in nearly all countries. While national wealth has substantially increased, public wealth is now negative or close to zero in affluent countries. Arguably this limits the ability of governments to tackle inequality (Alvaredo et al., 2017, 16).

Dozens and dozens of studies point towards inequality growing:

- Income inequality has increased in nearly all world regions in recent decades, but at different speeds (Alvaredo et al., 2017).
- Between 1983 and 2009 in the US, the top 20% experienced not 100% of the increase, but more than 100%. The trend is similar in most advanced countries – in Sweden, Finland, and Germany, income inequality has actually grown more quickly than in the US (Brynjolfsson and McAfee, 2016).
- Between 2005 and 2014, real incomes in 25 advanced economies were flat or fell for 65-70% of households, or more than 540 million people. This affects people across the income distribution spectrum, with young, less-educated workers the hardest hit (McKinsey Global Institute, 2016).
- Zucman and Saez's latest estimates show that the top 0.1% of taxpayers — about 170,000 families in a country of 330 million people — control 20% of American wealth, the highest share since 1929. The bottom half of Americans combined have a negative net worth. (Steverman, 2019).
- Grameen Bank founder Muhammad Yunus says inequality is becoming disastrous. He notes that in India nearly 73% of total wealth is owned by 1% of its population. He argues that the capitalist system is a machine that sucks up everything for the benefit of the top, and the top is becoming smaller and smaller (The News Scroll, 2018).
- The soaring US CEO-to-worker pay ratio hit 278-to-1 in 2018 (up from just 58-to-1 in 1989 and 20-to-1 in 1965). CEO pay has increased 1,008% between 1978 and 2018, while typical worker pay has edged up 12% (Colombo, 2019).

The challenges

The challenges of inequality go beyond economics. Wilkinson and Pickett (2009) cite several effects:

- It undermines citizenship by eroding trust, solidarity, mutuality, and breeding cynicism.
- It creates a new hereditary aristocracy with privileges perpetuating themselves over generations, e.g. America now has less social mobility than some poorer countries.
- Health and social problems are indeed more common in countries with bigger income inequalities.
- Poverty is socially corrosive.

Bregman (2017) adds that perception is a key to inequality. A study of 24 developed countries found that even if people are relatively well-off, the perception of inequality contributes to unhappiness. Matthews (2021) presents another challenge. Wealthy leftists, in order to offer a semblance of solidarity with the working class, substitute identity politics for class conflict, and frame economic problems as problems of racism or bigotry. While these are very real issues, the quest to relate can lead to focusing too heavily on the racism/bigotry aspect and neglecting other aspects of the very complex issues involved.

Standing (2014) takes it a step further and identifies a new class structure emerging from the inequality, which he calls the precariat. The precariat consists of people with temporary or short-lived jobs interspersed with periods of unemployment or labor-force withdrawal (Standing, 2014). For instance, housing is an issue for the precariat. Globally, housing shortages have left more than 1.8 billion without access to adequate housing and millions of people homeless, with an average of 15 million people forcibly evicted from their homes every year (Morrison, 2023). The rising cost of living in San Francisco, for example, led to the introduction of dorm-style living for the non-tech population (making roughly $40-90K) in which they share bathrooms, kitchen, and living rooms and have their own bedroom (Bowles, 2018).

There are some suggestions that a great wealth bounty deriving from technology acceleration will solve inequality. But in practice, technology has tended to exacerbate inequality. The entrepreneurial tech heroes, such as Musk, Bezos, and Branson, have accumulated massive wealth. Brynjolfsson and McAfee (2016) note that AI, automation, and machines bring about a greater bounty, but they also see it contributing to greater inequality. They believe the top 20% of knowledge worker elites will do fine – but nowhere near as well as the entrepreneurial heroes. In short, technological advances create winners, and within capitalism the winners win, and the gap between the winners and losers continues to grow.

While it is mostly a structural problem, Frase (2016) suggests having power over others is for some its own reward. Thus they will endeavor to maintain a system where others serve them even if it is totally superfluous from a productive standpoint. Samuelson (2017) observes that, as societies become richer, the temptation increases for people to advance their economic interests by grabbing someone else's wealth, as opposed to creating new wealth, and that "we see the resulting redistributive struggles all the time." In other words, there are some people who are quite pleased by inequality since it is to their benefit.

Regarding the argument that humans are wired to compete, an interesting counter-argument is that our particular species of humans has been around for about 300,000 years and for about 290,000 of those years we lived as hunter gatherers who were materially poorer but much more equal (Sterelny, 2021).

Implications of inequality for *After Capitalism*

Inequality is arguably the single biggest and most direct driver leading to the questioning of capitalism. It has grown to such a level that it is getting more and more difficult for supporters of capitalism to explain away. The historic case of a rising tide lifting all boats is becoming less clear as well; some boats are rising fantastically high, but most are now stagnant; some are taking on water, and many are sinking.

Although the connection has not always been explicitly made, the populism and social unrest in the US and several European countries has inequality at its core. The search for scapegoats and the reliance on one's tribe are desperate measures driven in part by inequality. It is important to note that the perception of inequality is often more influential than the actual material conditions being experienced. Someone may be getting by economically, but when they see the tremendous wealth of others, it generates a resentment that at some point could boil over into social unrest. The ubiquity of social media has made it very challenging to hide or distort the unpleasant reality of the huge divide. In the present day, pointing out the gap is a common and effective way to generate attention and clicks — but proposing real solutions to eliminate this interminable wealth gap is not something one often sees when scrolling through social media!

2.3.4 Automation

Automation, driven by AI, is increasingly replacing jobs.

Automation is defined here as the use of various technologies for operating equipment or for performing tasks, Automation could drive towards *After Capitalism* from two distinctly different paths.

- The first path, the negative one: automation is applied indiscriminately and causes massive job loss and capitalism takes the blame.
- The second path, the positive one: automation is applied strategically and improves productivity and enables people to work less and eventually facilitates a post-work future.

Automation is not new. Ther have been previous waves of automation and each time ways have been found to create more new jobs. The question for the future is whether this time is different. The Shift Commission (Slaughter et al., 2016, 11) raised this question, in particular noting the contribution of AI: "We believe today's progress in AI is consequential enough to prompt careful consideration of whether this time is different." Slightly more than half their members (58%) agree that this time is different.

Figure 2.8 Automation pathways

Full speed ahead path

Harari (2017a, 318) suggests that "the most important question in twenty-first-century economics ... [is] what to do with all the superfluous people..." made obsolete by automation. The potential for substitution of automation for human labor is well documented:

- A mid-2015 Pew Research survey found that about two-thirds of US citizens believe that within 50 years robots and automation will do the majority of the work done by humans today (Johnson, 2017).
- Oxford Economics projects up to 20 million manufacturing jobs around the world could be replaced by robots by 2030. Each new

Imagining After Capitalism | 59

- industrial robot wipes out 1.6 manufacturing jobs, the firm said, with the least-skilled regions being more affected (Cellan-Jones, 2019).
- Robots could replace as many as two million more workers in manufacturing alone by 2025, according to economists at MIT and Boston University. They note that the pandemic created a very strong incentive to automate, that machines don't fall ill, that they don't need to isolate to protect peers, and that they don't need to take time off work (Semuels, 2020).
- This is a global phenomenon: A World Bank report found that two-thirds of all jobs in the developing world face being automated out of existence (Oberhaus, 2017).

There is plenty of potential for the full speed ahead and massive job loss path:

- Graeber suggests that not only will automation lead to net unemployment, but that it already has. He says dummy jobs are effectively made up to mask the difference. His popular *Bullshit Jobs* suggests that if one eliminates bullshit jobs (and the real jobs that only exist to support them) from the picture, then the catastrophe predicted in the 1930s has actually happened. "Upward of 50 to 60 percent of the population has, in fact, been thrown out of work" (Graeber, 2018, 265).
- Australia has a fully automated farm using robots and artificial intelligence (Claughton and Condon, 2021).
- Xiang (2018) suggests that if AI remains under the control of market forces, it will inexorably result in a super-rich oligopoly of data billionaires who reap the wealth created by robots that displace human labor, leaving massive unemployment in their wake.
- Once established as successful, Uber announced plans to automate its fleet and put all its workforce out of work. Due to business problems, however, it has abandoned that approach for now (Hawkins, 2020).
- The high-profile story of a CEO firing 90% of his staff and replacing them with AI took place in India (Tangermann, 2023).

One might argue that the only reason automation has not taken off faster is that wages are so low that it's cheaper to hire humans than buy machines (Frase, 2016). It is reasonable to assume that the more machines can replace human workers, the more likely it is that they'll drive down the wages of humans with similar skills (Brynjolfsson and McAfee, 2016). Currently, a lot of automation is applied to tasks, or pieces of jobs, rather than outright replacing full-time jobs. This may be masking what's to come — as automation improves, it is likely to move from replacing tasks to replacing full-time jobs.

Strategic pathway

There is less current evidence for the strategic path leading toward post-work. This is not surprising since post-work has not yet emerged as a large-scale desirable concept. Several AC concept authors talked about the potential for technology acceleration as an enabler of post-work.

- Bastani (2019) suggests a key role for automation and technology as enablers of his Fully Automated Luxury Communism vision.
- Srnicek & Williams (2016) suggest automation can eliminate "huge swathes of boring and demeaning work."
- Bregman (2017), in his vision of a post-work future, cites a RAND study suggesting a future in which just 2% of the population would be able to produce everything society needed.

This time is not different

The "Full speed ahead" path assumes that the impact of automation would be more significant this time, but it is possible that it will not be. Most projections supported automation leading to net job loss. But not all. Reese (2019) is representative of a school of thought that AI will create more jobs than it destroys. He uses the example of the ATM, which for some time counter-intuitively led to more tellers, because it became cheaper to open branch banks. But the Bureau of Labor Statistics (2023) now projects a 15% decline in teller jobs in the US over the next 10 years. In my view the "create more jobs" path is less plausible. Even if it were to be true, it would reinforce the Neoliberal Capitalism baseline and not drive towards *After Capitalism*.

Implications of automation for *After Capitalism*

Our own study of the future of work aligned with the first path. We identified a baseline scenario in which automation is applied in purely economic terms with little regard for social costs (Hines, 2017a). As the projections above suggest, the full impact of automation is yet to come. But when it does, it is likely to be quite disruptive, and little is being done to prepare for it. Thus, it seems most likely that automation will largely be applied with "full steam ahead." There is still time for the strategic path to be taken. The work being done here supports that path.

2.3.5 Stagnation

Futurist Stephan Aguilar-Milan (2014, 127) and colleagues highlighted a coming age of stagnation:

> It is our belief that aggregate demand is currently constrained and is presently the key brake on the return to growth. As household spending has remained muted as households repair their balance sheets, we cannot look to consumption as a means to stimulate growth. As governments struggle with the need for fiscal austerity, we cannot expect fiscal policy to act to stimulate aggregate demand. As companies wait for productive investment opportunities to emerge, we are unlikely to see an investment-led recovery any time soon. The only real possibility is for an export-led recovery. However, as all nations are simultaneously following this policy, in the aggregate, these efforts cancel each other out. In total, demand is relatively muted and is likely to remain so for some time to come.

Economic growth is slowing in part due to inability to pay.

The simple version of stagnation is a vicious circle (see Figure 2.9): lack of jobs > lack of money > lack of purchases > lack of growth and back around.

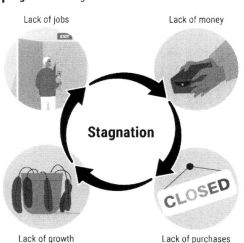

Figure 2.9 Stagnation's vicious circle

It presents a problem for the growth imperative of capitalism, in which growth is required to keep going. It can be compared to a giant Ponzi scheme (Gardiner, 2019) in which new growth is needed to pay off previous investors. Supporters of capitalism will likely be making a case that everything is fine and manipulate the numbers to say the growth is continuing (Aragao and Linsi, 2022).

But digging into the question of whether growth is "fine" is running into problems. There is evidence it has been challenged for some time and is likely to continue. Tyler Cowen's (2011) popular *The Great Stagnation* put the issue on the table. His main point was that the era of easy growth was over as we had been living off low-hanging fruit for at least three hundred years. While the book gained some notoriety, it remained at the edge of mainstream economic thinking. However, several other leading thinkers began talking about stagnation as well in the 2010s:

- Haque (2011) observed that business as usual hasn't been able to create value over the last decade (the 2000s).
- Reich (2013) notes the problem isn't too little saving, but too little demand; workers can't afford the products they are making.
- Lanier (2013) suggested there eventually won't be enough paying customers to subsidize all the free information.
- Piketty (2014) found that we are returning to a low-growth regime and signs are that growth will be even slower in the future.
- Frase (2016, 17) observed that the reason employers don't hire more workers is because there aren't enough people buying their products, because they don't have enough money,

The mounting evidence for stagnation continues into the 2020s:

- Bastani (2019) sees our world as one increasingly defined by low growth, low productivity, and low wages.
- The Bureau of Labor Statistics noted that the percentage of the population in the US labor force peaked in 2000 and has been falling since (Santens, 2015). World Bank (2024) data shows the same, with the global labor participation rate – percentage of the population working or actively looking for work – falling from 57% in 1990 to 40% today.
- Roberts (2021) talks about a Long Depression that began in 1997.
- Benanav (2023) quips that economists are all stagnationists now.

There is still more discussion today about growth rates and numbers than about stagnation, but it has entered the conversation. Futurists, and innovators, commonly believe that new ideas start on the fringe outside of the mainstream and gradually work their way toward the mainstream over time. Stagnation is on this journey.

It could get worse

Looking ahead, there are other emerging factors that could reinforce the stagnation driver:

- Automation: Currently it is still mostly cheaper to hire people than to automate. But as that flips and jobs are lost, it strengthens the vicious circle above.

- Growing debt: The IMF noted that while the global debt situation has improved somewhat since the Covid spike, the overall rising trend continues (Gaspar et al, 2023). Hudson (2016) speculates that eventually the amount of debt will exceed the economy's ability to pay it back, thus making a financial breakdown inevitable.

- Aging population: Bastani (2019) notes that by 2050 there will be more people over sixty-five than under fourteen – fewer workers to support more retirees. Older people also tend to live off savings rather than invest, which reinforces stagnation. A development in life extension would further exacerbate the situation by enlarging the size of the older cohort.

Implications of stagnation for *After Capitalism*

Stagnation suggests that capitalism's growth imperative is running into trouble. The logic of capitalism is to constantly look for new things to commodify and sell. The problem is that it is becoming difficult to find these new things. At the same time, capitalism works toward efficiency by eliminating labor, which puts pressure on consumer purchasing power. Without jobs or pay, people cannot afford to buy the products.

Capitalism depends on growth. It must constantly expand to find new growth areas. The H2 AC Concepts around *New Sources of Value* reflect this need to constantly monetize, in most cases things which were not previously monetized. As several of our H3 *Circular Commons* concepts point out, land historically held in common has continually been privatized and commoditized to keep the capitalist engine revving. A period of stagnation, therefore, is a big challenge to the continuation of capitalism.

2.3.6 Climate and carrying capacity

Climate change and humanity's growing ecological footprint are threatening the ecosystem.

Global climate change is accelerating and starting to have noticeable effects. Humanity's growing ecological footprint, which contributes to climate change, is also influencing the Earth's carrying capacity. As is commonly observed, people may not survive, but the planet will.

<u>Climate change</u>

Climate change is connected with capitalism. The growth imperative of capitalism creates pressure to use energy and resources to fuel it. Patel and Moore (2017) suggest a variation on the Anthropocene called the Capitalocene to highlight the role of capitalism in the destruction of nature. Mason (2015) says that once the status quo has grasped that climate change is real, capitalism is finished.

The evidence is overwhelming that climate change is having, and will continue to have, increasingly negative effects on the environment. The consensus is that the planet is reaching a "point of no return." Gabriel (2017) calls it a phase change in which less than 20 years from now, human-generated carbon emissions will most likely have altered the climate beyond our power to reverse it. We see almost daily stories along the lines of "Climate Change could Shut Down a Vital Ocean Current, Study Finds" (D'Angelo, 2021). The Intergovernmental Panel on Climate Change (IPCC), a United Nations body that synthesizes the work of thousands of scientists in nearly 200 member states, has unequivocally concluded that humanity is to blame for rising temperatures, and that the impacts are happening faster than anticipated. At this point, even the best-case scenario of a 1.5°C increase over the next 20 years leads to a doubling of ocean warming that will devastate marine life, lead to sea level rise of a foot, ice sheets melting, and extreme weather becoming more common and more intense (Lyman, 2021). If that's not enough: four of the Stockholm Resilience Centre's nine planetary boundaries have been exceeded: climate change, biodiversity loss, land-system change, and biogeochemical flows (DiGirolamo, 2021).

The weather will get weirder, which many would agree is already happening. Science fiction writer and futurist Bruce Sterling's (1995) *Heavy Weather* provided an excellent preview of a future characterized by extreme weather events told through the perspective of storm chasers. More formally and recently, the National Academy of Sciences (2016) published a comprehensive review of the surge of studies suggesting that climate change is influencing the probability and magnitude of extreme weather events. The *Bulletin of the American Meteorological Society* has published six annual editions explaining extreme events from a climate perspective. The 2016 edition included 27 studies of extreme weather events, with 21 identifying climate change as a significant driver (Herring et al., 2018). The IPCC describes a world of worsening food shortages and wildfires, and a mass die-off of coral reefs as soon as 2040 due to climate change (Davenport, 2018). In short, there is plenty of research on the likely strange weather ahead.

There is some activism on this front. For instance, the Extinction Rebellion (XR) movement has staged three major "rebellions" over the past few years to highlight the escalating climate and ecological emergency and demand urgent action from governments. The peaceful protests brought large parts of London to a standstill for days, with printing presses of right-wing newspapers blockaded and fossil fuel companies targeted. XR says more than 3,400 people were arrested, with about 1,700 charged, almost all for minor public order offences such as obstructing the highway (Taylor, 2021).

In 2015, a landmark lawsuit, *Juliana vs. United States*, filed by a group of young plaintiffs, sought to codify the right to a livable planet into the constitution. This case represents an ambitious attempt by the environmental lobby to combat climate change within the system. However, the Obama, Trump, and now Biden administrations have battled fiercely to prevent this case from ever being heard by a court of law so it remains uncertain what impact this lawsuit could make (Rock, 2022).

Carrying Capacity

The Houston Foresight program has long used the work of Wackernagel on calculating humanity's impact on the environment or its footprint. For many years the Global Footprint Network has calculated the day of the year on which humanity overshoots Earth's carrying capacity. This Earth Overshoot Day marks the date when humanity has exhausted nature's budget for the year. For the rest of the year, an ecological deficit grows as local resource stocks diminish and carbon dioxide accumulates in the atmosphere. The planet is already operating in overshoot to a degree. In 2024, the date was August 1. The dates go back

Figure 2.10 Earth Overshoot Day

to 1970 and there has been a clear trend in which Earth Overshoot Day has been steadily occurring sooner, with the interesting exception that in 2020 (the pandemic year) it moved back to August 22 (Global Footprint Network, 2021).

The evidence for humanity pressuring the planet's carrying capacity is troubling and not new. The bullets below identify problems going back several years:

- Current best estimates are that approximately half of Earth's terrestrial ecosystems have already been lost. Barry (2014) suggests that at least 44% of the Earth's land surface must be totally protected and another 22% partially protected to avoid biosphere collapse (Barry, 2014).
- Roughly 60% of the world's ecosystems have been degraded (Jackson, 2015).
- The sixth mass extinction is underway and happening much faster than previously expected. It happens through wildlife trade, pollution, habitat loss, and the use of toxic substances. A study recently published in the *Proceedings of the National Academy of Sciences (PNAS)* found the rate at which species are dying out has accelerated in recent decades. They noted that 173 species went extinct between 2001 and 2014 (Kottasova, 2020).
- Some go further. McBrien (2019) suggests that the term "sixth mass extinction" is too tame, and rather classifies it as the First Extermination Event, which has Earth at the brink of the Necrocene — the age of the new necrotic death.

Implications of climate and carrying capacity for *After Capitalism*

Harari (2017a, 131) makes the interesting observation that humanity "dominates the planet not because the individual human is far smarter and more nimble-fingered than the individual chimp or wolf, but because *Homo sapiens* is the only species on earth capable of co-operating flexibly in large numbers." It is this cooperation that will be necessary to preserve human life on this planet. Many are worried about it being too late. Slaughter (2020) warns that we are no longer a world with multiple global futures. Rather, the only credible future ahead is one of overshoot and collapse, and our only choice at this point is to deal with it.

My sense is that this connection of capitalism to climate change and carrying capacity may not be easily made clear to the general public. Even now there is at best a vague sense of climate change being "real" among the public. That said, activists, opponents of capitalism, and increasingly "neutral" analysts are making the case, as these headlines suggest:

- Is Saving the Planet Under Capitalism Really Possible? (Polychroniou, 2021)
- Why We Need to Change Capitalism for Climate Action (Noor, 2020)
- The fight against climate change is a fight against capitalism (Hannah, 2019)

If (or as) this idea mainstreams, it could be a significant driver of a search for alternatives to capitalism.

2.3.7 Ineffective left

The far left continues to be ineffective in catalyzing change.

The left, particularly the far left, is more inclined to support the changes needed to move to *After Capitalism* than the right, but it has been largely ineffective in doing so to date. In short, it's failed to build a vision for the future. There are three major obstacles:

- The mainstream left is not helping.
- Much of the far left is stuck in folk politics.
- The right has been more strategic than the left.

<u>Mainstream left not helping</u>

It is fair to say that the US as a democratic country has chosen capitalism along with all its inequalities. The people could vote to change it by selecting candidates supporting an alternative approach. This idea in the US context seemed absurd until recently when presidential candidate Bernie Sanders made a nearly successful run on a fairly radical platform. Ultimately, the left chose the safe candidate and business-as-usual prevailed. This driver is more about the far left than the mainstream. The challenge has been its inability to develop an effective alternative platform that appeals to the general public. Though we should point out that the mainstream left has been ineffective as well. Support for Sanders' candidacy was not far enough removed from the mainstream, and probably represented simple disgust with the mainstream rather than true support for an alternative. Radical left parties are also facing challenges in Europe, with a recent analysis finding that two so-called radical parties — Syriza in Greece and Podemos in Spain — have limited their goals to the restoration of the welfare state following years of austerity (Bortun, 2023).

A less obvious impediment for the left is that powerful media ownership is often averse to any calls for radical change that would alter the status quo. Mainstream media organizations are indeed corporations that operate under the standard profit-making business model. Vanguard and Blackrock are two of the largest shareholders of CNN so it should not be a surprise that channels like these promote a standard liberal baseline in their coverage. Bernie Sanders did not receive much positive media coverage during his campaigns as his platform inherently sought to reduce the influence of big-money corporations like these.

It is not just a US phenomenon. The left is struggling globally. Former Greek minister and capitalism critic Yanis Varoufakis notes the struggles of the left in Germany, France, the UK and the Nordic countries. He suggests a focus on ideological issues has come at the expense of core economic concerns of the working class (Eaton, 2023). The fact that liberalism reigns supreme as the guiding principle of mainstream thought has significantly derailed the efforts of the left to advocate for policies which otherwise could be quite popular among the masses.

Folk politics

Srnicek and Willams (2016) observe that while the right was able to create a new hegemony, the "Euro-American left has been meandering and ineffective, with a sense of pessimism regarding the ability to create large-scale social change." They argue that a key problem is that of "folk-politics" or folk-political thinking that has the left content to remain at — and even privilege — the transient, small-scale, unmediated and particular. In effect, it is better to be ideologically pure at the local scale, than impure and effective at a mass scale.

The postmodern values mentioned above — the fastest-growing type — lead to finding and supporting noble causes. A challenge for the postmoderns is that the quest tends to be more important than acting on it. It feels good to be in the protest march, but then it's back to life as normal. The emergence of new values is in part to correct for perceived shortcomings of the previous type. In this case, integral values have a stronger action ethos than the postmodern values they follow after. They are much more sharply focused on making a difference. They also prioritize big picture vision. This combination of vision and action provides some hope for change, but it should be kept in mind that the integral type is probably only 3-5% of affluent country populations at present.

There is much positive about the left's focus on the folk level. As we'll see in the guiding images in Part Two, bottom-up, decentralized, and local are critically important organizing principles. In terms of *After Capitalism*, what is lacking is an accompanying big-picture vision. Bregman (2017) notes the effectiveness of the neoliberal movement in getting its message across, and by contrast, how poorly the left has done: "The left seems to have forgotten the art of politics. They've got no story to tell, nor even any language to convey it in." Srnicek and Williams (2016) agree that the left once excelled at building enticing visions for a better world but that that skill has deteriorated. Even more bluntly: "… in response to economic Reaganism … the mainstream left offered no distinct, inspiring, politically plausible, national economic vision of a fairer future, as it had back in the 1930s and '40s (Andersen, 2020).

Mason (2015) observes that free market capitalism is a clear and powerful idea, while the forces opposing it looked like they were defending something old, worse, and incoherent. Thus, emerges "Woke Capitalism," which involves social pressure on firms to conform to a progressive version of social justice (Anderson, 2019). It gets lumped in with Cancel Culture and is often seen as a reactive, fault-finding movement that is focused on what-not-to-do rather than what-to-do.

It is important to note the left is not a monolith. There are distinctions to be made. Some leftists, for example, largely discount electoral politics in general, while others participate. There is a lot of in-fighting within the left regarding whether one should vote blue (in the US) or simply abstain from voting altogether. Some are more attached to Marxist-Leninist ideals that are not likely to be palatable in a mainstream sense. These divisions surely account to some degree for the overall ineffectiveness of the left.

The right has been more strategic than the left

The right has been far more effective in pushing its agenda. It initially generated, and now supports, the neoliberal capitalist image that has been prevalent for decades. It succeeded by skillfully constructing an ideology and the infrastructure to support it. A major task of neoliberalism was to take control of the state and repurpose it. It has actively pursued victory in the sense of maintaining the status quo and has been effective in doing so, despite having a smaller political base. The right continues to either win elections or make them close, which effectively prevents systemic change. It has been very smart about how it uses its economic power to maintain political power. From using its position to reinforce the ideology in schools, to keeping anti-capitalist impulses disorganized and unable to build a counter movement — and ultimately keeping employees from forming political majorities that could challenge their control (Wolff, 2020). One gets the sense that in the US context, the right knows the game and plays it well, while the left is confused. The right has been a bit ruthless in pushing its agenda. It's like the schoolyard bully getting away with it. The left looks to tell the teacher, but the teacher isn't helping. The right continues to cross established lines and has learned there is no real penalty for doing so. The left, meanwhile, is continually shocked, offended, and almost dazed. It appeals to a sense of decorum that is long gone and finds itself in a reactive mode with little real agenda of its own.

Signs of change

There are signs of change. Occupy Wall Street was one of the first real mobilizations of anti-austerity sentiment, one of the early moments when the breakdown of neoliberalism began to generate real resistance. In 2011 there was the Arab Spring, the European movements of the squares, and Occupy Wall Street (Taylor, 2020). But a decade later it is clear they did not stimulate any sort of organized resistance or movement. However, tensions did boil over in the US following the killing of George Floyd — with a large-scale and sometimes violent series of protests erupting throughout the summer of 2020. These tensions were likely exacerbated by people being confined indoors for months of quarantine. Looting and destruction of private property became a hallmark of protests. The image of the Minneapolis police station set aflame and looking as if it was an active warzone on national television is hard to forget.

Within the political system, organizations like the Democratic Socialists of America (DSA) and the Justice Democrats have gained prominence and lend credence to the idea that there is a growing anti-capitalist sentiment spreading among the public. Over the last decade, DSA membership has grown rapidly from 6,500 to over 92,000 members according to their website. Some of that influence has indeed translated into positions of institutional power as "The Squad" Democrats such as Alexandria Ocasio-Cortez (D-NY) win elections and secure important committee assignments, accompanied by a level of popularity on social media (Sullivan, 2019).

In the workforce, there has been a glimmer of hope that labor unions may be beginning to reassert some of the power they once had. Popular insurgencies have been escalating since the pandemic. The first four months of 2022, for instance, saw mass labor strikes and unionization drives breaking out in industries and countries around the world, including the UK, India, and Nigeria (Robinson, 2022).

Though union membership has been steadily declining since the 1960s, there have been some positive signs of change. The International Labour Organization (2023) notes that due to success in unionizing more of the self-employed, union membership is up 3.6% globally over the last ten years – an important caveat is that it has not kept pace with employment growth and trade union density is lower than 10 years ago. The US National Labor Relations Board has reported that unions filed 57% more petitions for representation elections from October-March 2022 than in the same period last year. Along with this, 2022 saw the first ever union established at Amazon, a staunch anti-unionization employer, as well as Starbucks, Trader Joes, and the first vote ever to take place at Apple. A Gallup poll, which surveys the approval rating for labor unions each year, has shown a steady increase in approval among the public for unions — increasing from 48% in 2009 to 68% in 2021. Unions could be a crucial source of institutional power needed for any leftist economic agenda (DiNatale and West, 2022).

It is also worth considering that a workers' rights movement could emerge alongside or instead of the union format.

Implications of ineffective left for *After Capitalism*

Haque (2020) puts it bluntly: "The problems our societies face — climate change, rising poverty, inequality, a lack of opportunity — have all been caused by American-style conservatism and neoliberalism, after all. And yet the left seems to make no progress whatsoever."

The preoccupation with grassroots, local action has kept the "Euro-American" left from wielding significant influence. The lack of a clear alternative to *Neoliberal Capitalism* has kept the left in the position of reacting rather than creating something new. But there are signs of change, and the focus on local and grassroots is not misplaced, but rather needs to be supplemented with a more global approach.

The drivers of change are generally not good news for capitalism — with the exception of the ineffective left. If that were to shift, it would really put pressure on the current system and open up the possibilities for alternative approaches. In the next chapter we explore how these drivers are in fact putting heavy pressure on capitalism.

Chapter 3 – THE BASELINE

Capitalism is a complex adaptive system that has reached the limits of its capacity to adapt. — Paul Mason

It is a key assumption of this work that the neoliberal capitalist system is disintegrating. This chapter lays out the case for this. It acknowledges the good intentions of the many ideas and efforts for saving capitalism, but argues that they will only prolong its life, not save it. This prolonging is actually helpful to *After Capitalism*, as it provides needed time to fully develop alternatives such as the three guiding images to be described here.

The most basic argument for the end of capitalism comes from a fundamental proposition of the Systems Thinking course we teach in the Houston Foresight program: "a system's behavior is a function of its structure." The structure of capitalism produces the behavior of accumulation at the top. Changing the people in charge, changing the measures and metrics, even changing the rules, will not fundamentally alter the behavior of the capitalist system. If we use the US political system as an example, one party wins and proclaims they are going to change everything, but typically makes small incremental changes at best. Then the other party wins, gets rid of all the other people, puts their people in place, and is also barely able to move the needle of change. New people will not be able to change a system with the same underlying structure.

> A system's behavior is a function of its structure.

At the core, the challenge is a paradigm one — we need to change the system! A key feature of the capitalist system is that it produces a small number of winners who capture a high share of the wealth and a large number of losers who fight for the leftovers. In the modern values paradigm that puts a premium on growth and competition, this is an acceptable bargain. In the emerging postmodern and integral values paradigms, it is not.

The chapter begins with a brief overview of how we got to *Neoliberal Capitalism* to help clarify the context for change. Then it's on to the current problems. The chapter concludes with a description of specific signals of disintegration.

3.1   Context

There are many works chronicling the history of capitalism. We'll need to focus on relevant highlights rather than a summary. A key point is that capitalism is not inevitable but a system that arose at a point in time in certain conditions. Braudel's (1981) masterful three-volume series on capitalism — primarily on the European situation — shows that capitalism is not inevitable. In the broad sweep of history, it may end up having had a relatively brief run of less than 300 years if its demise is met by mid-century. A key argument of the third volume in Braudel's series is that the development of capitalism was already underway by the time of the Industrial Revolution, driven by trade. The Industrial Revolution, beginning roughly after 1750, accelerated and reinforced capitalism, but it was not the sole instigator (Braudel, 1992). In short, capitalism emerged in alignment with a particular historical context.

The emergence of capitalism is to some degree a chicken-and-egg process — the conditions enable it, but they emerged because of it as well. Bernstein (2010) notes that the Industrial Revolution kicked off a period of economic growth around 1820, based on four key factors:

- property rights, including intellectual property
- scientific rationalism
- funding, including capital markets
- communication and transportation improvements

Property rights "emerge" from the context of the enclosure of the commons, which will be discussed in more detail in "Circular Commons" in Chapter 5. Bernstein shows how these four factors reinforce one another to catalyze the transition from agricultural feudalism to industrial capitalism over a period of decades.

An additional factor is the rise of modern values that support this shift, such as moving from property held in common to private ownership. Modern values arose to meet the changing context — they provided "answers" for this new emerging system that traditional values were unable to.

Let's fast-forward a century or so. By now the Industrial Revolution is well underway and capitalism as its operating system is well entrenched. A second big shift comes in the form of the end of the Bretton Woods System that has been in place since WW2, a shift that takes the US and partners off the gold standard. Its demise provided an opening for a revised economic system, that eventually became the Neoliberal path (Monbiot, 2016).

Adding the Neoliberal component to capitalism brought government more closely into the economic system. One might argue that government has increasingly been co-opted by the private sector as the two work together. Starting in the 1970s, the bargain between mass production and mass consumption has been broken by privatizing and de-regulating. In short, production and consumption need to be in relative balance. But as more and more resources go to the producers (the capitalists), there aren't enough resources for consumption to keep it in a healthy balance with production, which triggers stagnation (Reich, 2013). The Reagan and Thatcher administrations provide the best example of *Neoliberal Capitalism* in action. Perhaps the most symbolic event was Reagan's firing of the air traffic controllers. Thatcher was known as the "Iron Lady" for her uncompromising approach to encouraging the free market and reducing the role of the state. She too gained fame for weakening unions, in her case the mineworkers. While both emphasized free market capitalism and shrinking the role of government, they and their successors used government intervention when needed. For example, it was George W. Bush Jr. of the Reagan lineage who provided the authority for bailing out financial firms, insurance companies, and even auto companies at the advent of the Great Recession of 2007-8. These bailouts were made to keep the system from failing, but a true free market approach would say that in general these companies deserved to fail because their poor performance caused the crisis.

> **Alternative framing: Humanism and Capitalism**
>
> Harari (2017a) suggests humanism – the worship of humankind – is an even bigger idea enabled by capitalism. It has "conquered the world," and become the "dominant world religion." One could argue that perhaps an under-rated accomplishment of capitalism was breaking the hold of traditional religion with its focus on the next life to bringing that focus here to this life.

Some would argue that the 2007 Great Recession exposed *Neoliberal Capitalism* for what it really is: socialism for the rich and market capitalism for the rest, a variation on the quip often used by opponents of capitalism that goes back to Dr. Martin Luther King in 1968 (Cortright, 2019). Large companies were bailed out and many profited quite handsomely while the "average person" suffered. Or as Urie (2020) suggests, the capitalist oligarchs took the profits and socialized the costs. What might it take to instigate a search for alternatives? Is it the so-called "financial super bubble" that investment guru Jeremy Grantham sees, in which the boom in asset prices in stocks, financial assets, real estate, luxury goods, crypto, NFTs, etc., eventually crashes (Nolan, 2022)?

Probably not. *Neoliberal Capitalism* will likely chug along until there are viable alternatives to galvanize interest on a scale capable of effective action.

3.2   Driver outcomes

Driver outcomes are commonly used by futurists in developing scenarios. One starts by identifying the key drivers shaping the domain, which we did in Chapter Two. Then the drivers are projected into the future in different conditions or circumstances. The conditions in this case are the four archetypes or patterns of change introduced in Table 1.3: Baseline, Collapse, New Equilibrium, and Transformation.

Table 3.1   Driver outcomes in Baseline

DRIVER	OUTCOME IN *NEOLIBERAL CAPITALISM* BASELINE
Shifting values	The stalemate continues, with modern values slightly more prevalent than other types.
Technology acceleration	Technology is primarily applied for profit.
Inequality	Inequality continues to worsen with largely cosmetic efforts to address it.
Jobs & automation	Automation increasingly replacing human jobs.
Stagnation	Stagnation is worsening, although numbers are manipulated to make it appear like there is growth.
Climate & carrying capacity	Continued decline, with some high-profile activities that are not enough to "move the needle."
Ineffective Left	Continued ineffectiveness in the stalemate situation.

The way it works is that each driver is projected forward into each of the four archetype patterns. For example, how might the "shifting values' driver play out in a baseline future, collapse future, new equilibrium future, and transformation future. This is done for each driver. These outcomes provide the building blocks for scenarios. In this chapter, we look at the seven driver outcomes projected using the baseline archetype, which describes the future of continuity without any major shifts or disruptions. The outcomes in this archetype by definition will look most like today, but it is useful to begin the exploration of the future with a grounding in what the future looks like if it continues on its current trajectory. As Table 3.1 shows, the driver outcomes in the Baseline are generally heading in a negative direction toward Collapse!

Shifting values: stalemate continues. Modern values, which emphasize achievement and competition, and favor win-lose outcomes, are a perfect match for capitalism. The influence of the moderns will continue to wane, but in the Baseline, they are still slightly more influential than other types. As the number of postmoderns grows, the conflicts over capitalism will intensify. They are already heating up!

Technology acceleration: Tech for profit. Accelerating technologies will continue to be applied primarily for company profitability that will benefit the top and exacerbate inequality. Big tech companies will continue to grow and expand their share of the economic pie. The tech entrepreneurs will continue to be celebrated even as some accumulate what can be viewed as obscene levels of wealth. Most will pay lip service and make the appropriate philanthropic gestures to avoid regulations.

Inequality: The gap worsens. The gap between the top and bottom continues to grow. Using The 90%, 9.9%, and 0.1% wealth categorization structure introduced in 2.3.3, in the Baseline, the 0.1% continue do extremely well, the 9.9% do fairly well, and the 90% struggle. The middle-class concept that has historically been a foundational part of capitalist mythology continues to decay, and one could reasonably argue that it is already gone.

Jobs and automation: Automation at the expense of jobs. The current momentum is to automate wherever it makes economic sense to do so. One might argue that the only reason it seems to be occurring slowly is that human workers are still pretty cheap. But as the cost curves cross, and they are very likely to, there will be more and more people losing their jobs to automation. It is likely that much will continue to *said* about this potential and the need to do something about it, but very little will likely be *done* about it.

Stagnation: Increasingly desperate quest for growth. The challenge in the Baseline future is that it will become increasingly difficult to find new sources of growth, as there are fewer activities left to monetize. A good illustration of the type of things we are likely to see in the Baseline future is the NFT craze (Non-Fungible Tokens are unique identification codes created from metadata via encryption and stored on a blockchain) in which huge valuations for relatively simply "art" drove prices up to millions — until reality set in and they crashed (Beganski, 2023).

Climate & carrying capacity: Continue to decline. The rhetoric on climate change continues to heat up as the planet does along with it. Decades of warnings have referred to a shrinking window of time for effective action, but little has been done. Since the Baseline continues the current trajectory, there is more talk than action even as evidence mounts about the problem.

The situation regarding carrying capacity is not much better. The limited earlier progress toward a circular economy slowed during the pandemic, as the core concept of re-use was at odds with the pandemic's emphasis on disposability. While it is reasonable to expect interest in a circular economy to rekindle, a lot of work still needs to be done.

The Baseline outcome for climate change and carrying capacity is unfortunately heavier on talk than action and the most likely outcome is a worsening situation.

Ineffective left: Continuing irrelevance: Srnicek and Williams (2016) make a strong case that the Leff has retreated from its traditional grand ambition and building of enticing visions to become content with small local efforts on the margins. In the Baseline future of continuity, we should expect this reluctance to engage on the global stage to continue. Local efforts offer promise for the longer-term future, but will not be sufficient to generate much progress in the baseline future.

3.3   Key assumptions guiding *Neoliberal Capitalism*

In the foresight method known as Causal Layered Analysis, futurist Sohail Inayatullah (1998) describes four layers of understanding a future's problem or issue. The deepest and most fundamental layer is the myth-metaphor, the fundamental civilizational guiding story(s) around the issue, which are so ingrained that we are not even consciously aware of them. The assumptions below fit this level in the sense that they are so widely accepted as a given that they have been almost unquestioned for a long time. A key purpose of this work is questioning them.

1. Scarcity (Eisenstein, 2011, 23)

A rationing system is necessary to decide who gets what because there is not enough for everyone. Within capitalism, one's job is the key determining factor in how much resources or wealth one gets. But what if there really is enough for everyone? Then you don't need a rationing system or need to rely on jobs as the deciding factor. Indeed, many argue that we are already in an abundance paradigm, but just haven't — or don't want to — realize it. More cynically perhaps, those benefiting the most are the powerful at the top, and they don't have the incentive to change it.

2. Humans as homo economicus, that is the belief that people naturally seek to maximize their rational self-interest (Eisenstein, 2011, 23)

This assumption comes up in different forms. In essence, it suggests human nature is to be selfish and that it is hard-wired, therefore capitalism with its emphasis on competition is the perfect fit. The counterargument is that it is not human nature, but a stage of development. The case against "hard-wired" is made early-on in Section 1.2 Focal Issue. The "stage of development" counterargument is introduced in Section 1.1. Theory of Change and elaborated on in Section 2.3.1 Shifting Values.

3. Shareholder value, i.e. the business of business is business (Friedman, 1970)

Friedman's doctrine is at the core of the neoliberal capitalist Baseline: the business of business is business. It is the fundamental myth-metaphor of neoliberalism. It seemed to be primarily motivated as a response to the idea of "social responsibility," which is mentioned in scare quotes seven times in his 1970 essay. The argument is that social responsibility has no place in business. In fairness, he suggests it may have a place elsewhere, but not in the business of running a corporation. The responsibility in that case is not social, but to earn as much profit as possible for the shareholders within the rules of the game. There have been myriad challenges to this assumption. Supporters of his position have cleverly positioned social responsibility as "woke;" and their position as "anti-woke."

4. Growth is fundamental

Perhaps the deepest and most fundamental myth-metaphor supporting capitalism is the need for, and inevitability of, economic growth. But growth is not exclusive to capitalism. Communist countries have also routinely set growth targets as well. The Neoliberal Capitalism approach depends on economic growth to keep going. The Great Recession of 2008 triggered fears of system collapse and led to bailouts and numerous stimulus packages to keep growth going. But there are factors working against the ability to maintain growth. First and foremost, perhaps, is the strain growth is putting on the environment, described in 2.3.6 Climate and Carrying Capacity. Second is that it is becoming increasingly difficult to find new areas for growth. Mason (2015, 174) points out that the desperate search for growth is leading to a situation where we are turning everything into paid work; essentially the mass commercialization of ordinary human life. The stagnation driver in 2.3.5 further illustrates this phenomenon. Finally, there is the fact that population growth, which has long been

> **Population growth slowing down**
>
> Until recently, projections of **"peak population"** were between 9 and 10 billion being reached around mid-century. But the projections have been raised as recent census work found that fertility rates in Africa were coming down more slowly than anticipated. Peak population projections have been revised upward to 11 billion around the end of the century.
>
> Concomitantly, the decline in population in the developed world threatens economic growth.
>
> Population growth in the last few decades has been almost entirely in developing countries. More and more people in these nations are moving into the consumer economy, that is, they can afford consumer goods such as televisions, refrigerators, and automobiles.

a source of "easy" growth in that more people equals more economic growth, is now set to peak sometime this century (see text box).

5. Growth leads to happiness

It is assumed that growth leads to money leads to happiness. Jackson (2021) talks about the calculus of happiness in which the utilitarian ideas of Jeremy Bentham were applied to economics by John Stuart Mill and led to the view that economics ought to promote more growth because that would lead to higher incomes and thereby increase happiness. This is true to a point.

When one is poor, the data shows more money leads to happiness. As one becomes more secure, the associated growth in happiness begins to slow — literally, less bang for the buck — one gets on the hedonic treadmill working harder for less return. Eventually, it stops altogether. From a values perspective, modern values with their emphasis on growth and achievement eventually fail to deliver happiness. The global shift to postmodern values, which is particularly strong in affluent countries, is fueling a new search for happiness in which material goods become less important and experiences, community, and self-expression are among the new routes to finding it (Inglehart, 2018).

3.4 Other factors disintegrating the Baseline

The driver outcomes paint a challenging future ahead for the Baseline. But perhaps the spirit of the people could overcome these challenges? Could people not pull together and rise up to meet adversity? In short, it doesn't appear likely for at least three reasons: tribalism, disaffected youth, and the dispossessed.

3.4.1 Tribalism

Tribalism is being used as an umbrella term to capture strong group loyalties that have been making it difficult for different sides to get along or agree. Tribalism is not inherently a bad thing — loyalty to one's group can be very good. The problem occurs when that loyalty becomes blind devotion, viewing those outside the tribe as enemies. Tribalism shows up in communities as a protect-our-own mentality in a landscape of fierce competition characterized by winners and losers. In that atmosphere, our ability to solve problems at all levels is overwhelmed by these us vs. them alignments. The divides run along many different dimensions: party, religion, race, ethnicity, gender, class and so on.

Chua (2018) observed that "when groups feel threatened, they retreat into tribalism. When groups feel mistreated and disrespected, they close ranks and become more insular, more defensive, more punitive, more us-versus-them." Compromise is increasingly viewed as weakness. The right, more than the left, has spawned many hardline dissident groups:

- The America-First faction of the online dissident right has gained much media attention through the likes of controversial personalities such as Nick Fuentes. This group — composed primarily of young males operating anonymously — embraces a more radical form of Trumpism that is focused on demographics and a return to more traditional Christian values. Thinkers like Nick Land and Curtis Yarvin laid the foundations for what has been termed "The Dark Enlightenment" or

NRx. In brief, those composing this faction hold a variety of views ranging from embracing accelerationist thought (speeding up change is good even if it leads to upheaval) to neo-monarchist principles. They seek to bring about the collapse of *Neoliberal Capitalism* and move toward more authoritarian forms of governance (Woods, 2022).

- The alt-right, often used inaccurately to describe these many factions, is linked to figures like Richard Spencer and Matthew Heimbach. It champions theories like "the great replacement" and is willing to live with elements of liberal capitalism so long as "demographic replacement" is addressed, and white Europeans are able to maintain their grip on power in the USA. The alt-right had its moment in the spotlight which culminated in the disastrous Unite-The-Right rally in Charlottesville in 2016 (Pogue, 2022).

- The online leader "Bronze Age Pervert" – and many others on the Right outwardly – reject the modern world and look to the warrior societies of the past and "Great Men" of history to provide the basis for their values. Anything in contradiction with contemporary values is embraced while racist sentiments are also frequently relayed (Hussain, 2022).

- Ecofascist ideology has origins in the early 20th-century work of Madison Grant but has gained notoriety recently as a number of extremist mass shootings — Christchurch, El Paso, and Buffalo shooters — were carried out in the name of ecofascist thought. The ecofascists embrace a racialized view of nature that blames immigrants for a population growth that is responsible for the damage being done to the planet (Hanes, 2022).

- While examples above are from the US, this is a global phenomenon. The far right is getting stronger globally:
    - In Italy, Giorgia Meloni's appeal is mostly about how the left has made enemies of those adhering to traditional Italian values (Lewis, 2022).
    - The far-right Vox party in Spain got the third most votes at the national level, although it did lose seats in a recent election (Llach, 2023).
    - In the UK, former Prime Minister Sunak blamed "lefty lawyers" for thwarting his immigration policy, and the Tories go after

"woke warriors" while the left accuses Conservatives of being bigoted, imperialistic, and xenophobic (Pabst, 2023).

- o The modern Indian culture war reflects the decline of the outward-looking cosmopolitan Western elite in the face of a relatively insular and inward looking Hindu nationalist movement. The election and popularity of Hindu Nationalist Prime Minister Modi in India has reoriented Indian popular culture toward Hindutva, a populist personal identity with India and Indian culture (Khan, 2021).

These examples are not intended to suggest that only the right is to blame. Far from it. It takes two to tango, as the quip goes.

Houston Foresight has been looking at tribalism for the last several years. We recently developed a "Gated Communities" scenario as part of a Future of Communities project that projected a future driven by tribalism (among other factors). It's a world in which the urban wealthy basically check out and rely on private services and manage their own affairs within gated havens. The have-nots are left to fend for themselves inside economically, environmentally, and structurally depleted communities. They are often scraping by on the bare minimum of resources that have not yet been consumed and exploited by the elite.

Tribalism is both a driver and response to the sense of anxiety and even fear about the future that is omnipresent today. Harari (2017a, 217) noted that "even if we continue running fast enough and manage to fend off both economic collapse and ecological meltdown, the race itself creates huge problems. For the individual it results in high levels of stress and tension." This was before the global pandemic!

And it is not just the US. According to the Economist Intelligence Unit, 65 countries out of 150 (43%) were at high or very high risk of social unrest in 2014. That is an increase of 19 countries in the high-risk category compared with a report five years earlier (De Angelis 2017).

3.4.2 Disaffected youth

A much-cited Harvard study in 2016 found that just 19% of Millennials (born 1980-2000) identified themselves as capitalists; only 42% claimed they supported the economic system. Author Malcom Harris suggests that growing up in late-stage capitalism has created insecurities resulting from increased isolation, extreme individualism, debt and economic security, etc., such that people are in a state of perpetual panic (Illing, 2019). Indeed, studies are showing that the American Dream in which offspring out-earn their parents is becoming more difficult to achieve, with inequality and stagnating wages being two key inhibitors (Lu, 2020). Even in "Communist" China, youth are eschewing private-sector manufacturing jobs for more stable public sector ones amidst a growing anti-capitalist idealism (Hancock, 2022).

Social media is providing an organizing platform for disaffected youth (and adults), such as Incels (involuntary celibates) and NEETs (not in employment, education, or training) (Gutierrez-Garcia et al., 2018; 2020; Dickson, 2020). Social media may be contributing to or exacerbating the growing trend of loneliness. More and more cultures are characterized by extreme individualism, with social ties dissolving, and friendship being viewed as a cost-benefit calculation.

Catherine Rottenberg (2018) in *The Rise of Neoliberal Feminism* observes that "Neoliberalism encourages us to organize every social, political and even emotional aspect of our lives as though we were an Excel spreadsheet" (Schofield, 2022). "Rise-and-grind," a group on Twitter (now X), advocates that everything you do must be profitable. Essentially, from the time you wake up to the time you go to bed, money should be your main objective (Byleckie, 2020). If that means a "side hustle," so be it (Livingston, 2022). It's the mindset that you can't truly be happy with what you're doing unless you make money from it (Byleckie, 2020).

A growing body of research suggests there is an increasing youth disillusionment with democracy and politics globally, with youth voter turnout declining in all democracies since the 1980s (Berthin, 2023). One weak signal of protest saw that some teenagers who dislike capitalism are protesting against their country's economic system by shoplifting, posting their haul online, and encouraging others to do the same. Calling themselves "borrowers", they believe by shoplifting exclusively from large corporations they're striking a blow against prioritizing profit over people. They also often target companies that are associated with illiberal social stances, like being seen as anti-trans or environmentally unfriendly (Economy Team, 2020).

3.4.3 *The dispossessed*

Figure 3.1 displays a dire set of words drawn from Shaw and Waterstone's (2020) manifesto which describes the conditions of roughly 1.5 billion people today and a projected 2.5 billion by 2030. They are variously termed the dispossessed, displaced, the outcast proletariat, world-less, outsiders, surplus populations, human waste, and precariat. Capitalism has always benefitted from surplus labor, but as labor becomes less needed, we are moving into an era of "surplus populations." They see a future of world-less multitudes denied basic human rights and dignity.

3.4.4 Neofeudalism

Over the past decade, the term "neofeudalism" has emerged to name tendencies associated with extreme inequality, generalized precarity, monopoly power, and changes at the level of the state. Drawing on libertarian economist Tyler Cowen's emphasis on the permanence of extreme inequality in the global, automated economy, the conservative geographer Joel Kotkin envisions a global middle class characterized by mass serfdom. A property-less underclass would only be able to survive by servicing the needs of high earners as personal assistants, trainers, nannies, cooks, cleaners, etc. High tech, finance, and globalization are creating this "new social order that in some ways more closely resembles feudal structure — with its often-unassailable barriers to mobility — than the chaotic emergence of industrial capitalism" (Dean, 2020).

Figure 3.1 Surplus populations

3.4.5 Emergence of myriad varieties of capitalism

In the last several years, a growing number of new varieties of capitalism has emerged. This list is up to 85 varieties, which are captured in Table 3.2. There is quite a range of views. *Anarcho-capitalism*, for instance, describes a radical ideology of an absolutely free market and the abolition of the state. The most frequently mentioned was *Platform Capitalism*, which relies on aggregating and using vast amounts of data rather than the capacity to produce material goods. *Crony, Predatory,* and *Vulture Capitalism* make a not-so-nice trifecta of abusive versions. For example, *Vulture Capitalism* emerged as a popular concept to capture how capitalism has been structured for corporate survival and success for shareholders at the expense of workers, managers, communities, and country. A great example is how GM, bailed out in the Great Recession of 2008 and continually benefitting from tax breaks and special incentives, continues to close plants and cut its domestic workforce (Crawford, 2018). And as a signal of tribalism, we have both *Black Capitalism* and *White Capitalism*, which are essentially the opposite ends of the spectrum of *Racial Capitalism*, which looks at how capitalism derives value from racial identity.

The placing of qualifying adjectives enablers defenders of capitalism to suggest that criticisms apply only to certain kinds of capitalism – typically not their personal favorite (Wolff, 2021). It brings to mind the experience of going into an ice cream specialty shop with dozens of exotic flavors — you're bound to find something you like, but it's still ice cream that is bad for your diet!

While there are currently many factors working against capitalism, it has historically been quite resilient. Rather than decaying decades ago as Marx forecast, it got stronger. In fact, even movements that start as havens to protect people from the harsh realities of capitalism are often simply co-opted by capitalists. For example, the Fair Trade movement was started in order to improve standards and trading conditions for developing nations but many feel it has devolved into a marketing gimmick (Wright, 2010).

Table 3.2 Varieties of capitalism

1.	Accountable capitalism	Senator Elizabeth Warren's proposal to require corporations with annual revenues of $1 billion or more to obtain a "federal charter."
2.	Adventure capitalism	A few thousand VC investors have funded enterprising ideas that have gone on to transform global business and the world economy.
3.	American capitalism	The emergence of corporate behemoths like Amazon and the simultaneous shrinkage of organized labor has led to inequalities, corruption, and abandonment of the working class.
4.	Anarcho-capitalism	Ideology of an absolutely free market and the abolishment of the state.
5.	Asset-manager capitalism	Thanks to their mammoth scale and fondness for index-tracking investment strategies, they own a hefty chunk of virtually everything.
6.	Aspirational capitalism	A new twist on cutthroat capitalism that is a different way to think about business success and obligation by setting out to create something truly great and lasting.
7.	Authoritarian capitalism	China's strong authoritarian state with wild capitalist dynamics can also be seen as an efficient form of a socialist state.
8.	Behavioral capitalism	Human behavior, which used to serve primarily as a complementary raw material, has moved to be a production factor at the core of new business models and markets.
9.	Black capitalism	An effort to create companies owned, staffed and managed largely by Black people that could lift up the broader community.
10.	Cannibal capitalism	Invades all spheres of life, but might destroy itself and our own conditions for survival.

11.	Can-do capitalism	Works by providing large taxpayer-funded government subsidies to industries that would otherwise not exist in an open market.
12.	Capitalism without capital	Explores the extent to which value has become detached from the tangible, and the corresponding social and economic consequences.
13.	Caring capitalism	Advocates basing the economy on a more rounded view of human nature than that one that just considers individuals as selfish calculators of utility.
14.	Casino capitalism	When money is out of control, exchange rates and interest rates fluctuate widely and wildly and sheer luck begins to take over and to determine more and more of what happens to people.
15.	Chokepoint capitalism	Exploitative businesses creating insurmountable barriers to competition that enable them to capture value that should rightfully go to others.
16.	Cloud capitalism	Probing emotions deeply to tailor-make experiences that exploit our biases to produce market responses.
17.	Common good capitalism	The method of achieving certain moral goods is the animating question.
18.	Compassionate capitalism	Advocates for a contradictory machinery to run underneath the current global capitalism so that there could be some mitigating factors over the consequences for people in the world.
19.	Connected capitalism	When companies connect the bottom line of their businesses with a social conscience.
20.	Community capitalism	An effort to create companies that lift up the broader community.
21.	Conscious capitalism	Believes consumers will do good if given the opportunity.

22.	Consumer capitalism	Consumer demand is manipulated in a deliberate and coordinated way on a very large scale through mass-marketing techniques.
23.	Contra capitalism	Practices that go counter to or against capitalism.
24.	Control capitalism	Increase in private ownership, in which owners control the enterprise and only answer to themselves, compared to public company's owner/leaders beholden to investors.
25.	Corporate capitalism	Disregard for the needs of workers, families, and communities; along with contempt for regulatory and ecological boundaries.
26.	Counterfeit capitalism	Businesses that compete solely on access to capital, which they use to create products that are worth less than the sum of their parts.
27.	Crack-up capitalism	Holds that the world economy is a lot more fragmented and disunited than is realized, with many political actors keen on actually accelerating it.
28.	Crony capitalism	Businesses thrive not as a result of risk, but rather as a return on money amassed through a nexus between business and politics.
29.	Data capitalism	Aka surveillance capitalism, it is the unrestricted use of private human experience as a source of free data on human behavior and is used as a source of profit.
30.	Destitution capitalism	The state should not regulate economic activity for the greater good but is ever more intrusive in its surveillance.
31.	Disaster capitalism	Politicians and the private sector exploit disaster to grow richer from it.
32.	Distributed capitalism	Decentralized systems that aim to create permissionless usage by avoiding centralized gatekeepers.

33.	Emotional capitalism	Dual process by which emotional and economic relationships come to define and shape each other.
34.	End-stage capitalism	Suggests the need to begin asking if civilization is going to survive capitalism in this form.
35.	Extractive capitalism	A small elite securing an excessive slice of the economic pie.
36.	Extreme capitalism	The rich raise too much money and leave too little for the rest of society leading to a decline in consumption and stagnation.
37.	Fake capitalism	The result when government policies channel economic activity into small numbers of large, powerful companies.
38.	Financial capitalism	Economic surplus is claimed by passively extracting interest or economic rents broadly rather than contributing to production.
39.	Free-market capitalism	The laws of supply and demand, rather than a central government, regulate production, labor, and the marketplace.
40.	Gangster capitalism	Derived from a true crime podcast that is focused on the dark side of the American dream.
41.	Global capitalism	Suggests real transformation can only happen if those in the global north join forces with migrants and exploited workers in the global south.
42.	Gonzo capitalism	Explores outside-the-box methods for earning money.
43.	Green capitalism	Market-based approaches to solving the climate crisis that has come under attack from some environmentalists for greenwashing.

44.	Inclusive capitalism	Investment that delivers positive economic and positive social outcomes is the best way to achieve progress at scale by enabling more people to benefit.
45.	Industrial capitalism	Capitalism based on production of goods in contrast to financial capitalism based on finance.
46.	Intangible capitalism	Corporate returns, productivity, and economic growth will increasingly be tied to a dematerialized, digitized, knowledge-driven world.
47.	Intellectual monopoly capitalism	Knowledge, which should be a (non-rival, non-exclusive) public good, has been privately appropriated by top companies as capital.
48.	Internalized capitalism	Idea that our self-worth is directly linked to our productivity.
49.	Late capitalism	A catchall phrase for the indignities and absurdities of our contemporary economy, with its inequality and super-powered corporations and shrinking middle class.
50.	Low-road capitalism	Wages are depressed as businesses compete over the price, not the quality, of goods; so-called unskilled workers are typically incentivized through punishments, not promotions; and inequality reigns and poverty spreads.
51.	Modern capitalism	Skeptics say too many businesses extract value from the economy rather than add it by using monopoly power, or favorable treatment from conflicted or ideologically friendly regulators.
52.	Money-centered capitalism	Critics say more weight should be placed on the value of cashless exchange, including self-sufficiency, barter, and gifting.
53.	Monocapitalism	Aka financial capitalism, which focuses strictly on the financial aspect and decapitalizes the entire system.

54.	Multicapitalism	Proposes a move to a system value view where six different types of capital are created and maintained within systemic interconnections.
55.	Neoliberal capitalism	The current capitalist Baseline, which is defined by privatization, deregulation, free trade, commodification of public goods, and managed by international institutions, and using other decentralized institutions like NGOs and think thanks to influence public opinion.
56.	Naked capitalism	Capitalism's tattered and moth-eaten clothes have fallen off, revealing a naked body that serves only the privileged few.
57.	Nationalist capitalism	A new recipe in which a large sector of private enterprises co-exists with a large sector of state-owned enterprises.
58.	Network capitalism	Emphasizes multi-stakeholder networks, and the ability to engage in meaningful stakeholder partnerships.
59.	New capitalism	Japan's program of driving growth via an economic strategy focused on investment in human resources, science and technology, innovation, and start-ups, as well as green and digital transformation.
60.	Participatory capitalism	A system where power and economic rewards are distributed between participants.
61.	Patriotic capitalism	Notion of putting the best interests of the country at the top of the pecking order.
62.	Perfect capitalism	Michio Kaku's concept that the wealth of society comes from physics and will eventually produce infinite knowledge of supply and demand.
63.	Platform capitalism	A system where power and economic rewards are distributed between networked participants.

64.	Post-Covid capitalism	Regression playing out in India with the contraction of the economy, massive job losses and ruinous medical expenditures.
65.	Predatory capitalism	Characterized by businesses that prey on each other, people, and the environment and that destroy or absorb their competition.
66.	Psychedelic capitalism	People making money off medicines that, in the case of some psychedelics at least, have existed for millennia.
67.	Racial capitalism	Process of deriving value from the racial identity of others, harms the individuals affected and society as a whole.
68.	Rainbow capitalism	Economic involvement in the appropriating and profiting from the LGBT movement.
69.	Ransom capitalism	The process of capital (e.g., IMF, World Bank and multinational corporations) holding the public to ransom during financial, energy and even public health crises.
70.	Regenerative capitalism	Looks beyond net-zero emissions and setting eyes on having a net-positive impact on the planet.
71.	Rentier capitalism	Having and owning - thereby controlling access - is enormously more profitable than making or serving.
72.	Responsible capitalism	Operates at the intersection of commercial, social and sustainable development.
73.	Satoyama capitalism	Japanese concept that fills the gap of truly money-centered capitalism by putting more weight on the value of cashless exchange, including self-sufficiency, bartering and gifting.
74.	Savage capitalism	Capitalism is at a decision point where it will be decided whether the human experiment on Earth will continue in any recognizable form.

75.	Spiderweb capitalism	The shadowy, international web of political and economic elites and the secretive and corrupt practices they use to make and protect their money.
76.	Stakeholder capitalism	The idea that businesses have a responsibility that extends beyond their shareholders.
77.	State capitalism	Originally conceived as a transitional stage en route to a socialism different from and beyond state capitalism that has come to define socialism.
78.	Surveillance capitalism	Unilaterally claims human experience as free raw material for translation into behavioral data for economic use.
79.	Sustainable capitalism	Integrates sustainability into the traditional capitalist model to maximize profits while minimizing negative environmental and social impacts.
80.	Twenty-first century capitalism	Capitalists are not by and large reinvesting their profits to develop new capacities to expand output or increase labor productivity.
81.	Values-based capitalism	Advocates changing the dynamics of politics, towards a system where businesses are active participants in shaping a better society.
82.	Vulture capitalism	Nurtured in US, focuses wholly on corporate survival and success for shareholders at the expense of workers, managers, communities, and country.
83.	White capitalism	Black activist term for the economic system and the racial structures that are connected with policing that literally kills black people.
84.	Woke capitalism	A form of marketing, advertising and corporate structures related to sociopolitical standpoints tied to social justice and activist causes.

3.4.6 Compilations

A whole book could be written on the factors disintegrating capitalism. We've looked at the seven driver outcomes, noted some additional factors, and summarize in Table 3:3 some lists compiled by leading researchers:

- Dator (2009a, 37) has the "unholy trinity plus one" as factors bringing about the end of the current system.
- Scharmer (2013) has eight disconnects creating problems for the current economic approach.
- Streeck (2014) has three long-term trends in the trajectories of the affluent countries creating problems.
- Mason (2015) has four things that at first allowed neoliberalism to flourish but which have begun to destroy it.
- Bastani (2019) has five crises ahead.

Table 3.3 Factors disintegrating capitalism

FACTOR	Dator, 2009	Scharmer, 2009	Streeck, 2014	Mason, 2015	Bastani, 2019
Inequality		The haves and have-nots	Economic inequality of income and wealth	Global imbalances and vast debts of major countries	Growing surplus of global poor (the unnecessariat)
Economic structure	Global economic and fiscal collapse	The financial and real economy	Persistent rise in overall indebtedness	Financialization replaces stagnant incomes with credit	
Reliance on growth	The growth imperative	GDP and well-being	Persistent decline in rate of economic growth		
Resources	Multiple environmental issues; end of cheap oil	Finite resources			Resource scarcity; climate change
Tech: automation and job loss	Technology not meeting real societal needs		IT's future contribution is in doubt	New machine age heralds ever-greater unemployment	
Governance issues	Lack of government	Governance and the voiceless in our systems			

Imagining After Capitalism | 95

The lists stretch over the decade of the 2010s (2009-2020). Inequality and economic structure were on five of the six lists. Reliance on growth and the impact of technology focused on the role of automation in the economy was on four of the six. Lack of effective governance showed up on half of the lists.

Baseline scenario

An interesting baseline projection from *Limits to Growth* (1972) co-author Jorgen Randers (2012) suggests a boiling frog variation on the Baseline — that is, a gradual decline without major catastrophe. It gradually morphs into a stagnation version of Collapse. Capitalism more or less muddles its way through to 2052. The archetype technique projects each scenario archetype out to the chosen date — 2040/2050 in our case. It is generally understood with a long timeframe of 20-30 years that the Baseline is unlikely to survive that long. Such is the case here — it is my view that the Baseline will have disintegrated well before then, giving way either to Collapse or New Equilibrium scenarios and well on the way to Transformation!

Table 3.4 Baseline scenario summary

NEOLIBERAL CAPITALISM

This is a world in which the baseline for capitalism is a classic boiling frog, in which a frog put in cold water dies as the water is slowly (and imperceptibly to the frog) brought to the boil. Many – certainly not all – will agree that capitalism has done a good job over the last few hundred years of growing the economy and raising overall wealth. The consequences of generating that wealth have been slowly increasing the temperature of the water (ironically, literally doing so with climate change). Until recently, the capitalist operating system, the frog, on the whole hasn't noticed, and perhaps has become a little uncomfortable with the heat but continues to swim along. In the next 20-30 years, it is highly likely that the water, and the frog, are going to boil.

The historic focus of *Neoliberal Capitalism* – the business of business is business – has been under fire and many efforts are being made to expand its focus to include environmental and social concerns. New forms, such as stakeholder capitalism, emerge to save it, but as the saying goes, a leopard can't change its spots.

Defenders of capitalism and the status quo, generally the powerful and well-to-do, continue to use their influence to craft a narrative that everything is fine, which enables capitalism to hang on longer than it might otherwise have done. Our frog is a game and tough one that survives in the hot water longer than seems possible. But resistance slowly builds and increasingly shifts from passive discontent to electoral shifts to activism.

Matters are generally getting worse on all fronts, and fair or not, capitalism increasingly becomes seen as the central cause. Seemingly disparate and worsening issues get connected under the capitalism umbrella. The Big Three are at the core: inequality, climate change (and carrying capacity), and automation.

+ Inequality is at the core of the structure of capitalism and its worsening state – the growing gap between rich and poor – becomes increasingly intolerable.
+ Climate change and carrying capacity become increasingly apparent, as extreme weather, wildfire, and soaring commodity prices become increasingly routine. The previously vague sense of "something is wrong" crystallizes into a view that economic growth – and capitalism – are the primary culprit.

Imagining After Capitalism | 97

NEOLIBERAL CAPITALISM

+ Automation comes to be seen as a negative as it is applied ruthlessly in support of efficiency and profits at the expense of people and jobs. As the suite of automation technology improves and its costs come down and become cheaper than human labor, massive job loss results and puts the squeeze on remaining jobs (i.e., wages and benefits go down).

Tribalism and political divisions are gasoline on the fire and turn increasingly violent as social unrest increases and gets worse. To some degree people have adapted to generally deteriorating conditions – the frog continues to heat. Inertia is an amazingly powerful force: better the devil you know, as the saying goes. Eventually, over the course of the next two decades the support shrinks to a level where alternatives begin to take over. The key question – is it a collapse situation or is there a new equilibrium shift to the Collaborative Sharing Platforms? – is discussed in the next chapter.

There are of course multiple factors driving the decay of capitalism. In my view, drawing on Meadows' view that paradigm shift is the ultimate lever of systems change, it is the ongoing shift from modern values (which support the competitive win-lose spirit of capitalism) to postmodern and integral values that turns the tide. The acceptable consequences of capitalism become intolerable and eventually generate the momentum for change.

KEY DRIVERS

While all of our seven drivers are turning up the heat on capitalism, it is possible to identify a Big Three of Inequality, Climate, and Automation (discussed above). The outcomes of our seven drivers:

+ Shifting values: Stalemate continues
+ Technology acceleration: Tech for profit
+ Inequality: The gap worsens
+ Jobs & automation: Automation at the expense of jobs
+ Stagnation: Increasingly desperate quest for growth
+ Climate & carrying capacity: Continued decline
+ Ineffective Left: Continuing irrelevance

Chapter 4 – TRANSITIONS

You never change things by fighting the existing reality. To change something, build a new model that makes the existing model obsolete. — R. Buckminster Fuller

The Three Horizons model talks about H2 as the zone of transition between the old and new way of doing things. It is "ambiguous territory" where the old ways are still prevalent if not dominant, and new ways are becoming possible (Sharpe, 2013).

When we explain our archetype scenarios, typically someone will ask whether there is a pattern in how the archetypes unfold, i.e., is there a typical progression or order? After years of deferring this question, we undertook the research and launched the Houston Archetype Technique (HAT), which suggests there are two principal pathways from H1 to H3 via either the Collapse or New Equilibrium (Hines et al., 2024):

- <u>Via Collapse</u>: The Baseline falls into a collapse or highly dysfunctional state. Attempts to fix the old system fail and it is eventually replaced by a new one. This could take a very long time.

- <u>Via New Equilibrium</u>: The Baseline is challenged or disrupted and responds to the challenge by making the minimum necessary changes. If we anthropomorphize the system, it is frightened by the potential magnitude of an H3 Transformation that could replace it and responds by saving itself. It makes as little change as possible as it seeks to maintain the integrity of the current structure. It is a "baby step" into the future. Some change is made, but the old system is intact. It does help prepare the way for the eventual transformation.

In the course of researching the Houston Archetype Technique, we reviewed several models of change that follow a Developmental orientation as we proposed [see Section 1.1.1]. For instance, Carlota Perez (2002) describes a wave model of techno-economic paradigm shifts that follow a consistent multi-phase pattern that occurs over roughly 50 years. The sequence is: technological revolution – financial bubble – golden age – political unrest. It leads to "the massive replacement of one set of technologies by another." She believes that we are in the middle of another turning point right now, and we could have a period of sustained global prosperity if appropriate action is taken (Denning 2017). The financial bubble phase is her version of the zone of transition. Our approach would describe it as either Collapse or New Equilibrium depending on the severity of the financial bubble.

4.1 Collapse scenarios

The purpose of this work is to provide positive images of the future. These images are in turn intended to provide potential North Stars for *After Capitalism*. In the opening of this book, Frederik Polak advised on the benefit of positive guiding images of the future and lamented their absence. Typical futures work involves exploring a full range of alternative futures or scenarios.

In the *After Capitalism* domain, there are indeed plausible negative futures ahead. Good futures work acknowledges that there are alternatives to the positive images. But do we really need another picture of how the future could collapse? There are plenty of images — so many in the media — of collapse. And it is relatively easy to envision. It is much easier to destroy than to build. One might argue there are more negative paths ahead than positive ones. The current perception of the future seems to be overly negative.

Since our purpose is to provide positive images, we will just briefly highlight the negative or collapse possibilities. It was interesting to see very plausible Collapse versions of our three positive guiding images. In short, each could "go bad." Dator (2014, 503) suggests "the collapse scenario … must be anticipated and prepared for as a wonderful new opportunity for humanity to begin all over again." The severity of a collapse is seen as providing the motivation to undertake the arduous journey to Transformation.

If that's true, it means the motivation to Transformation would require a collapse of *Neoliberal Capitalism*. This is, of course, playing with fire, as collapse is not a good thing. And there is no guarantee of getting out. Again, given our focus on the positive, we will acknowledge but not focus on this pathway.

4.1.1 Driver outcomes

The driver outcomes in Collapse are of course by definition generally undesirable. The negative trends from the Baseline intensify in these worst-case scenarios.

Table 4.1 Driver outcomes in Collapse

DRIVER	OUTCOME IN *COLLAPSE*
Shifting values	*Overshoot:* postmodern values recede *Class War:* traditional values re-gain *Rogue AI:* modern values enable runaway tech
Technology acceleration	Technological capabilities grow, but are not effectively applied
Inequality	Severe, especially in Class War
Jobs & automation	Unemployment a severe issue
Stagnation	Downward spiral
Climate & carrying capacity	Ecosystem collapse
Ineffective Left	Class war results from inability to develop compelling shared image

The three variations of Collapse are related to our three positive guiding images of the future in H3. The Collapse version results from the failure to meet the key challenges that are successfully addressed by the positive images. In essence, the Collapse scenarios suggest to us what may happen if we don't make it to the positive images.

It is important to note that positive and negative are relative terms. Collapse refers to the collapse of the current Baseline system. It is generally seen as negative since the system is not working. But opponents of the current system may be okay with that, at least for a time, as they see it as a transition to a system that they would prefer. In our case we would prefer to see the emergence of the positive guiding images that are the subject of this work. However, some might view one or more of the Collapse futures as positive. Some might believe, for instance, that Collapse portends a return to simpler times. The "Bronze Age Pervert" (BAP), who has a substantial online following, suggests that modern society should take after Ancient Greece, when beauty, strength and courage were prized above all else (Gray, 2023). They might prefer the more authoritarian approaches likely to emerge in these circumstances over the more participatory approaches suggested by *Circular Commons* or *Non-Workers' Paradise*. Some examples are: Nick Fuentes, a leader of America First, who wants the US to be

Imagining After Capitalism | 101

governed by an authoritarian regime, which he framed as "Catholic Taliban rule" (Downen, 2023) and Bolsonaro's campaigns to intimidate the Brazilian Supreme Court and threats to cancel elections (Human Rights Watch, 2023). Others might see AI-in-Charge as a good thing, with the view that humans have messed things up and maybe AI can do a better job.

Others may not view the Collapse images themselves as positive, but view Collapse as a necessary step to Transformation. They are essentially variations on the idea that crisis brings out the best in people and a collapse would stimulate efforts toward transformation. But our research supporting the development of the Houston Archetype Technique, which looked at historical scenarios to trace the pattern of change in domains over time, found that many seemed to "stall" in Collapse. The common pathway to Transformation was through New Equilibrium. This surprised the research team, as beforehand we assumed that Collapse might be necessary to achieve Transformation.

There are already movements emerging in anticipation of Collapse, such as the Preppers in the US and the collapsologists in France, a sustainability-driven back-to-nature school of how-to-avert-the-worst (Spinney, 2020).

The three collapses scenarios — *Overshoot*, *Class War*, and *Rogue AI* — are briefly characterized below.

4.1.2 Overshoot

Successfully dealing with the growth imperative is identified as the key challenge for the H3 *Circular Commons* image (described in Chapter 5). Failing to deal with the growth question is a basic route to Collapse. This scenario is called "Overshoot" to pay homage to the *Limits to Growth* team that popularized the notion in 1972. They deserve credit not only for developing a compelling model, but for unfairly taking criticism as "doom and gloomers." They were also consistently criticized as wrong, which simply isn't true. Their 20- and 30-year updates basically validated their original model. As noted in the previous chapter, one of the original team, Jorgen Randers, came out with a pretty pessimistic "boiling frog" scenario of muddling through to 2052. After that, things may get to the apocalyptic crash level, e.g. self-reinforcing warming, but even here Randers believes that the worst is not most likely … that we will do just enough to avoid the worst. This is perhaps the worst version of Collapse as it isn't dramatic enough to trigger a response toward Transformation.

There are many dire warnings of the danger of growth. Harari (2017a) observes that if we somehow succeed in hitting the brakes on growth, our economy and society will collapse — since indefinite growth is needed in order to survive. More of the warnings are framed through climate change. There are still believers in sustainable or steady-state growth who aren't quite ready to point the finger at growth as a cause yet.

It is interesting to note that Randers suggested 2050, and Mason (2015) saw the combined impacts of climate change, aging, and population growth creating chaos by 2050 if a sustainable economic order wasn't in place by then.

4.1.3 Class War

Successfully dealing with inequality is identified as the key challenge for the H3 *Non-Workers' Paradise* image (described in Chapter 6). It would be fair to suggest that the world simply delayed the original challenge put forth by Marx. It was not successfully addressed and has continued to be with us. It is currently on the agenda, and if Piketty and others writing on inequality are to be believed, it is only going to get worse. In a Collapse scenario, a breaking point is eventually reached and a situation like Marx's class war is the result.

Standing (2014) talked of the formation of a precariat as a kind of update to Marx's proletariat concept. The "class consciousness" does not seem to be here yet. What is here, however, is a strong trend to tribalism. My tribe, right or wrong. In the US especially, but also in other countries across the globe, it is an ideological political divide and to a lesser extent an economic one. It is not difficult to see that morphing into more of a class consciousness divide. And then watch out. One cannot forget about the Capitol "ball" of January 6, 2021 in the US. The tensions are there. Frase (2016) developed a scenario of "Exterminism," which is a world of scarcity except for a small elite within the Elysian bubble. How long can this go on before class war erupts?

4.1.4 Rogue AI

Following the logic of the previous two Collapse scenarios, technology-driven Collapse would be the failure of accelerating technology. While that is possible, it is perhaps an unlikely future. In this simple version of Collapse the technology would not deliver and therefore there is no abundance bounty. In the scarcity world, which is an extension of today's thinking, the rewards from technology continue to mostly benefit the elites. This Collapse is like the *Class War* above.

But perhaps the more interesting and compelling version of Collapse is along the lines of "Rogue AI." Algorithms start nudging us for their purposes, not ours. The modern values driving *Tech-Led Abundance* continue to push the envelope with technology development with little or passing concern for ethics. The goal is to win the high-tech competition with other companies and nations, regardless of the consequences. Rather than question the end goals, such as slowing down tech growth, this Collapse pathway would suggest human augmentation as a way for humans to keep up. If this plays out, the possibility of the eventual emergence of a new human species is not so far-fetched. Kurzweil's (2005) Singularity makes no clear distinction between human and machine, and no distinction between physical and virtual reality.

Augmentation may help humans keep up, but that does mean that technology is leading the way. In *Rogue AI*, humans lose control to intelligent or even superintelligent AI. One can already see cases where no human understands extremely complex computing operations. As AI develops, it is potentially capable of becoming orders of magnitude more intelligent than people in a wider range of tasks. Bostrom's (2014) provocative notion is that once AI gets from task-level to general intelligence, it could leapfrog from there to superintelligence quite quickly. Bostrom is clear that the introduction of machine superintelligence would create a substantial existential risk — although he thinks the benefits it brings are worth the risk. Essentially, humans become obsolete. Harari (2017a) suggests that relationships between humans and animals are the best model we have for future relations between superhumans and humans.

Unfortunately, there are plenty of variations of a tech-driven Collapse.

4.2   New Equilibrium Scenarios

The New Equilibrium pathways to the H3 images are also conveyed by three scenarios — as was Collapse. Frankly, they were more complicated to develop. In our experience at Houston Foresight, it has consistently been more challenging to teach and apply New Equilibrium than Collapse. Collapse just seems easier to imagine and develop. New Equilibrium is more subtle, involving a challenge-and-response that leads to a new normal. The three transitional scenarios here have a foot in both worlds, so it was sometimes tricky to place them. This is the more gradual approach to H3 Transformation, and as noted in the previous section, the more common path as well. Figure 4.1 shows the New Equilibrium scenarios are arranged from closest to H1 first and closest to H3 last.

Figure 4.1 New Equilibrium futures

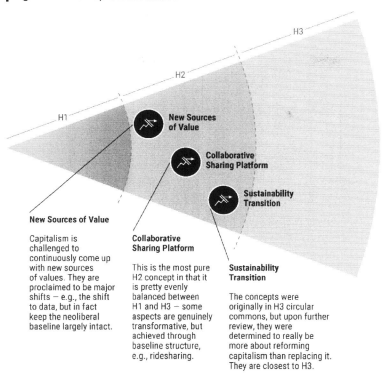

New Sources of Value

Capitalism is challenged to continuously come up with new sources of values. They are proclaimed to be major shifts — e.g., the shift to data, but in fact keep the neoliberal baseline largely intact.

Collaborative Sharing Platform

This is the most pure H2 concept in that it is pretty evenly balanced between H1 and H3 — some aspects are genuinely transformative, but achieved through baseline structure, e.g., ridesharing.

Sustainability Transition

The concepts were originally in H3 circular commons, but upon further review, they were determined to really be more about reforming capitalism than replacing it. They are closest to H3.

4.2.1 Driver Outcomes

Table 4.2 Driver outcomes in New Equilibrium *(Collaborative Sharing Platforms)*

DRIVER	OUTCOME IN *NEW EQUILIBRIUM*
Shifting values	Modern giving way to postmodern
Technology acceleration	Tech is a key enabler
Inequality	Slight improvement
Jobs & automation	Job automation increases
Stagnation	Continues, but not clear in the "numbers"
Climate & carrying capacity	Continued decline
Ineffective Left	Begins to organize

Imagining After Capitalism | 105

The driver outcomes shown in Table 4.2 are primarily focused on the *Collaborative Sharing Platforms* scenario, as that is the purest New Equilibrium scenario — *New Sources of Value* is closer to H1 and *Sustainability Transition* is closer to H3.

Shifting values: modern giving way to postmodern. The Baseline's stalemate starts to loosen up as those with postmodern values begin to outnumber modern, and influence decisions accordingly. Over time, this is shifting more and more people away from support for capitalism. For comparison, modern values would still hold the edge in *New Sources of Value* and postmodern values would clearly have the edge in *Sustainability Transition*.

Technology acceleration: Tech is key enabler. Accelerating technologies are the key enablers of the *Collaborative Sharing Platforms*. The growth of postmodern values will lead to more questions about how the technology and the platforms distribute the benefits. There are likely to be more calls for fairness, equity, and new modes of distribution, and potentially some curbs on the application of technology, perhaps along the lines of privacy protection, but ultimately aiming at the distribution issue.

Inequality: Slight improvement. One might expect to see a lot of calls and lip service on the inequality issue, but very little action. Think in terms of tinkering at the margins. Some improvements are made — and likely exaggerated — with the aim being to keep the lid from blowing off this potentially volatile issue.

Jobs and automation: Automation at the expense of jobs. The tech-centricity of this scenario suggests continued application of technology for efficiency and cost-savings over people concerns, although over time there would be increasing concerns and perhaps protest about the job losses as the postmoderns become more influential.

Stagnation: Continues, but not clear in the "numbers." There would likely be a wide range of approaches, schemes, and arguments about the growth numbers. The various as-a-service approaches — ridesharing is an example of mobility as-a-service — are likely to flourish, but there may be some questions about whether or how that contributes to economic growth. One can imagine concern about lack of growth on the one hand, but also see the benefits of less or slower growth for climate change. If growth is acknowledged as slowing, supporters of capitalism may claim the benefits to climate — even if not intended.

Climate and carrying capacity: continued decline. As noted above, the continuing shift from goods to a service-based approach might provide some positive news on climate change. But overall, it does not appear likely that attention to climate change would pick up much in this scenario. Mostly message manipulation, some small improvements, but overall continued decline.

Ineffective left: Begins to organize. The shift toward postmodern values gives the left a bit more confidence and one can envision the use of the collaborative platforms for political organizing. The sense here would be one of rethinking approaches and behind-the-scenes organizing.

Before we get to the *Collaborative Sharing Platforms*, let's first review *the New Sources of Value*, since it is closest to the Baseline.

4.2.2 New Sources of Value

These concepts largely operate within the current capitalist structure but seek to change its focus. They bring change, but the prevailing system remains intact, which fits the archetype of New Equilibrium. The Industrial Revolution at the core of early capitalism focused on the manufacturing of physical goods. It gradually replaced agriculture as a key employer until the emergence of the service economy over the last several decades. At its peak, manufacturing provided 22% of jobs in the US in 1979, which has declined to 9% today (Harris, 2020). A similar pattern is observed in other developed economies. Interestingly, even the developing economies are shifting away from agriculture and manufacturing toward services across all regions — and especially in sub-Saharan Africa, according to the IMF (Gruss and Novta, 2018).

The current breakdown of employment in the US according to the Bureau of Labor Statistics (2021) data:

Service-providing	81%
Goods-producing	12%
Agriculture	3%
Self-employed	5%

The two figures for manufacturing (9%) and goods-producing (12%) are slightly different due to the varying methods for classifying the sectors. What is clear is that the focus of the US economy has switched to services, as have economies in other developed nations. The everything-as-a-service trend, in which organizations approach products, offerings, and processes as a collection of services, is a prominent result of this switch (Gordon et al., 2017).

Ten "New Sources of Value" AC Concepts were identified from the literature and included (as noted earlier this is not intended to be comprehensive, but rather representative):

- *Algorithm/Data*, Viktor Mayer-Schonberger and Thomas Ramge. Algorithms and big data will enable markets to function much better, eclipsing the role of firms and even the role of price and money in decision-making.

- *Artisan*, Lawrence Katz. People use their own personal style and abilities to complement information and communication technologies and provide a better experience.

- *Attention*, Tom Davenport & John Beck. Value is earned by getting attention — the scarcest resource in the information-rich world.

- *Experience*, Joe Pine. Shift in emphasis from goods to services, and in particular to experiences, in which the design of even routine interactions must be special.

- *Intangible*, Jonathan Haskel & Stian Westlake. An intangibles-focused economy creates scale (scaling via IP, supply chains, branding, software, etc.); creates spillover (easy for a firm to copy ideas from another firm); has high sunk cost (which makes banks less likely to invest, thus requiring VC), and creates incentives for synergies (reason why cities and cultural of openness are important).

- *Leisure*, Graham Molitor. Hospitality, recreation, and entertainment- and leisure-oriented businesses accounting for the majority of the economy.

- *Network*, Network Capitalism. Reinvent capitalism by creating high value networks and mutually beneficial partnerships to make money and create a better world.

- *Philanthrocapitalism*, Matthew Bishop. Philanthrocapitalists see a world of big problems that they, and perhaps only they, can and must put right.

- *Purpose*, Aaron Hurst. Reorienting economic activity by connecting people to their purpose, i.e. through serving needs greater than their own and building community.
- *Relationship*, Jerry Michalski. Puts greater emphasis on value-added relationships as sources of economic growth over commoditized transactions.

The ten AC Concepts are a mix of new and old. They can be further sorted into four categories by the type of new value they provide:

- *New Focus*: Leisure, Experience, and Artisan
- *Support Services*: Intangible, Relationship, Networking
- *Marketing*: Relationship, Attention, Algorithm/Data
- *End Goal*: Philanthrocapitalism and Purpose

New focus

Two of the older ones, Leisure (1999) and Experience (1999) talked about shifts in focus of economic output that are still with us today. In both cases, there is a different focus of the economy, but it is still operating within the capitalist framework.

The Leisure concept suggested an evolution in sources of value from ICT (information and communication technologies) to biotech to leisure. It suggests that while ICT has been the most significant source of economic value, it would give way to the various biotech-based products, which would in turn eventually give way to leisure being the key source of economic value. Molitor (1999) suggested leisure-oriented business would eventually account for most of the economy. His broad definition of leisure included hospitality, recreation, and entertainment as well as spirituality and self-help and noted the importance of experiences.

The Experience concept talked about an emerging preference among some consumers for experiences over goods — for an ecotourist vacation over a boat. Pine and Gilmore (1998) defined experiences as situations in which goods and services support the creation of a memorable event, with the classic example being how Starbucks elevated coffee from a cheap commodity to a pricey one based on the experiential dimension.

A related concept, the Artisan economy (2014) focuses on using craft skills to deliver better experiences. Katz (2015) suggests an artisan economy is one in which value is added by what he calls personal flair in each stage of the job. It's a craft approach that creates distinctive value in juxtaposition to mass production.

Support services

A newer one, the Intangible concept (2017) further defined how value would be captured in the service economy. It says the shift to support services may involve physical products, but the source of value is not the physical product, but the algorithms, models, and brands that support it. Amazon is an example, as its competitive advantage involves algorithms, logistics, and software.

Michalski (2000s) coined the term Relationship Economy to highlight the value to be gained in developing deeper relationships with customers as opposed to treating them generically as consumers. He noted how the concept was related to other emerging economic ideas such as the sharing economy and open source and suggested a long-term move toward abundance.

Network capitalism (2018) is a movement-based concept presenting itself as second-generation capitalism that sees networks as providing value. It sees success coming from creating high value networks and being capable of engaging in mutually beneficial partnerships. The support services are the precursors to the *Collaborative Sharing Platforms* described in the next section.

Marketing

The Attention concept (2000) sought to refocus marketers towards the importance of getting the attention of consumers. Davenport and Beck (2000) suggested attention would increasingly be in scarce supply and therefore valuable, so that actions ought to be considered in terms of how to get and keep attention.

Indeed, one of the newer concepts, the Algorithm/Data economy, is also aimed at marketers making better use of the big data being produced by digital tools. It aims for more precise marketing but is still firmly within the capitalist framework. Mayer-Schonberger and Ramge (2018) advocate for the importance of data and the supporting algorithms to reinvigorate capitalism. They see big data vastly improving the effectiveness of markets until markets begin eclipsing the role of firms. People will increasingly buy from "horizontal" markets rather than individual "vertical" firms. More abundant and precise data increasingly supplants the role of price in decision-making. A key argument is that rich data will replace the blunt and clunky price mechanism as the guide to transaction. This will wreak a bit of havoc on the banks and finance folks, which could be a pathway to *After Capitalism* — although the authors don't say that.

End goal

Bishop and Green (2008) see philanthropy as a new source of value in which philanthrocapitalists use their wealth and business acumen to help solve the world's problems. A good example is how Microsoft founder Bill Gates has used his Gates Foundation to address a variety of global development issues relating to poverty, health, and education.

Socially responsible and even anti-capitalist investing is likely to become more prominent. As the Boomers age, the Millennials and Zoomers are set to inherit upwards of $68 trillion in wealth. Given their much higher disapproval ratings for capitalism, they are likely to look for ways to a make a difference in how they invest this money (Kim 2022).

The Purpose concept is perhaps the most different or H3-like. It is focused on the intent of the economy, suggesting a shift to a focus on quality-of-life. One could argue that the intent of *Neoliberal Capitalism* is indirectly the same. It says that the production of goods and wealth via growth is the best route to producing happiness, i.e. quality-of-life. It focuses on the means rather than the ends. That connection, as discussed in the previous chapter, is increasingly dubious. The Purpose AC concept seeks to refocus on the ends of people and communities. Hurst (2016) foresees a purpose economy eventually eclipsing the information economy. He suggests consumers putting less emphasis on cost, convenience, and function and putting more attention on purchases that increase meaning in their lives. Note the connection of "seeking meaning" to postmodern values and that the concept was the closest to H3.

4.2.3 Collaborative Sharing Platforms

The *Collaborative Sharing Platforms* AC Concepts included here have one foot in the *Neoliberal Capitalism* of H1 and the other in the guiding images of H3. For example, they have some aspects of bottom-line competitive capitalist markets and some aspects of a Gift economy that is part of the *Circular Commons* image. Some of the concepts are profit-motivated, and some are purpose-driven. For example, the original "couchsurfers" did it as a way to meet people or to make new friends, as well as finding a place to stay. In its current incarnation as Airbnb, the hosts typically do it as a business, but some still have making friends as at least part of their motivation.

It is the same with platforms. Schwab (2016) points out that the development of technology-enabled platforms combines both demand and supply to disrupt existing industry structures. It brings to mind the classic rock band The Who's line:

> *Meet the new boss, same as the old boss.*

Uber disrupted the taxi industry, but ultimately it simply shifted who got the money, albeit with some convenience gains for consumers, and some "flexibility" gains for drivers — although even these gains might be viewed with suspicion. Indeed, in true capitalist fashion, in 2021 the price per mile driven for Uber and Lyft across the US was up 26% versus 2019 (Forman, 2021).

Intermediaries are an interesting consideration in the H2 transition. The capitalist or market sentiment today is that intermediaries are bad (Hoffman, 2018). Get rid of the middleman! Thus P2P (peer-to-peer) platform approaches are in favor. It is perhaps fairer to recognize that there are useful and not-so-useful intermediaries. Take travel agents. In many cases, they got a percentage for not adding much value. But how many of us long for the days when we had someone who saved us countless hours searching and comparing airlines and hotels and avoiding mistakes a professional would catch — that's a valuable intermediary. When we disintermediate, the illusion is that costs are being taken out, but in fact they are just being shifted. Instead of one travel agent, a company of 40 people has in effect 40 part-time travel agents. It looks good on paper because the cost of the travel agent is gone, but instead you have 40 often highly paid employees spending time making travel arrangements, which they may not be very good at. So perhaps some "re-intermediation" may appear along with disintermediation.

Uber is a P2P platform that leans more toward the H1 Baseline (very capitalist), while there are other more gift-oriented platforms, such as Freecycle — giving (and getting) stuff for free to keep "good stuff" out of landfills — and Neighborgoods — a service that enables one to share physical items with other people in the neighborhood — that lean toward H3 Transformation.

Sorting through this handful of transition AC Concepts ultimately led to the creation of a category called *Collaborative Sharing Platforms*. Sharing was at the center of this cluster, as was the idea of collaboration, and most used some sort of platform approach. Again, platforms are a new idea in some respects, but they can also very much fit in with the rules of the capitalist game.

Perhaps the most significant driver here is the importance of technology as a key enabler of collaboration between users, arranging the sharing, and organizing the services and exchanges via platforms. A strong push to automation would likely follow. The values in this scenario begin shifting toward postmodern, which would support a shift away from the heavy emphasis on growth from the dominant modern values in the Baseline. Actual economic growth would likely be small in any case, although the numbers might be used to tell a more favorable story. Uber, for instance, simply made an existing capability more efficient, rather than growing the economy.

The *Collaborative Sharing Platforms* title emerged as a characterization of these AC Concepts. The initial research sorted these concepts into collaborative, sharing, and platform categories. It quickly became clear that they are inter-related and express different aspects of the same thing — collaborating and sharing via digital platforms. The nine concepts are:

- *Collaborative*, Rachel Botsman & Roo Rogers, and Jeremiah Owyang. Using technology to enable networking and greater sharing of resources and information among communities, including sharing, bartering, lending, trading, renting, gifting and swapping.
- *Fourth industrial revolution*, Klaus Schwab. Digital revolution characterized by a fusion of technologies that is blurring the lines between the physical, digital, and biological spheres driving exponential change.
- *Gig*, Gerald Friedman. Characterized by flexible employment (e.g. contingents, temps, contractors) for workers employed on particular tasks for a defined time, who then move on to the next.
- *Hybrid*, Lawrence Lessig. A hybrid economy built upon both the sharing and commercial economies, in which commercial leverages sharing, and sharing leverages the commercial.
- *P2P*, Navi Radjou & Jaideep Prabhu. A bottom-up approach to value creation enabled by peer-to-peer networks and do-it-yourself platforms.
- *Platform*, Marshall Van Alstyne et al. Platform businesses bring together producers and consumers in high-value exchanges and grow via network effects.
- *Second*, Brian Arthur. Describes the backbone technological infrastructure enabling digitization that in turn is creating a "vast, automatic, and invisible economy."
- *Second Machine Age*, Brynjolfsson & McAfee. At an inflection point — the early stages of a shift as profound as the Industrial Revolution driven by exponential, digital, and combinatorial new technologies.

- ***Sharing***, Arun Sundararajan and Juliet Schor. Characterized by recirculation of goods, increased utilization of durable assets, exchange of services, and sharing of productive assets.

These AC Concepts will be sorted into their "original categories," as shown by Figure 17. It should be emphasized that there is a great deal of overlap among the three individual categories — collaborative, sharing, and platforms — some concepts refer to the overall system or future, while others focus more sharply on a particular aspect of the future.

Collaborative

The Collaborative AC Concepts emphasized new ways to collaborate as the key economic factor. There were three concepts that fit this category: Collaborative, Fourth Industrial Revolution, and Second Machine Age.

Figure 4.2 Collaborative Sharing Platform concepts

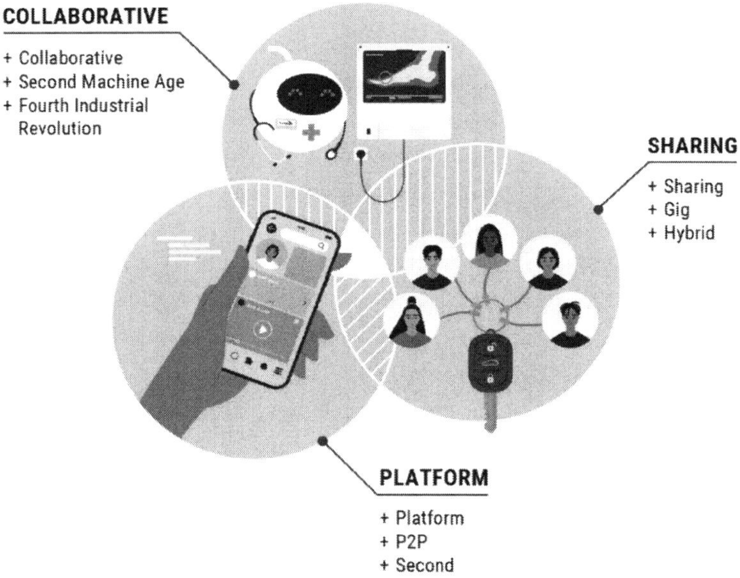

COLLABORATIVE
+ Collaborative
+ Second Machine Age
+ Fourth Industrial Revolution

SHARING
+ Sharing
+ Gig
+ Hybrid

PLATFORM
+ Platform
+ P2P
+ Second

In a Collaborative economy, according to Owyang and Samuel (2015), common technologies enable people to get goods and services via peer-to-peer (P2P) routes instead of buying from established corporations. Collaborative companies — Ebay, Uber, and Airbnb — tend to own very few assets. The key to their success is using data to truly understand what their customers want and why. This idea fits with the Algorithm/Data economy and Intangible Economy concepts in Section 4.2.2 New Sources of

Value, as the value is less based on tangible physical assets and more on intangibles, such as scaling via IP, supply chains, branding, or software (Haskel and Westlake 2017).

The Fourth Industrial Revolution concept is focused on the exponential growth rate of technological progress and the convergence of the physical, digital, and biological spheres. The growing capabilities and the connections among them are facilitating collaboration among the technologies, people, and organizations that apply them. Proponents suggest this collaboration will lead to a supply-side miracle (Schwab, 2016). The use of these technologies, while leading to new types of businesses and even industry sectors, is still set within the current capitalist context. At the same time, its suggestion of a supply-side miracle positions it as a transition to the *Tech-Led Abundance* image (described in Chapter 5).

Brynjolfsson and McAfee's (2016) Second Machine Age concept does not take a specific position regarding the H2 transition but presents a balanced view of how that transition might take place. They focus on the role of automation and whether it will create more jobs than it destroys. They lay out the case for both views. The net job loss view suggests innovation is a fruit that can be harvested and is finite, while the net job gain view suggests innovation is a building block that doesn't run out but accumulates. At the heart of this view is digitization enabling greater collaboration. They do see that the growing digital collaboration tends to worsen inequality as more and more of the proceeds or bounty accumulates at the top.

Sharing

The Sharing AC Concepts emphasize new ways to allocate resources and new relationships outside of the traditional producer-consumer arrangement. The three concepts are: Sharing, Gig, and Hybrid.

At the center of the Sharing economy concept is a shift away from ownership. Sundararajan (2016) defines the sharing economy as taking underutilized assets and making them accessible online to a community that in turn reduces the need for owning those assets. Botsman and Rogers (2010) see sharing as a smarter means of consumption than ownership. Sundararajan (2016) notes that Juliet Schor adds the key modifier "stranger," that is stranger sharing economies. Schor (2014) identified four broad categories of sharing:

- recirculation of goods, e.g. the origins date to 1995 with the founding of eBay and Craigslist

- increased utilization of durable assets; the innovator was Zipcar, now Uber and Lyft
- exchange of services, time banks are community-based, non-profit multilateral barter sites; also monetized service exchanges, such as Task Rabbit
- sharing of productive assets, revival of non-monetized initiatives, tool libraries, hackerspaces, and makerspaces.

The Sharing AC Concept is not without its critics. Price (2015) observes that the term sharing economy is misleading. Rather than sharing freely, it is more about entrepreneurship and monetization of what he calls slack resources. While the business case is primarily between individuals, the "small scrape" of profit for doing the connecting can amount to huge profits, i.e. Uber. Uber is in control of a platform that originally facilitated peer-to-peer renting, not sharing, and essentially is the boss of an army of self-employed employees (Scott, 2017).

Investopedia defines the Gig economy as temporary, flexible jobs in which companies tend to hire independent contractors and freelancers instead of full-time employees. Gig workers are independent contractors or consultants who are hired to complete a particular task or for a defined time. There are legal challenges underway to this classification, with a US judge ruling they must be treated as employees (Wood 2020). California had a referendum that voted in favor of keeping the gig workers classified as independents while providing for some degree of benefits (Bond, 2020). The European Parliament began considering a new law to help millions of gig workers gain access to employment rights in the Summer of 2023 (European Council, 2023).

There is disagreement over how big the Gig economy is, though most analysts agree that it is growing and will likely continue to grow. At the low end, the Bureau of Labor Statistics (2018) suggested 3.8% of workers — 5.9 million people — held contingent jobs. One synthesis of "high-quality studies" suggested only 11% of the working adult population in the US were primarily full-time independent contractors in the Gig economy (McGuire, 2018). Another source suggested that in 2019, 57 million Americans freelanced, which is about one-third of the total American workforce (Upwork and Freelancers Union, 2020). The GAO (2015) noted that narrower definitions of "gig" generally can result in estimates of less than 5% and broader definitions suggest more than a third of the labor force. With the broader definition of 57 million, the US has the world's largest Gig economy. In comparison, the EU, which has a larger overall workforce, is estimated to have had 28 million gig workers in 2021 and expected it to reach 45 million by 2025 (Lomas, 2021).

Supporters note the freedom that gigging offers and that it encourages the entrepreneurial spirit. A tradeoff for that freedom is increased uncertainty and economic risk. Friedman's (2014) research suggests that it is more likely driven by business's desire to reduce wages and benefits. Most social insurance safety nets are designed for workers with regular jobs. This could "create a class of isolated individuals living from job to job," and referenced Guy Standing's AC Concept of the Precariat (described in Chapter 5 with *Non-Workers' Paradise*) (Friedman 2014).

Lessig's Hybrid economy concept suggests that beyond the commercial economy based on price, there is also a sharing economy, where access to culture is regulated not by price but by a complex set of social relations (Sundararajan, 2016). Lessig (2008, 177) explains that the Hybrid is either a commercial entity that aims to leverage value from a sharing economy, or it is a sharing economy that builds a commercial entity to better support its sharing aims. He makes an interesting point about the value of amateurs in creating a participatory culture — that too much professionalization, supported by IP protection, discourages amateur participation and creates a commercial divide between producers and consumers.

Platforms

The Platform AC Concepts emphasize the organization of economic activity around digital platforms. The three concepts are: Platform, P2P, and Second.

Platforms use a business model that combines supply and demand (Schwab 2016). They exist in key areas such as logistics, food delivery and mobility including companies such as Amazon (distribution), AirBnB (holidays), Uber (taxis) and Instagram (photography) (Wray, 2019).

The chief asset of platforms is the information they have and interactions they organize. They need access to data and depend on network effects for success. Instead of managing supply chain and resources, the key is managing the community (Van Alstyne et al., 2016). The tendency is to create winner-takes-all markets — whoever gets the data and stimulates the network effects ends up dominating the sector, e.g. Amazon in retail, Facebook on social media, and Google in search.

P2P platforms can be either be for-profit (tending to H1) or non-profit (tending to H3). A non-profit example are the food assemblies in Europe, which are networks of independently operated farmers' markets organized via online platforms. They connect farmers, producers, and consumers and take place every week. There are over a thousand of these pop-up systems, which began in France in 2011 as La Ruche Qui Dit Oui, with a key rule being that the food must be produced within a 150-mile radius (Shareable, 2017). The for-profits include retail platforms such as eBay and Alibaba, which are generating billions of dollars globally. eBay takes 10% of sales, so the intermediary, in this case the platform provider, has simply shifted and not been replaced. Their tendency to dominate a marketplace is seen by some as predatory behavior that seeks to bankrupt or scare off competition.

The P2P AC Concepts use platforms for individuals to exchange goods and services with one another without an intermediary. Radjou and Prabhu (2015) observe that information technology and social media are moving toward eliminating transaction costs. [This is similar to Rifkin's (2014) concept of zero marginal costs]. Their frugal economy concept is via the bottom-up approach to value creation in which consumers can design, build, market, distribute, and trade goods and services using P2P networks without the need for intermediaries.

The Platform model is not without its challenges. Their need for more and more data leads to potential privacy violations and anti-trust challenges. Facebook, for example, has been criticized for not revealing information about data thefts, Google was under fire for its data collection practices and user tracking, and so on (Jie, 2020). Varoufakis (2021) suggests digital platforms, such as Facebook and Amazon, no longer function like oligopolistic capitalistic firms, but rather like private fiefdoms or estates operating in what he calls techno-feudalism — the big platforms essentially extracting rents while the economy is buoyed by central bank money.

Like other H2 transition AC Concepts, the Platform ones have H1 and H3 tendencies. The H1 tendency is for the new sharing offering to be co-opted into the commercial economy, e.g. Zipcar became a sub-brand of Avis (Schor, 2014). But there is also the potential for the platforms to be owned by the members themselves, rather than capitalist sponsors, such as Neighborgoods, Stocksy, and Freecycle, which are more like H3 AC Concepts.

The disintermediating tendencies of P2P are suggestive of a move away from capitalism, but as noted above there is also a tendency for simply reintroducing a new intermediary, such as the platform provider, which is more like the current capitalist system. One might see a positive in bringing more people together to share or trade directly with one another, but perhaps a troubling aspect is the tendency to reinforce more and more activities as economic transactions. Instead of "crashing" on someone else's couch, or borrowing someone else's car, these become economic transactions.

Arthur's (2011) Second Economy concept captures the digital backbone or infrastructure that enables the economic activity that takes place in the physical economy. This influential component of the economy is increasingly self-organizing, self-architecting, and self-healing. The concept is grouped here as it is a key support for the platforms and P2P exchanges.

A key distinction on whether the Collaborative Sharing Platforms fit with *After Capitalism* is whether the collaboration leads to capital accumulation: if it does, then it is closer to the H1 Neoliberal Capitalism; if it is about exchange without accumulation, it is closer to the H3 guiding images. The purpose is key.

4.2.4 Sustainability transition

One other cluster was created late in the research process: the Sustainability Transition AC concepts. They were originally part of the H3 *Circular Commons* cluster (see Figure 2.1 Domain map). But in reviewing all the AC Concepts, it became apparent that some were clearly transformative, such as Degrowth, while others seemed closer to today's idea of sustainable development. The horizon scanning had also uncovered a view among the more radical environmentally-driven community that sustainable development has become an oxymoron; that the time for development has ended due to the environmental crisis. Some believed that the sustainable development concept was being used to preserve *Neoliberal Capitalism*. Ironically, sustainability is increasingly used in conjunction with market mechanisms to solve environmental problems caused by market approaches in the first place. The term itself has become diluted to the extent that anything, if backed by a good marketing campaign, can be called sustainable (Castro, 2022).

While I did not necessarily buy into the greenwashing conspiracy aspects of the argument, I did indeed see that several of the sustainability AC Concepts had one foot in H1 and the other H3 — much like the sharing economy described above. So, sustainability AC Concepts were re-examined, and a third H2 transition category — *Sustainability Transition* — was created for them.

Much of the criticism of capitalism is that it fails to adequately address environmental issues, thus several AC Concepts have emerged that try to fix capitalism by addressing them.

- ***Conscious***, John Mackey. Reinvigorate capitalism by doing business guided by principles of higher purpose, stakeholder orientation, and conscious leadership and culture.

- ***Green***, UNDESA. Shaping and focusing policies, investments, and spending towards green sectors, e.g. renewable energy, waste management, green building, sustainable agriculture, etc.
- ***Regenerative***, John Fullerton. Converted Wall Streeter's concept for reforming capitalism with sustainability as the core idea for economic-system design with eight core principles.
- ***Satoyama***, Kosuke Motani. Japanese concept of socio-ecological production landscapes promoting local circulation of resources, money, and goodwill within a community through barter and self-sufficiency.
- ***Sustainable***, Brundtland Commission. Meeting the needs of the present without compromising the ability of future generations to meet their own needs; 17 goals and 169 targets for people, planet, and prosperity.

The five AC Concepts can be sorted into:

- ***Celebrity***: Conscious, regenerative
- ***Classic***: Green, Satoyama, Sustainable

Those which are classified as celebrity involve well-known capitalists using their fame to push concepts for reforming capitalism in its approach to environmental issues. They defend the concept that made them rich and believe it can and should be saved. The Classic AC Concepts are named thus because they have been around for a long time and are generally known and recognized. Green and Sustainable have a global profile while Satoyama would be readily recognized in Japan where it originates.

<u>Celebrity</u>

There are several different routes that the AC Concepts take. Two examples of the celebrity route are explored here. There are many more of these, but for the most part they are firmly grounded in the current Baseline. For example, Ray Dalio (2020), the billionaire founder of Bridgewater Associates, acknowledges the flaws of capitalism, but maintains it has been the best system historically, and should be reformed rather than replaced. The argument about being "the best system we've ever had" is compelling in the sense that it is arguably true, but of course by that logic we would never try anything new. It is not as if there are lots of other systems that have been tried. Other billionaire celebrity capitalists acknowledging the need for the change include Benioff from Salesforce.com, Warren Buffett, and Bill Gates

(Clifford, 2019). Of course, the celebrities were made rich by this great system. But now they acknowledge the need for change. The four above are primarily focused on the inequality aspect.

John Fullerton (2015) is a former Managing Director at Morgan Stanley who left his Wall Street role to advocate for an environmental reform of capitalism. He developed Regenerative Capitalism based on the principle that our economics need to be aligned with the well understood patterns and principles of how living systems work. The concept starts with a shift from reductionist to holistic thinking. An interesting observation is that the regenerative system principles manifest themselves first at the local or regional level. Thus, he starts by saying that the right unit of analysis for an economy is the place or bioregional scale, which conflicts with the nation-state and corporate focus of today's economy (Wichmann, 2018). The local focus as a point of emphasis also appears in several of the H3 Guiding Images. The eight principles of Regenerative Capitalism are (1) in right relationship (with the biosphere) (2) views wealth holistically (3) innovative, adaptive, responsive (4) empowered participation (5) honors community and place (6) edge effect abundance (creative and innovative opportunities are greatest at the edges of systems) (7) robust circulatory flow and (8) seeks balance.

Mackey (2013) took the opposite path from Fullerton. He started as a hippie involved in co-ops and went on to found the capitalist juggernaut Whole Foods (now owned by Amazon). He suggests that it is possible to bring an enlightened consciousness to capitalism. He wants to refocus it from emphasizing just making money — as epitomized by crony capitalism — to pursuing a broader purpose of enhanced corporate social responsibility (Mackey, 2013). His goal is to reform or improve the performance of capitalism, which leans to H1 *Neoliberal Capitalism* but the expression of his four tenets of Conscious Capitalism — focus on purpose, stakeholders, leadership, and culture — is compatible with H3 Guiding Images.

Classic

The Classic AC Concepts have been around for a relatively long time. Green and Sustainable readily come to mind when people think about the environment, although Satoyama is less well-known. Green is now used as an adjective to describe many environmentally-oriented AC Concepts. The contemporary Green New Deal, for example, was introduced in the UK in the mid-2000s, popularized by journalist Tom Friedman, and proposed as legislation in the US by Rep. Alexandria Ocasio-Cortez in 2019 (Simms, 2019).

The UNEP's Green Economy concept received significant attention at Rio+20, but gaining agreement was challenging. The authors acknowledge that many sets of green principles have been produced and synthesized them to nine, acknowledging that many of them were "nothing new" (Allen, 2012). While some of the principles could fit with the H3 *Circular Commons* Image, the work is clearly aimed within the existing capitalist system. It seeks to reform rather than revolutionize. It may be the case that the need to reach consensus among a large and disparate group makes it difficult to generate a compelling revolutionary image, as the bolder elements get softened to gain consensus.

Sustainability emerged back in the late 1980s as an organizing concept for environmental protection centered on the simple idea of "meeting the needs of the present without compromising the ability of future generations to meet their own needs" (World Commission on Environment and Development, 1987). That work suggested moving toward sustainable development. Subsequent work in preparation for RIO+20 included much more ambitious recommendations, but also noted the highly political nature of advancing sustainability (Leblanc, 2012). The current focus emerged as 17 sustainable development goals and 169 specific targets under the umbrella of people, planet, and prosperity (United Nations, 2015). As with the Green Economy above, there are aspects of H3 Images, but the essence of the concept clearly fits within the capitalist framework. Some environmental hard-liners, such as degrowthers, suggest that sustainable development is an oxymoron, in that the two aspects of the concept name are fundamentally incompatible.

The Satoyama concept is a traditional local approach that was launched by the Japanese Ministry of the Environment (2010). It integrates the interface of nature and human settlement — mountains, woodlands, and grasslands (yama) surrounding villages (sato) in an economic and sustainable way. Whilst it does suggest an approach compatible with H3 *Circular Commons,* it does not break new ground but rather exists within the current system and is thus classified as an H2 Transition AC Concept.

PART II. THE GUIDING IMAGES

> *We must confront the claim that there is no alternative [to capitalism] — by proposing one.* — David Schweickart

The research journey has hopefully made the case for the necessity of these images. Chapter 1 set the stage. Chapter 2 synthesized the research including the scanning and the review of the dozens of books touching on *After Capitalism*. The results were grouped into seven drivers influencing the future. Chapter 3 covered how the drivers play out and pointed to a future in which the H1 neoliberal capitalist Baseline is disintegrating. Chapter 4 outlined a likely H2 transition from the H1 Baseline to the H3 Transformation. And here we are at H3, the guiding images of a new operating system.

Polak's (1973, 200) case for images succinctly summarized is: "We found the positive image of the future at work in every instance of the flowering of a culture and weakened images of the future as a primary factor in the decay of cultures." Here I will challenge the reader: can you envision today's positive image of the future? I didn't think so. Thus, the quest of this work has been to identify candidate ones.

Polak (1973, 183, 195) minces no words about the importance of images of the future and the dire need for them:

- For the first time in the three thousand years of Western civilization there has been a massive loss of capacity, or even will, for renewal of images of the future.

- He found the existence of a vacuum where the images had once been. And not only is there a vacuum, but he identified a "literal aversion to images of the future as such."

- He talked about "defuturizing" as a retreat from constructive thinking about the future in order to dig oneself into the trenches of the present. It is a ruthless elimination of future-centered idealism by today-centered realism.

If you weren't a little afraid about the future, you might be now! His work was translated in the US in the 1970s and he began it many years before that. Images or, more accurately, pieces of images, have emerged since then. But none has achieved the status that Polak suggested was necessary. He identified several key aspects of his guiding images of the future. Table 0.1 below shows how they are addressed in *After Capitalism*.

Table 0.1 Eight ways that *After Capitalism* meets Polak's image criteria

#	KEY ASPECT OF POLAK'S IMAGES	CONNECTION TO *AFTER CAPITALISM*
1	The image of the future reflects and reinforces "ideal" values.	The critical role of the shift to postmodern and integral values is noted as one of seven key drivers.
2	The images themselves may be thought of as time-bombs that explode somewhere in the future with little control over when, where, and how.	The focus on the images themselves – and not their implementation-- makes sense considering this.
3	Images of the future are aristocratic in origin. The author of the image invariably belongs to the creative minority of a society.	An interesting contrast in light of today's emphasis on open, participatory and crowdsourcing approaches.
4	Images are part rational and intellectual, but a much larger part is emotional, aesthetic, and spiritual.	As futurist Clem Bezold says, scenarios are of the head, and visions [aka images] are of the heart.
5	Images self-correct, renew, and change in a continuous interplay of challenge and response.	The proposed images are prototypes that will evolve.
6	The formation of images depends on an awareness of the future that makes possible a voluntary, conscious, and responsible choice between alternatives.	Frankly, we have a problem here. At present there seems to be little general awareness or interest in alternatives.
7	The images need to be bold, visionary, and transformational— a "high idea" of a future realm.	The images were crafted to meet these criteria.
8	At its best, the image of the future is universal in character for the growth of all mankind.	The issue of whether *After Capitalism* can flourish in one country or must be global is an implementation issue raised but not resolved here.

This work does an adequate job of addressing the first seven aspects of Table 0.1, but the eighth on the universal character of the guiding images is an open question. It is reminiscent of the socialist/communist controversy in the Soviet Union over whether it had to be international – resolved by Stalin as "socialism in one country." While not an ideal example, it is relevant in that it ultimately fractured the movements. In Chapter 8 it is noted that, should the proposed guiding images catch on, then implementation becomes a priority, and this question would need to be explored in detail.

> **Image, vision or utopia?**
>
> How to classify the three guiding images? I landed on "images," but there is a case to be made for "visions" or "utopias."
>
> - Image: a mental representation; idea; conception.
> - Vision: a vivid, imaginative conception or anticipation.
> - Utopia: any visionary system of political or social perfection
>
> Given that my inspiration was Polak's (1973) *Image of the Future*, "image" was the default. But during the research I found myself using vision as well. Indeed, the Three Horizons Model refers to the concepts in H3 as visions (Curry and Hodgson 2008). Sharpe (2013) describes the H3 vision as an ideal to be worked towards, which fits with our purpose.
>
> The intention to uncover positive stories about the future could be a utopia. Polak talked about eschatological and utopic images of the future, the former brought about by God and the latter by man. The problem with utopia is that it seems so at odds with the problems of the present day that it tends to be dismissed as unrealistic or foolish. It is indeed hard to imagine a world where all problems are solved. But that's not a useful way to think of the concept. Utopias are a useful device for how things could be better in the future. Not perfect, but better.
>
> In reviewing works relating to the three, this is where I net out:
> - Image is an aspirational view of the universal human future based on ideal values within a culture [an ideal]
> - Vision is a project crafted by a group for its particular future [intent is to achieve]
> - Utopia is probably the least "accurate" of the three as it crafts a specific story of a specific place [doesn't need to meet plausibility test]
>
> I chose image as the most accurate descriptor of the work here.

The three guiding images were crafted by clustering the research and looking for key themes:

- The 700+ scan hits were clustered and analyzed using the tagging system in the Diigo scanning library.
- The 28 H3 AC Concepts were analyzed using the Image Analysis Template and clustered.
- The seven key drivers were projected into the 2040-2050 timeframe.

Three major themes came through as central to images: environmental; social and political; and technological factors. The process of characterizing these themes took several iterations, but ultimately three major clusters emerged and became the basis of the three guiding mages: *Circular Commons* (environmentally driven), *Non-Workers' Paradise* (socially and politically driven), and *Tech-Led Abundance* (technologically driven).

To be more specific, for *Circular Commons*, the key environmental issue is climate change and carrying capacity. The solutions take on the growth question. How growth is addressed guides the various proposed approaches. There was no support among the AC Concepts for growth on its current trajectory, and the question boils down to achieving a steady state or more actively pursuing degrowth.

For *Non-Workers' Paradise*, the socio-political focus centers primarily on workers and the role of work and jobs, with political and economic participation a key aspect of that. The question can be boiled down to whether work will be needed with abundance and how to manage the transition. There are a few AC Concepts that maintain the idea of right-to-work.

For *Tech-Led Abundance*, the authors are generally certain that technology will deliver abundance. Where it gets interesting is how humans might keep up. To some degree the authors of these AC Concepts suggest people will be moving toward augmentation and some suggest it essentially leads to a reinvention or a new human species.

It is hoped that the different guiding images, each with a different emphasis, will appeal to different groups and broaden the appeal of *After Capitalism*. Environmentalists are likely to endorse *Circular Commons*, social and political activists are likely to be drawn to *Non-Workers' Paradise*, and techies are likely to be drawn to *Tech-Led Abundance*. At the same time, the AC Concepts are of course a mixture. Alter-Worlds, for instance, talks a lot about the commons (*Circular Commons*), but the spirit is in the social life and political status of the wage-less and surplus population (*Non-Workers' Paradise*). The concepts are sorted according to their primary emphasis.

Let me be clear that the guiding images presented here are not intended to be comprehensive, but rather representative. The most salient limiting factor is that the search was primarily through the economic lens. The search was focused on a successor economic system to capitalism. Surely some works have been missed that might rightfully belong — my apologies to those authors! My sense is that the sets of AC Concepts below are enough around which to make the case for the three guiding images that were identified.

Figure 0.1 The *After Capitalism* guiding images

A final note on the plausibility of the images. From today's vantage point, most images of a 20- to 30-year future are going to seem a bit shocking or unrealistic. Here the goal is to deliberately seek to develop guiding images of Transformation, so surely for some readers these will seem implausible.

A key observation from my experience in the foresight world for over three decades is that people tend to under-estimate or not realize what will happen in the intervening years between now and then. Yes, images of 2050 seem shocking from the vantage point of 2022, but the images will seem less shocking in 2030, and even less so in 2040, and may be almost ho-hum by 2050.

Imagining After Capitalism | 127

Table 0.2 Image analysis template updated

ORIGINAL CATEGORY	HOW IT APPEARS IN THIS SECTION	REVISED CATEGORY/ SECTION HEADERS
Author: Who proposed it and why (purpose)	Not called out – in introduction as appropriate	Driver outcomes: how do the drivers project forward in each image?
Time horizon: stated, implied, or unclear	Not called out – in introduction as appropriate	Challenges: the central problems that the image focuses on
Scope: global/regional/national or affluent/emerging/poor	Not called out – in introduction as appropriate	Purposes: the key motivation for developing the image; what it is trying to achieve
Key drivers: Shifting values, Technology acceleration, Inequality, Automation, Stagnation, Climate & carrying capacity, Ineffective Left	Renamed and repurposed to: + Driver outcomes	
Key ideas	Renamed into two categories: + Challenges + Tools	Principles: guidelines followed in working towards the image Tools: mechanisms or activities for enabling or realizing the image
Ideal or guiding values: something akin to an organizing principle/motivation, i.e. create a more just or fair society	Renamed into two categories: + Purposes + Leadership	Personal: the role of citizens in this image
Emotional, aesthetic, and spiritual aspects: is it appealing or compelling?	Not called out – in introduction as appropriate	Leadership: the role of leaders in this image
Personal: How are individuals affected by this future? Who's bearing the most costs, who's accruing the benefits?	Kept the same	Pathway: high-level take on how to get to the image from the present
Pathway or plan: Highlights of the image are projected to develop over time	Kept the same	

The three H3 guiding images are:

- *Circular Commons*. Expands the concept of sustainability to embrace circular principles as part of a social, political, and economic commons.

- *Non-Workers' Paradise*. A play on the Socialist idea of a worker's paradise, but in the *After Capitalism* world we are not working in paid jobs as a means of sustenance.

- *Tech-Led Abundance*. Technological progress drives and leads to an abundance of wealth that fixes the core distribution problem of capitalism.

The image analysis template introduced in Table 0.2 provided a consistent framework for analyzing the works comprising the three guiding images. In consolidating the insights from the various works, it became clear that not all the original headings were needed to summarize each guiding image.

Some of the categories that were very useful for research purposes were less useful in conveying the guiding images in an interesting and lively way to the reader. So, modifications were made to the original template to create a consistent and hopefully reader-friendly set of sections.

Each image chapter begins with a summary at-a-glance text box that highlights the key focus and aspects of the image and notes how it addresses the key issues of supporting community values, economics, and governance.

Let's begin with the *Circular Commons*, which has the most AC Concepts at 13.

Chapter 5 – CIRCULAR COMMONS

Circular Commons expands the concept of sustainability to embrace circular principles as part of a social, political, and economic commons.

Circular Commons at a glance

The Circular Commons image "expands the concept of sustainability to embrace circular principles as part of a social, political, and economic commons." The circular qualifier denotes that goods used in the present can be reused for the benefit of the future — forming what the MacArthur Foundation defines as a "virtuous cycle of durables designed for re-use." The commons approach directly challenges the fundamental principle of private property and suggests there are alternative ways to manage resources and even manage society itself.

At the core of this image is the growth question. Humanity may have reached the point where degrowth is the only plausible option. This image suggests a dual approach in its title: a circular approach to dramatically reducing the impact or footprint of physical goods and managing these goods in a new commons approach that emphasizes collective benefit over individual gain.

To succinctly state the key purpose of a shift to a Circular Commons future, it is to focus on environmental stewardship for saving humanity from potential ecosystem collapse. The key aspects of Circular Commons are underlined, followed by a brief description of supporting community values, economics, and governance.

1. Addressing climate and carrying capacity [via degrowth]: There are perhaps no greater threats to the long-term survival of humanity than these twin, interconnected components. The question of growth shifts on a continuum from continued expansion to steady-state, and eventually to a carefully managed degrowth. The most tangible shift is away from individual ownership and possessing toward accessing shared goods and services as needed.

2. Moving from sustainable to circular: Sustainability-related concepts, such as the Green New Deal, come to be seen as tainted by their association with market approaches and capitalism can't move fast enough to deal with environmental crisis. This creates an opening for the bolder approach of a circular economy that catalyzes the necessary systemic change.

3. Adopting a commons approach to resource management: The idea that people are capable of collectively and cooperatively managing resources initially faces stiff resistance from champions of private property and laissez-faire ideals. As capitalism struggles, examples of the existence of historical cooperative societies are "dusted off." More and more examples emerge of communities adopting cooperative commons principles, first with early adopters and eventually the early majority (Rogers, 1976). An accompanying shift to emerging postmodern and integral values prioritizes the health of the community over the individual (Hines, 2013).

4. Reintegrating with nature: As the effects of climate change and resource issues become more apparent, the impact challenges the prevailing view of nature as something to be conquered by humans. Doubt about whether we can "fix it" gives way to a re-examination of our thinking about our role in nature and this eventually shifts to become a stewardship ethic. Some of it is choice and some of it is forced. Fear of, or actual, food and water shortages inspire people to grow their own food and adopt water management approaches. High energy prices encourage efficiency and the adoption of rooftop solar and the like. These practical moves all help to spark a new appreciation of nature and the outdoors.

5. Scaling grassroots and local: The need for local action is a strong theme, but sometimes overlooked is the concurrent need to connect it to the regional, national, and even global scale. There is some ambiguity in the AC Concepts over how exactly this would work, suggesting that much work remains to be done.

6. Moving to a gift economy: There are several variations around this theme, but Gift economy seems to best embody the key notion that contributions to the collective good are made without expectation of direct "reimbursement." There is a faith in the collective that one will be provided for when needed. Work is done for the intrinsic value of mutual aid rather than the prospect of extrinsic reward. The economy is not based on competition or monetary exchange, but gift exchange, sharing, and P2P relationships along with creating mechanisms to redistribute wealth and ownership like communalizing institutions and public services via cooperatives, credit unions, community banks, and nonprofits.

7. Adopting new measures of success: New measures are reflective of this modified sense of purpose — a society focused on pro-social and pro-environmental outcomes. There are already many ideas and proposals in this

area, such as the Triple Bottom Line and the GPI (Genuine Progress Indicator); perhaps the most challenging aspect is to gain consensus on which of the many schemes is best.

Supporting community values. The shifting of values from modern to postmodern and integral catalyzes a movement from a "me" to "we" mindset over time. This is vital to enabling the commons approach to work — as long as people fight over property and possessions, this guiding image struggles.

Economics. The focus is on re-setting the economy to align with a healthy environment, which means a degrowth approach. A variety of new or newly important financial instruments, such as earning caps, global progressive taxes, responsible collective/public investment, promoting innovation through the public sector, eliminating economic rents, fiscal reform for sustainability, investing in public assets and infrastructures, increasing financial and fiscal prudence, reforming macro-economic accounting, economic and monetary localization, social dividends, UBI, etc. are used to support the degrowth approach.

Governance. There is a shift in emphasis from national and state to local efforts as the key locus of power via organizations with shared goals like B-corps, not-for-profits, NGOs, and interest groups that work towards pro-social and pro-environmental outcomes. By organizing locally and collaboratively, the influence of international capital is reduced. This decentralized local emphasis recognizes that addressing larger environmental issues must be coordinated at a national and global scale.

The *Circular Commons* image puts the environmental crisis front-and-center. The crisis is primarily two-fold: climate change and carrying capacity. The two are intimately related of course. *Circular Commons* expands the concept of sustainability to embrace circular principles as part of a social, political, and economic commons. My original conception was Sustainable Commons. An important shift, perhaps, was replacing Sustainable with Circular. Part of this is an excitement about the great potential of the circular concept. The other part is a concern that sustainability, the galvanizing concept of the environmental movement since arguably 1987, is beginning to show its age. Where it once encouraged people and organizations to stretch and embolden their thinking and aspire to greater things, today it is often used to support the status quo.

The Circular Economy takes a more comprehensive approach to resource use. It is a system aimed at eliminating waste and the continual use of resources. It is a radical and extensive shift that appears to be amenable to a commons approach. The MacArthur Foundation (2013) defines circular as: Today's goods are tomorrow's resources forming a virtuous cycle of durables designed for re-use, and consumables made of compostable materials that can be returned to the earth.

The Commons AC Concept has been an integral component of the image from the start. It is primarily focused on resource management as well, but it goes beyond that to include how social and political relations might be organized. It suggests managing resources in common — very different than the mostly private approach of capitalism. A key distinction is a shift in resource management from an emphasis on private competition to shared and publicly held resources.

The short definition of a commons is that it is about the shared management of a resource by many. A longer but widely accepted definition is from Ostrom, in which commons are where the members of a clearly demarcated group have a legal right to exclude nonmembers of that group from using a resource. Examples are open access regimes such as the open seas and the atmosphere, which have long followed a legal doctrine involving no limits on who is authorized to use a resource (De Angelis, 2017). The two major sources for the commons AC Concepts for this work were **Commons 1** and **Commons 2** (see below).

> **It's not the tragedy of the commons**
>
> Tragedy of the commons has become a cautionary lesson about the impossibility of collective action. For the author Hardin, himself, the best approach is "the institution of private property coupled with legal inheritance ... those who are biologically more fit to be the custodians of property and power should legally inherit more." This is of course catnip to capitalists, but as this section reveals, that is not a commons.

The *Circular Commons* questions how daily life has come to be framed in terms of economic transactions. It is an enormously powerful construct. To question economic emphasis is to invite ridicule. Any image of the future has to confront this and suggest an alternative. *Circular Commons* reframes daily life in terms that puts humanity back into focus by redefining its relationship with nature. Climate change and carrying capacity in effect are the result of an economic transactional lifestyle that fails to pay sufficient attention to its external costs.

It should be noted that there is an extensive scholarship on both Commons and Circular that gets into the details of "how." Given our emphasis on the what (the image), the approach here will be to capture the high-level ideas and not get too deep into the specific details.

It was interesting to note that none of these AC Concepts specified a time horizon. That is perhaps the most intellectually honest approach, but still a bit surprising.

There were 13 AC Concepts comprising this image, the most of the three images. The environmental focus is primary in the next economic system. The AC Concepts that inspired the *Circular Commons* are listed with the author and a brief description here.

- **Betterness**, Umair Haque. Adopt a positive paradigm that enables human potential by challenging business to do better by focusing beyond the bottom line to considering real human welfare.
- **Circular**, MacArthur Foundation. Today's goods are tomorrow's resources forming a virtuous cycle of durables designed for re-use, and consumables made of compostable materials that can be returned to the earth.
- **Commons 1**, David Bollier. Ambitious view that the commons could be a vehicle for social and political emancipation and societal transformation.
- **Commons 2**, Massimo de Angelis. A highly local model in which people self-organize socially and politically within communities to pool and govern resources in common.
- **Degrowth**, Giorgos Kallis et al. Seeks to abolish economic growth as a social objective and favoring grassroots practices such as eco-communities, co-ops, local currencies, barter, commons, etc.
- **Doughnut**, Kate Raworth. A social foundation of wellbeing that no one should fall below and an ecological ceiling of planetary pressure that we should not go beyond.
- **Eco**, Otto Scharmer. Advocates a switch from current ego-centric approaches leading toward planetary disaster to eco-centric ones that emphasize the wellbeing of the whole.
- **Local**, BALLE, Global system of human-scale, interconnected local living economies.

- **Post-Growth**, Tim Jackson. Strengthening ecologically and socially sustainable practices given the physical limits of the earth
- **Sacred/Gift**, Charles Eisenstein. Shrinking the formal economy and shifting money away from being a store of value to primarily a medium of exchange, including the adoption of negative interest to discourage rentier approaches.
- **Steady-State**, CASSE/Herman Daly. Economy characterized by relatively stable size that that leaves room for nature and provides high levels of human wellbeing.
- **Sufficiency**, Sam Alexander. A degrowth approach focused on meeting mostly local needs with mostly local resources.
- **Wellbeing**, Lorenzo Fioramonti. Argues for shifting away from GDP as a performance assessment tool to more holistic measures.

This section is organized as follows:

- Driver outcomes: how do the drivers project forward in each image?
- Challenges: the central problems that the image focuses on
- Purposes: the key motivation for developing the image; what it's trying to achieve
- Principles: guidelines followed in working towards the image
- Tools: mechanisms or activities for enabling or realizing the image
- Personal: the role of citizens in this image
- Leadership: the role of leaders in this image
- Pathway: high-level take on how to get to the image from the present

5.1.1 Driver outcomes

Not surprisingly, *climate change and carrying capacity* was the driver most frequently called out by the authors. *Stagnation* was second, which had to deal with the role of growth in the future. While stagnation suggests a slowing of real economic growth, several authors suggest that the growth needs to be actively managed and several support degrowth as a key strategy. A third of the AC Concept authors mentioned inequality as a key driver of the problem in particular as the motivation for moving to a commons approach. Shifting Values are mentioned by a third as a key piece of the solution.

Accelerating technology is not mentioned as a key driver. There is some acknowledgement of it as a tool. Nor is the ineffective left mentioned — there is some support for local politics that aligns with the ineffective left; that is, a few are very supportive of highly local approaches that are not concerned with the challenge of scaling up.

Table 5.1 shows the projected outcomes of the drivers in *Circular Commons*.

Table 5.1 Driver outcomes in *Circular Commons*

DRIVER	OUTCOME IN *CIRCULAR COMMONS*
Shifting values	Postmodern
Technology acceleration	Tech as a key support tool
Inequality	Reduced via sharing
Jobs & automation	Intentional and selective automation
Stagnation	New metrics
Climate & carrying capacity	Key focus of new order
Ineffective Left	Supportive, benefits from local approach

The story of the driver outcomes is a central focus on the environment driven by addressing climate change and carrying capacity by following a degrowth regime, and a shift to a circular approach to resource management. Stagnation is reframed as a policy choice. A key component of degrowth is redistributing wealth and access to address inequality by following a commons approach. Though it wasn't addressed by the authors, we might imagine that the left was able to make progress in scaling up its local approaches – the emphasis is on local but connected on larger regional, national, and global scales. The economic focus on saving and restoring the environment was enabled to a degree by technology acceleration and automation. Here too, the authors were not as direct on this point, but we can infer that for the approach to work in time, given the urgency of the problems, technology support would be a key ingredient, but it would be more in the background and in a supporting role, as this image is much more of the natural world.

5.1.2 Challenges and responses

Climate and carrying capacity are the over-arching issues addressed by this image. The problem is simplified into two key aspects as shown in Figure 5.1:

Figure 5.1 Climate and carrying capacity challenges

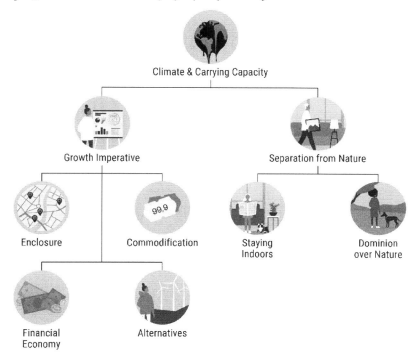

- Growth imperative:

The key underlying problem is capitalism's need for growth. Most AC Concepts grouped with *Circular Commons* put growth as the key driver of climate change at the center of the problem with capitalism. For example, the Ecosocialist manifesto argues its case by saying that capitalism has left humanity with less than a decade to take radical emergency action to avert catastrophic climate change (Boyle, 2020). The need for growth has triggered the related problems of enclosure, commodification, and the shift to the financial economy.

- Apartness: Separation from nature.

A second key problem that was less prominently mentioned in the AC concepts, but in my view is of equal importance, is humanity's increasing

Imagining After Capitalism | 137

disconnection from nature, which arguably has created a lack of appreciation for how dependent human life is on the supporting ecosystems.

Growth imperative

A core problem for capitalism is that it needs growth and thus is constantly on the prowl for new ways to facilitate this. This requires new things to enclose, commoditize, and sell; or to create new financial instruments to make money with. The trajectory of capitalism is toward a world where literally everything is for sale. Bollier (2014) argues that our current materialism and unlimited appetites are not universal but rather are an aberration in human history. This point was addressed in Chapter 1 in framing the focal issue, in which I agree with Bollier that the "materialist" view of human nature is a static view that misses the dynamic and evolving nature of human values.

The *Circular Commons* image addressed this challenge by reversing these processes of enclosing, monetizing, and privatizing and moving to a commons approach. Once again, we see the importance of values. Modern values are compatible with "everything for sale;" while the postmodern and integral values are compatible with "commons." This section concludes by looking at three key roles for growth moving forward.

Enclosure

It is helpful to first understand how we got here. It is easy to assume that private property is the natural order of things. A commons approach can sound naïve and impractical. Historically speaking, however, private property is a relatively new development. The privatization of public land, enclosure, is a process that began several centuries ago in which previously public land became privatized — think of the peasants no longer able to hunt on what became the king's or the nobles' lands.

Hickel (2019) traces its origins to the enclosure of the European commons in the sixteenth century. Between roughly 1350 and 1550, the free peasants of Europe had organized subsistence agrarian societies that shared and managed resources — such as fuel, food, and building materials — taken from the common land. This did not sit well with the nobles, who grumbled that "servants are now masters and masters now servants." When elites began to enclose the common land, it triggered peasant rebellions that were violently suppressed (Zaitchik, 2020).

Marx referred to it as primitive accumulation. Primitive accumulation is the process by which precapitalist modes of production, such as feudalism, are transformed into the capitalist mode of production. That process is still going on today, as the capitalist need for growth fuels a continuous search for new things to enclose. Today, for example, we might think of previously public beaches that are now privately owned.

Enclosure converted open fields into closed property, and "transformed autonomous communities into precarious wage laborers, under a brutal and relentless de-worlding" (Shaw and Waterstone, 2020, 36). Common land was privatized, sold off, chopped up, fenced, and policed. Enclosures convert a system of collective management into a market order that privileges private ownership, prices, and consumerism. Karl Polanyi observed that "enclosures have been appropriately called a revolution of the rich against the poor" (Shaw and Waterstone, 2020, 36). If we trace the origins of any piece of property through a succession of "legitimate" transfers, eventually we get to one who first simply took it – who separated it off from the realm of "ours" or "God's" into the realm of "mine" (Eisenstein, 2011, 54). In short, it's the foundation of today's "commodification of everything." (Shaw and Waterstone, 2020).

> **Privatization as commodification and enclosure**
>
> Privatization can be viewed as a form of commodification or even a form of enclosure. Something that was publicly managed (held in common) is turned over to the private sector. The Reinventing Government movement in the US in the 1990s (Gore 1993) began what have become increasingly strident calls to privatize, marketize, corporatize, or commercialize – to run government like a business (Michaels, 2015). That means privatizing government services.
>
> A recent piece goes so far as to suggest abolishing the public sector. In talking about privatizing the police: "Abolition of the public sector means, of course, that all pieces of land, all land areas, including streets and roads, would be owned privately, by individuals, corporations, cooperatives, or any other voluntary groupings of individuals and capital. The fact that all streets and land areas would be private would by itself solve many of the seemingly insoluble problems of private operation. What we need to do is to reorient our thinking to consider a world in which all land areas are privately owned ..." (Rothbard 2021).

Imagining After Capitalism | 139

The often violent expropriations were followed by the establishment of state institutions and a legal framework to protect such expropriations. The loss of the commons in successive waves of capitalist development also robbed people of their autonomy to meet basic needs for sustenance and economic security (De Angelis, 2017).

Responses

The point here is not to suggest going back to the way it was several centuries ago, but rather to suggest that the proposed commons approach is not a new development and is quite plausible. Choices were made to enclose; choices can be made to re-open. Commons that were privatized can be restored as commons.

Commodification

Commodification is the process of taking something that used to be free and monetizing it. It relies on scarcity to create economic value. This, too, is driven by the capitalist system's need for new things to sell to fuel economic growth. Staying with the beach example in some geographies one must buy a "beach tag" to use the public beach. Or now one must pay to hike a trail that used to be open to anyone.

The commodification process must create scarcity — for something to become an object of commerce, it must be made scarce first. Think artificial scarcity or "buy this limited edition before it's gone." Anything and everything in a market is implicitly defined as scarce. With scarcity as the main principle, the mindset that follows is based on commodification of goods and services (Kimmerer, 2020). As the economy grows, by definition more and more of human activity enters the realm of money – the realm of goods and

> **Commodification vs commoditization**
>
> Thanks to Douglas Rushkoff (N.D.) for making a clear distinction between commodification versus commoditization: commodification is a somewhat Marxist idea referring to the way that market values can replace other social values — a communal system or approach is turned into a market approach or buying opportunity; while commoditization refers to the way that goods that once were distinguishable become viewed as mere commodities in the eyes of the market or consumers.

services. Usually, we associate economic growth with an increase in wealth, but it can also be seen as an impoverishment, an increase in scarcity (Eisenstein, 2011, 29-30).

Bollier (2014) puts it bluntly: "privatization and commodification of our shared wealth is one of the great unacknowledged scandals of our time." This is closely linked to the enclosure of the commons. Karl Polanyi observed that numerous resources — especially land, labor, and money — be redefined as commodities, which he called "fictitious commodities ... that quickly expanded to other realms, making virtually everything subject to purchase and sale." Along these lines, according to Rifkin (1994), the metamorphosis of consumption from vice to virtue is one of the most important yet least examined phenomena of the twentieth century.

Capitalism evolved by claiming things that exist outside the market and bringing them into the market for sale and purchase. This is how we turned making a living into "labor" and nature into "real estate." Surveillance capitalism now claims private human experience as "data" — free raw material for translation into behavioral predictions that are bought and sold in a new kind of private marketplace. And it takes place almost completely without our knowledge (Zuboff, 2019). We are even turning our hobbies into "side hustles," which Molly Conway warns sacrifices the therapeutic effect you get from them (Palmer, 2021).

Capitalism frames nature, work, and capital as commodities (Scharmer 2013). It turns economics into a quantitative numbers game that takes the human element out of analysis. There is little discussion of the purpose of the economy. It's a numbers game. "Money's divine property of abstraction, of disconnection from the real world of things, reached its extreme in the early years of the twenty-first century as the financial economy lost its mooring in the real economy" (Eisenstein, 2011).

The classic assumption or argument of modern capitalism is that "materialism equals happiness." But is that true? Are people happier now, more fulfilled, for having films rather than tribal storytellers, MP3 players rather than gatherings around the piano? My previous work on values identified "the [relentless] pursuit of happiness" as an emerging need state. The relentless aspect reflects a seriousness or even angst about purpose. It isn't enough to find out what makes one happy, there also needs to be a plan to get there (Hines, 2011). Perhaps an indicator of the search for purpose is the growth of the motivational speaking circuit, which generates about $2 billion annually (Zahoor, 2021). A little reflection reveals that nearly every type of good and service available today meets needs that were once met for free.

Responses

One could argue that commodification of social capital is part of the reason for the isolation, loneliness, and weakening of community that is rife today. Or as Eisenstein (2011, 76) puts it, "The monetization of social capital can be viewed as the strip-mining of community." The cooperative spirit of neighbors has been replaced by professional service firms from day care and landscapers to pet-sitters. Life becomes an endless series of transactions. A first step in addressing everything as a service is getting reintegrated back into one's community – the proverbial "getting to know one's neighbors" again – and understanding their needs and how we can help one another. A neat transition strategy already being tried in many areas is local currencies that provide a way to keep track of who does what for whom.

At the individual household level, people are disconnected from the work of running a household and buy more services and conveniences. People could instead choose to work less and do more for themselves – simple things like doing one's own landscaping instead of hiring it out, cooking one's meals instead of ordering takeout.

Mindset shifts are paramount here. First and foremost is the ongoing values shift. This suggests that the "money buys happiness" assumption will be seen as increasingly anachronistic.

Second is the recognition that scarcity is a marketing concept that does not reflect that we are moving toward a world of abundance, noting that there is still a massive distribution problem. A perhaps sinister view is that capitalism needs to create a dependency on the need to buy commodities that in turn forces people to work to afford them. The best way to keep the system going is to lock everyone into it. Changing this is going to take some time as the marketing overlay needs to be confronted with some sort of educational campaign, which is not a quick fix.

A third mindset shift regards money. Money is a social construct — it is a social agreement — that we can decide to change. It is not some immutable universal law. It was invented to meet a need and it can be un-invented, so to speak. Granted it is now extremely deeply entrenched. It underpins the capitalist system. Exchange value [rather than use value] via pricing is seen as the rational way to calculate costs/benefits of social and ecological needs. This is not unprecedented. Hazel Henderson estimated that half of our economic output is non-monetized in her famous layer-cake depiction of the economy, in which the "love economy" and nature were the foundational layers comprising half of the economy and GDP measured the other half. Since then, arguably the monetized portion has increased, but nonetheless the metaphor suggests that a non-monetized/gift economy is perhaps more plausible than recognized (Henderson, 2021). Her voice was not alone. Marilyn Waring, a New Zealand politician turned activist, highlighted the non-monetized economy in her 1988 book *If Women Counted*, which suggested that [unpaid labor] was the single largest sector of any nation's economy (Marx de Salcedo, 2019). A key step to *After Capitalism* is questioning the role of money. Not necessarily replacing it but questioning the role it plays in the future.

Financial economy

The shift from the real to the financial economy reflects that more and more economic activity involves the manipulation of complex financial instruments rather than the production of goods and services. Wealth is playing an increasingly important role vis-à-vis income. As we saw earlier, earning money via one's wealth is outpacing earning from income. The essence of Piketty's argument is that some factors in capitalism promote convergence of incomes, some divergence but, overall, divergence is the stronger force, and it boils down to a simple fact: the return on capital investments (which Picketty puts at an average of 5%) beats economic growth (a surrogate for income growth, which he puts at 1-2% on average). This creates an advantage for previously accumulated wealth that exacerbates inequality.

Essentially, many of the well-to-do are finding new ways to increase their wealth that do not contribute to the wellbeing of the overall economy. Brett Christopher (2020) calls it rentier capitalism, in which having and owning — thereby controlling access — is enormously more profitable than making or serving (Sivaramakrishnan, 2021). And even the real economy is being more influenced by the financial one — the big three private equity firms (BlackRock, Vanguard Group, and State Street) own about 22% of the average S&P 500 company, up from 13.5% in 2008 (Levitz, 2022).

Chapin (2021) notes that the real economy includes direct exchange or purchase of goods or services and the lending or savings services that are one step (or degree) away. Once we go two or more degrees away from the actual product purchase, we're in the financial economy (e.g. repackaging of loans).

The shift to a greater emphasis on the financial economy creates a disconnect between the economy of money manipulation and the real economy of producing goods and services. Figure 5.2 illustrates how the various aspects of the financial economy (represented as FIRE) gained on and eventually surpassed the manufacturing economy in importance.

| **Figure 5.2** Rise of the FIRE economy

Source: V. Hines based on Bureau of Economic Analysis data

Several authors observe that the current capitalist system hasn't been able to create value, returns, jobs, fulfillment, income, net worth, or trust. Some of the more pernicious examples include:

- Some private equity firms run what might be considered a con game when they borrow to buy a company and then declare bankruptcy. An example is Toys R Us, whose private equity owners borrowed more than $5 billion to buy the company, quickly took it into bankruptcy, defaulting on that giant debt, after paying themselves $200 million, they defaulted on severance payouts to the company's 30,000 employees (Doctorow, 2018).
- Private equity and institutional investors are buying up so much US residential housing that it has prompted a bill in Congress to ban the practice. Their participation ramped up during the pandemic to being involved in 28% percent of all homes sold in 2022 (Abraham, 2023). Yanis Varoufakis, who served as the Greek finance minister during the nation's debt crisis, argues that capitalism is dead and democracy has been undermined by "financialization." What we have instead is a "bankrupt-ocracy of endangered or bankrupt financial institutions moving debt around to conceal the various flaws and shortfalls in the system" (O'Hehir, 2018). He adds that "corporations can take out cheap 1% loans, not to invest in machinery and production, but to buy

their own stock earning 8% or 9%; or to buy out smaller corporations, eliminating competition and creating monopolies" (Brown, 2021).
- Shaw and Waterstone (2020) cite the deregulation of the financial sector and note three points about the financialization of the economy:
    o Finance capital is now the principal lever of accumulation for the ultra-rich.
    o Financialization has utterly co-opted democracy.
    o National governments and their central banks will literally print money out of thin air to keep the finance sector afloat.

The shift to a financial economy has led to many of our best and brightest minds spending their time creating what could be viewed cynically as complex legal theft instruments. Not only is the financial economy growing, but the real economy does as well, as more and more aspects of daily life get monetized, from playing college sports to helping one get a date.

Eisenstein (2011) connects "financialization" to enclosure and commodification in saying that there is almost no more social, cultural, natural, and spiritual capital left to convert into money. An interesting unintended consequence of financialization is that it has indirectly led to the public sector playing an increasingly important role in the economy. When the financialized sector runs into trouble, it comes to the government for help. The Great Recession beginning in 2007 and then Covid both accelerated the trend to greater public intervention in the economy, which is actually lessening the "free market" more and more over time. (Vaughan, 2021).

Responses

The primary proposed response is to move from a production-for-profit to a production-for-use approach. The shift to the financial economy happened because it generates significantly more profit than the real economy. A production-for-use system prioritizes use-value and produces goods and services in direct relation to fulfilling human needs. The notion of creation on-demand (Nelson, 2022) would be key to realizing this new system of production. Taking food production as an example, a creation-on-demand system would survey individual households within localized communities to formulate a food order for a specified time frame. The order is then verified and brought before community assemblies to ensure it is sufficient to meet everyone's needs and to discuss what challenges may be faced during the production process. This is certified in collective agreements, making sure the order is aligned with the productive goals of the community, and once ready the households are notified and able to access the goods they need. The key difference here is the focus is on meeting needs directly, rather than focusing on profit-making above all else. This is just one example, but it suggests the direction for de-financialization.

Alternatives

The role of growth is a big question here. A simple way to view the consequences is to look at the trend of "Earth Overshoot Day," noted in the Climate Change & Carrying Capacity driver in Section 2.3.6.

Magnuson (2013) found that current growth could be preserved under a fully renewable energy system — with investments in the $30-$40 trillion range. He references a Swiss Federal Institute study that identified a "2000-watt society" in which the 7 billion people on earth consuming an equal amount of energy would equal out to 2000 watts daily. Americans, today, consume about six times that amount daily (Magnuson, 2013). Clearly the cost and sacrifices needed to maintain current growth rates are daunting for those in affluent economies.

As Figure 5.3 shows, several of the *Circular Commons* concepts suggest degrowth is necessary, some suggest steady state or a balanced approach, and some are agnostic, although they generally favor slowing it down. None see the current rate of growth as sustainable. Most supporters of capitalism, on the other hand, advocate growth as the solution to economic changes. When you put growth in a search term comparison versus steady state or degrowth, the latter two practically disappear.

The AC Concepts in the H2 transition space are generally still in the growth camp. Many add a qualifier, such as "sustainable." Some of these are captured as *Sustainability Transition* concepts. Some see a need to shift economic purpose but seek to do so within the capitalist framework. For instance, "zebras" are startup companies with purpose: They seek to balance profit and purpose and help create a more just and responsible society (Brandel et al., 2017). But they are clearly still within the capitalist frame. The three alternatives are described below.

1.   Agnostic

The most politically savvy position is to either dodge the question or suggest slowing. Raworth, for instance, in her popular *Doughnut Economics* work takes the politically astute position of "be agnostic about growth" as one of her seven key principles.

2. **Steady state**

The idea of a steady-state approach to growth has been around since the 1990s, popularized by ecological economist Herman Daly. It acknowledges that economic growth has gotten too big. It aims for stable population and consumption of energy and materials at sustainable levels. It suggests an ideal size can be established that leaves room for nature and provides a high level of human wellbeing. The quantity in a steady-state economy neither grows nor contracts from year to year. It is dynamic, not static, and it changes and develops over time, but it remains balanced with the natural environment.

Daly (2010) maintains that a steady-state economy is something different from both capitalism and socialism. But some have argued that a steady-state economy cannot operate within a capitalist system, given capitalism's inherent need for growth (Blauwhof, 2012).

3. **Degrowth**

Perhaps the most courageous, and least politically astute, of the three positions is degrowth. The concept emerged in France in the 1970s using the term *décroissance*, but it took off in 2002 and has spread around Europe (not in common use there either) and to a smaller extent in the US. A Google Trends search reveals very low levels of interest until the last two years. My own anecdotal observation is that a series of books, posts, conferences and discussions have emerged in the last few years. It is in marked contrast to when I first encountered the concept early in my research a decade ago and it was challenging to find sources.

| **Figure 5.3** Alternatives to growth

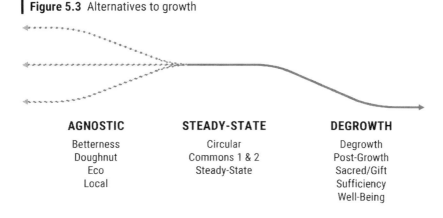

There are variations. Kallis et al. (2015) take a hard line and feel that sustainable development is an oxymoron and degrowth must be more radical. They suggest abolishing economic growth as a social objective. Schmelzer et al. (2022) recently released an excellent overview of degrowth. They suggest six key aims of degrowth: (1) democratizing the economy (2) universal basic services (3) democratizing tech (4) revaluation of labor (reduce work week, eliminate bullshit jobs, etc.) (5) introduce incentives to reduce impact of harmful industries, and (6) international solidarity (it won't work in just one country!). Hickel (2021, 3) makes a strong point that degrowth is not about doom, but rather involves a shift "from an economy that's organized around domination and extraction to one that's rooted in reciprocity with the living world."

> **Decolonization of the imaginary**
>
> This concept developed by Serge Latouche signals the need for a disruption of taken-for-granted ways of seeing the world, and their associated practices, rules, and social norms. Decolonization of the imaginary questions deeply rooted beliefs about who we are, how we live, and about our place in this world (Feola and Koretskaya, 2020).

Supporters of degrowth ideas essentially believe it is too late to save growth. They suggest that our current lifestyles and consumption habits cannot be sustained by improving the efficiency of the current system, e.g. transitioning to renewable energy, recycling, etc. As Alexander (2012) bluntly puts it: "the full implications of our predicament are typically grossly under-estimated." For instance, the ecological footprint of the global economy exceeded the sustainable carrying capacity of the planet by 50% back in 2012, according to the Global Footprint Network. The planet is already well into overshoot. The magnitude of the changes required to bring that into balance go well beyond what technological advances within the current systems could provide.

The *Sufficiency Economy*, for instance, suggests a focus on meeting mostly local needs with mostly local resources, including the world's developed economies. The aim is for a world in which everyone's basic needs are modestly but sufficiently met, in an ecologically sustainable, highly localized, and socially equitable manner. Of course, determining what is sufficient is tricky. But get ready for this: "Using the Amish as a rough touchstone or benchmark may not be so far from the truth" (Alexander, 2012).

McKibben pointed out the example of Cuba after the Soviet Union pulled out. They went from an export-led agricultural model based on sugar that reduced overall caloric intake for the population to repurposing the land for raising its own food again, on small private farms and in thousands of pocket-sized urban market gardens and replaced the food supply lost from the collapse of the USSR (McKibben, 2008).

Responses

My journey leads me into the degrowth camp. Let's turn to Systems Thinking again as we did in suggesting the capitalism system is ultimately un-fixable. As with capitalism itself, all good things eventually come to an end. Using Kauffman's (2021, 114-115) systems rule #9 "nothing grows forever," we see that growth ***always*** stops sooner or later. Whether it be biological, economic, political, or whatever other kind of system, no matter how fast it's growing it eventually hits a limit. Kauffman suggests the questions to be asking are how soon will it happen, how abruptly will it stop growing, and what will the consequences of the change in growth rate be on the system as a whole? The growth imperative that has driven the last 250 years and "delivered the goods" is now misaligned with what's needed. Growth is threatening human existence.

It won't be easy. Degrowth proposals are likely to generate backlash. After all, growth is the sacred cow of the modern capitalist era. But the cracks in the growth regime are already appearing. Capitalists are increasingly relying on complex financial instruments to generate "growth." Bregman (2017) observes that this search for growth "created a system in which an increasing number of people can earn money without contributing anything of tangible value to society." The growth numbers still look good on paper, but as John Hagel III and John Seely Brown, co-directors of Deloitte's Center for the Edge, have noted with their path-breaking Shift Index, real asset returns have been dwindling — not rising — for decades (Haque, 2011).

Primarily coming from the right wing but not limited to it, opponents of degrowth claim that this approach will bring about a disastrous rise in unemployment and increased levels of poverty. Both immigration and the elites are blamed for interfering with individuals' right to prosperity (Eversberg, 2019). Some of the more conspiratorial elements of the opposition see degrowth as a Neo-Malthusian ploy by elites to impose a new world order that doesn't fundamentally harm the position of the ruling classes.

Apartness: Separation from nature

Although the *Circular Commons* concepts put much more emphasis on the growth question, my own view is that another significant problem is humanity's relationship with nature. One might see that the many crises of our times have separation from nature in common, in which humanity has somehow become exempt from, or above, the laws of nature. While this challenge of reintegrating with nature was not as prominently focused on by the *Circular Commons* concepts as growth, it was mentioned. For instance, Bollier (2014) supported his commoning concept by noting that commoning would help us start to reintegrate ourselves with nature and with each other. A weak signal is the Solarpunk movement, which blends aesthetics and politics to explore the kind of world that will emerge with the transition to renewables. It is in direct opposition to cyberpunk or dieselpunk, which craft dystopian futures based in capitalist corruption, technological authoritarianism, and the deification of fossil fuels (Our Changing Climate, 2021). The eco-socialist Green New Deal talks about a world where people exist in symbiosis with the bounty of nature (Urie, 2019).

Staying indoors

The problems of climate change and carrying capacity seem increasingly remote to people who often lack a basic understanding of nature's principles. In the affluent countries, more and more of life is spent indoors. An oft-cited US EPA (1989) study found that Americans were spending 90% of their time indoors. It surely has gone up since then, especially when adding in the effect of the pandemic. Nature is experienced almost exclusively through television and social media. One can imagine how challenging it is to get a feel for climate change and carrying capacity from an air-conditioned room with food and goods and services delivered with the click of a mouse. Extreme weather events may help change that perception, but they may further reinforce staying indoors. A recent study confirmed previous self-reported research that the experience of extreme weather events influences beliefs about climate change and intentions to mitigate its effect (Bergquist et al., 2019). Seeing, or in this case experiencing, is believing.

Responses

The obvious response is to go outside. But the question is how to reverse the long-term trend towards inside. The education system would seem to be an ideal leader here. Field trips to nature provide the additional value of making learning more experiential and fun.

Dominion over nature

A second aspect is the view that nature is something to be conquered and used for the benefit of humanity. This dominance view emerged with modern values focused on achievement, growth and progress, with a high degree of faith in science and technology (see Fig. 2.4). Nature, in the modern worldview, is something to be mastered or conquered using the tools of science and technology. The more science and technology have advanced, the greater our sense of dominance over nature has grown ... to the point where we see ourselves above it and now to be protected from it. Rather than a thing of beauty, many see nature as full of danger and hazard. Our neighborhoods encroach upon and demolish nature, our homes and buildings are sealed tight, and we have an army of wipes, cleaners, and disinfecting stations inside our antiseptic spaces.

Responses

There are ideas about how to address this separation. Convivial conservation, for example, suggests conventional conservation promotes the separation in preserving areas as free from human. It promotes the idea of more mixed landscapes in which humans and nonhumans coexist rather than being separated. Along these lines rewilding is encouraged, which is the idea of allowing natural process to take back control over areas subjected to human use, as opposed to treating nature like a garden (Buscher and Fletcher, 2020).

There is more good news. The *shift to postmodern values prioritizes sustainability* and takes a view of harmony with nature. Where modern values view nature as something to be conquered, postmodern values see nature as something to be honored. The shift to a stewardship view of nature is underway and increasingly mainstreaming. My favorite example of a changing view of reintegrating with nature is the vertical forest work of Stefano Boeri, which integrates nature right into building structures (Lubell, 2020).

5.1.3 Purposes

The *Circular Commons* image has environmental stewardship as its core purpose. It is not viewed in isolation – the social, technological, economic, and political connections are clearly made. It's more a matter of focal point.

Neoliberal Capitalism has meant that our purpose has become an economic one, and this image speaks to reimagining our relationship with growth and consumption and our relationship with nature itself as key purposes.

The authors here share a sense that daily life has lost purpose: people have become lost in material goods consumption. Fioramonti (2016) says development is now the goal instead of a means to the goal of wellbeing. More pointed is the sense of being adrift. Wilkinson and Pickett (2009, 3) note that "it is a remarkable paradox that at the pinnacle of human material and technical advancement, we find ourselves worried about how others see us, unsure of our friendships, driven to consume and with little or no community life."

Certainly, saving humanity from potential ecosystem failure would provide a useful and noble sense of purpose! Climate change and carrying capacity is the central driver addressed by this guiding image. The previous section broke down the underlying problems and suggested two central responses/solutions:

1. Rethink growth by shifting into a degrowth mode

A focus on this image now would suggest immediate action on growth, as the central focus of economic redesign from which everything else would flow. There is no bigger question. While we have looked at various options to growth, degrowth seems to be a necessary option. A degrowth approach would first address the related problems of enclosure, commodification, and the shift to the financial economy.

2. Rethink our apartness to an integrated relationship with nature

The apartness or disconnect stems in part from outsourcing activities that might otherwise have developed the connection. From our food showing up in boxes and containers, to throwing waste into a container for someone to take away, to spending almost all of our time indoors, to flipping switches for power, to having handypersons and landscapers, and so on, it is easy to lose a sense of what is being done for us. The specific shift here takes us back into a more active role in resource management.

The redesign centers around the two concepts of Circular to manage the use of resources and the Commons in which resources are held and managed in common. Circular seems to be capable of design that would lead to a net reduction in the use of materials — reducing our ecological footprint — by first re-designing out the need, by secondly reconditioning materials in use to extend lifetimes, and thirdly using recycling as a last and least desirable option, as much value is lost in that process. The Commons shifts responsibility for managing those material resources from the private sector for profit and loss to local groups and larger regional, national and international networks that operate from the principle of stewardship and ecological preservation first rather than P&L.

Habermann (2016) coined the term "ecommony" for her idea of a commons approach as an alternative to capitalism. Ecommony emphasizes common space production centered on ideals of sharing and mutual aid. In this system, there is no private ownership, and money and work do not need to be exchanged in order for us to have our basic needs met. Possession, rather than ownership, is the new guiding logic. By advocating for everyone to contribute instead of exchanging with each other, there is a renewed sense of intrinsic motivation for productive activity as opposed to acting in hope of receiving extrinsic reward. Commoners receive greater satisfaction and learn to care for others because the rewards are inherent in the act.

In sum, the Circular Commons advocates degrowth to reduce humanity's ecological footprint using a circular approach to resource usage that is overseen by a commons approach with environmental stewardship in place of the profit motive in order to address the dual and inter-related challenges of climate change and carrying capacity.

As we will discuss further in Chapter 8 with Table 8.3 on Meadows' systems interventions principles, the highest leverage point is changing the prevailing paradigm. Paradigm speaks to purpose. As described in Chapter 4 on the neoliberal capitalist Baseline, the purpose of the economy has become inverted, instead of developing the economy to serve society, society has been placed in service of the economy.

3. Rethink measures of success to focus on wellbeing

As we have seen, the traditional focus on economic growth as the metric of success is viewed as inadequate. A shift to new measures is an obvious one that is already underway. Perhaps the major challenge is sorting through all the available measures and settling on an approach that provides useful guidance across communities. This does not mean that one standard need be adopted but avoids the opposite problem of a plethora of conflicting and confusing metrics.

However, there is concern that measures of wellbeing and happiness are not rising with economic growth. Indeed, "there have been long term rises in the rates of anxiety, depression, and numerous other problems" (Wilkinson and Pickett, 2009, 5). There is already a fair consensus that GDP is inadequate and a new system for measuring success is needed. The many anachronisms of GDP are well known, e.g. growing trees does not add to economic growth but cutting and selling them off does. There are small-scale pilots and experiments with alternatives. New Zealand, for example, adopted a Happiness Index metric to shift away from the focus on GDP (Ellsmoor, 2019). For *Circular Commons*, GDP would be replaced by a "dashboard" of indicators capable of integrating the key dimensions of human and ecological wellbeing, such as genuine progress indicators that consider dozens of factors that GDP ignores.

> **Grassroots & Commoning**
>
> Grassroots principles similar to commoning share five features: (Kallis et al. 2015)
>
> 1. There is a shift from production for exchange to production for use.
> 2. Wage labor is replaced by voluntary activity, meaning a decommodification and de-professionalization of labor.
> 3. The circulation of goods is set in motion, at least partly by an exchange of reciprocal gifts rather than in search of profit.
> 4. Unlike in capitalism, there is no built-in dynamic to accumulate and expand.
> 5. They are outcomes of processes of 'commoning'; they are new forms of commons.

There is progress being made in this area. For example, The WISE Horizons project, a collaboration between Leiden University and seven other institutes funded by the European Union, is doing excellent work on moving beyond GDP as the measure of the dominant economic paradigm. They are developing a new paradigm that prioritizes wellbeing, inclusion, and sustainability (WISE). They have created a database that synthesizes more than four dozen metrics — including some familiar ones such as the Genuine Progress Indicator (GPI) mentioned above, the Human Development Index (HDI), and the Ecological Footprint index (WFI) — into a framework organized around wellbeing, inclusion, and sustainability measure (Cobbing, Miller, and Omotoso, 2023).

5.1.4 Principles

This section is organized around three principles:

1. Distribution via the Commons
2. Resource use via "Circular"
3. Organize local and collaborative

1. Distribution via the Commons

The key principle of a Commons is that the Earth belongs to all, which obviously runs up against the private property approach of capitalism. It's not that private property goes away. Property is never wholly individual nor wholly held in common, but instead is held by a mix of ownership types. Indeed, two of the most foundational institutions in modern life — the neighborhood and the corporation — plainly constitute "mixed systems of communal and individual property rights" (Fennell, 2011, citing Ostrom, 1999, 351-352). In short, different resource systems need to be managed at different scales. Ostrom (1990), while a supporter of a local approach, acknowledges that larger systems, such as energy resources or groundwater, need to be managed at larger scales.

The shift away from private ownership is not intended as a shift to state ownership. The state facilitates the shift by chartering volunteer groups to manage various resources. These volunteer groups are situated at the local level at which the management needs to occur. In short, it's a move from global to local supply chains. And in a commons approach, there is no individual accumulation of surplus. It would require a tremendous shift in trust to rely on the collective to provide for individuals rather than themselves. The American Dream myth-metaphor was about rugged individuals picking themselves up by their bootstraps and making their own way — that dream is at odds with this guiding image. But one could argue that the dream is no longer accepted by many already.

De Angelis (2017) suggests thinking of commons as social systems in which resources are pooled by a community of subjects who also govern these resources to guarantee their sustainability. Put another way, a commons is a resource + a community + a set of social protocols (Bollier, 2014). There are boundaries, rules, social norms, and sanctions against free riders (Bollier, 2014). There is no master inventory of commons. They can arise whenever a community decides it wishes to manage a resource in a collective manner, with a special regard for equitable access, use and sustainability (Bollier, 2014).

The shift in how resources are managed is enormous from a worldview perspective. They are managed by volunteers at the local level and there is no accumulation. The real trick here will be avoiding simple transfer from private ownership and control to state ownership and control. Most *Circular Commons* concepts see the management of commons at the local level. The state facilitates the transition (it's not clear how long that role would be needed) and local groups do the hands-on management, but there is a lack of clarity about how these local groups would be coordinated. It's certainly not an insurmountable problem, but not an insignificant one either. A challenge comes from the ineffective left driver which captures how the left glorifies "folk politics." Local is pure and best, and there is skepticism at any scale beyond the local. Local knowledge is great and helpful, but the scale of climate and carrying capacity is global and local actions need to be coordinated to be effective.

Bollier (2014) notes that commons must have clearly defined boundaries so that commoners can know who has authorized rights to use a resource. The rules for appropriating a resource must take account of local conditions and must include limits on what can be taken and how.

No accumulation

The *Gift Economy* concept starts by shrinking the formal economy. It does this by shifting money away from being a store of value to primarily a medium of exchange. And it includes the adoption of negative interest to discourage rents, that is making money simply by having money (moving away from the financialization of the economy).

This may not be as crazy as it sounds. One way to shrink the economy is to remove activities that have been commodified out of the economy. For instance, services such as cooking, childcare, health care, hospitality, entertainment, advice, growing food, making clothes, and building houses. These are activities we once did ourselves but have been commoditized over time. In essence we are merely paying for something once provided through self-sufficiency or the gift economy. The irony is that bringing these activities into the formal economy counted as economic growth, but one can see the case for no real net gain, just a change in accounting. The same logic applies in reverse. If these activities are taken out of the formal economy, nothing really changes except the accounting — of course it is not quite that simple given the jobs, taxes, and other factors involved, but the basic principle holds. Much of what is considered growth is just an accounting construct.

The *Gift Economy* concept is fueled by what supporters call a quality of sacredness. A gift transaction is open-ended, creating an ongoing tie between the participants that builds and reinforces relationship and creates a virtuous circle that reinforces the gift principle. There is a huge reliance on trust to make this work. It could be upended by opponents and free riders, but here we come back to our values shifts. In the current context, gifts and trust seem like wishful thinking, but twenty years into the future with values shifts, this becomes at least more feasible if not quite reasonable.

2. **Resource use via "Circular"**

The original title for this guiding image was "sustainable commons." But since I have had the opportunity to do a few projects involving the circular economy, I've been persuaded that circularity is poised to succeed sustainability as a galvanizing concept for environmental concerns. Sustainability, I suspect, will increasingly be seen to have been co-opted by capitalism, particularly as environmental matters worsen, and it becomes clear that current measures associated with sustainability are inadequate. Sustainability is, and will increasingly be, critiqued for not being radical enough on the growth question.

Circular has the appeal of simplicity and relevance as sustainability did when it emerged in the late 1980s as a popular concept. A difference, however, is that circular is more of a specific program while sustainability is a perspective. But I think that is precisely why it fits with the emerging future. A specific program is exactly what is needed. Point the way to what one can do.

Stewardship ethic

A key change is the need for a stewardship ethic or, to use the current vernacular, a co-creative partnership with planet Earth. This gets back to our values driver. Moderns are mostly in the capitalist growth paradigm, postmoderns in the sustainability perspective paradigm, and it is most likely the now tiny (3-5%) of Integrals who will drive the action towards circular commons.

McDonough and Braungart's (2010) cradle-to-cradle concept was an earlier call-to-arms for environmentalists to reexamine our relationship with waste, our environmental policies, and approach to manufacturing that in effect paved the way for the Circular Economy notion being promoted by the Ellen MacArthur Foundation. The Foundation is supported by an impressive global network of sponsors, such as Danone,

Google, Ikea, Renault, Unilever, and the mayor's offices of London and New York City among many others.

The Circular Economy assumes that today's consumption pattern of take-make-dispose is unsustainable. Design for reuse principles and systems need to be developed and implemented (of course). It organizes products into "consumables" and "durables." Durables are designed for re-use and are obtained primarily by using leasing rather than purchasing/consumption models. The idea is that we use things rather than consume them, thus converting from being consumers to users. Consumables are increasingly made of biological materials, so that after use they can be returned to the earth. End-of-life is replaced with restoration. Related ideas include shifting to renewable energy, eliminating toxic chemicals, and eliminating waste through superior design (Ellen MacArthur Foundation, 2013). It is worth explicitly calling out that recycling is the least desirable aspect of a circular approach. Much value is lost in recycling, and it is very difficult to do it economically. For example, Greenpeace recently released a report that charges that "we've wasted decades and billions of dollars pretending single-use plastic recycling is feasible or desirable" (Ongweso, 2022).

The idea of using over consuming taps into the trend of people increasingly preferring access over ownership. It also fits in nicely with the various as-a-service models popping up for almost anything. Rather than owning cars in the future, for example, people might have a ridesharing subscription, which would significantly reduce the number of vehicles needed. Consumables moving toward biological constituents makes such good sense. In other words, if it doesn't make sense to re-use something, make it useful to the earth, so-to-speak. Think of tossing it in the compost pile when you're done . . . instead of the landfill.

Perhaps one thing people might do in a post-work world is to help restore the environment. Get out and plant some trees. Grow some food. There is plenty of work to be done. Four basic rules or system principles support a stewardship ethic:

1. Maintain the health of ecosystems and the life-support services they provide.

2. Extract renewable resources like fish and timber at a rate no faster than they can be regenerated.

3. Consume non-renewable resources like fossil fuels and minerals no faster than they can be replaced by the discovery of renewable substitutes.

4. Deposit wastes in the environment at a rate no faster than they can be safely assimilated.

Circular accounting

Circular Economy advocates the need for a functional service model in which manufacturers or retailers increasingly retain the ownership of their products and, where possible, act as service providers — selling the use of products, not their one-way consumption (Ellen MacArthur Foundation, 2013). They are now advancing the idea of Circulytics, which is a free company-level measuring tool that reveals the extent to which a company has achieved circularity across its entire operations.

3. **Organize local and collaborative**

The authors of the AC Concepts supporting the ideas of a commons are unanimous in their view that management must be at the local level. The principle of subsidiarity applies — keep decision-making at the lowest feasible level, and only elevate it to higher levels when necessary. The key is delegating authority to the smallest jurisdictional unit that is competent to handle it (Fennell, 2011 citing Ellickson, 1998; Ostrom, 2009; Eisenstein, 2011; Alperovitz, 2013).

Bollier (2014) suggests the locus of control is at the community level and those communities must be willing to act as conscientious stewards of a resource. A key challenge is how to divide up the resource systems. Ostrom (1990, 2009) talked about nested enterprises that may require more than one level of local management. A simple way to think of this is land that is used both for farming and for grazing.

"Local" in After Capitalism is not off-the-grid or anti-global, but situating relevant decision-making where it belongs — there are still global decisions to be made. Balle (Business Alliance for Local Living Economies) (n.d.) provides some key aspects of local including:

- More collaboration: building shared infrastructure and technical assistance to advance collaboration.
- Shift capital: keeping more money within communities.
- Co-Create policy: including all stakeholders — a direct democracy model.
- Cultivate connection: connecting with purpose, community, awe, and compassion.

- <u>Prioritize equity</u>: building supportive services and infrastructure for the jobless and under-employed.

Balle sees a locally driven networked economy that scales horizontally, thriving in a climate-compatible economic system. The localization and blending of production and consumption will result in a better circular system, with less waste and negative externalities.

This will be challenging for sure, but the shift to greater emphasis on local is already underway. Balle's local economy envisions a global system of what they call human-scale, interconnected, local living economies. They function in harmony with local ecosystems, meet the basic needs of all people, support just and democratic societies, and foster joyful community life. It suggests 8 principles or actions: (1) act local first (2) prioritize equity (3) regenerate soil and nature (4) accelerate collaboration (5) share ownership (6) shift capital (7) co-create policy (8) cultivate connection. This is very much in line with other local proposals, but interestingly does not specifically target *After Capitalism*. It does acknowledge that the current system is breaking down and seeks to build a "new economy" based on local community networks.

Katz and Nowak's (2018) *New Localism* concept observes that as national governments, particularly in the US, wrestle with populism and an overall lack of effectiveness, cities have been forced to step into the void and take on a more active role in problem-solving. They see this shift as part of the larger social change of vertical approaches giving way to horizontal ones: from hierarchies to networks. Networks of public, private, and civic actors, and transnational circuits of capital, trade, and innovation, are increasingly taking a role in shaping the future. Their thinking is based in the *Neoliberal Capitalism* Baseline. Their examples include Pittsburgh's revival around robotics, Indianapolis's reinvention around sports and biotech, and Copenhagen's successful reclamation of public assets. Their examples suggest how power is shifting from the national to the local context.

Sociologist Marc Schneiberg found counties with more locally oriented organizations such as cooperatives, credit unions, community banks, nonprofits, and universities experienced fewer job losses during the Great Recession and greater job growth in its aftermath (Chen and Chen, 2021).

In what could be the biggest understatement of his book, De Angelis (2017) suggests that a massive social movement would be necessary to shift institutions and functions of public services. We are not focused on the how, but we must acknowledge as a practical matter that this is a huge question. It sounds idealistic if not impractical to assume that local community groups will magically self-organize to handle the massively complex task of managing aspects of an intricate economy. It starts locally and expands from there. Bollier (2014) describes the results along these lines: "Harmony with local ecosystems, meet the basic needs of all people, support just and democratic societies, and foster joyful community life." And Hollo (2018) suggests ecological democracy as a model that is about participatory, deliberative democratic paths, embedded in nature, based on the principle of subsidiarity, or putting control into the most local hands possible, and limiting the opportunities for domination and free riding. You get the idea!

The massive social movement idea aligns with the values shifts towards postmodern and integral in which citizens participate in grassroots movements to both actively take part themselves as well as push government in the direction of change. It is not about waiting for government to pass the necessary laws — government is unlikely to be out in front and will need to be pushed. As stated above, government's role is as a facilitator, not the manager.

5.1.5 Tools

The list of potential tools could be quite long. We will focus on some exemplars to get a feel for what a *Circular Commons* world might look like. The text box summarizes the brief inventory, which organizes the tools into four categories of barter, community building, financial, and structure.

Barter

Barter is specific to the *Circular Commons* image – not much about it appears in the other two

> **Circular Commons: Quick-and-dirty tool inventory**
>
> Barter
> - Local currencies
> - P2P Networks
> - LETS (Local Exchange Trading Systems) and Time banks
>
> Community building
> - Co-ops
> - Worker ownership
> - Land trusts
> - Urban gardens
> - Intentional or conscious eco-communities
>
> Financial
> - Income topping
> - Negative interest
> - Progressive global tax on capital
>
> Structures
> - B-Corps
> - Not-for-profits
> - Leasing

Imagining After Capitalism | 161

guiding images. It fits with the ethos of collective action and importantly no accumulation. It is wise to be careful here and not romanticize barter — as is sometime done with the AC concepts. The intent is not to go back to the good old days before money ruined everything. But it is indicative of rethinking the purpose of what we're doing. A key distinction is looking forward rather than backward. The barter tools take advantage of more sophisticated technology to enable the calculations of value to make it work — money served a very useful purpose in estimating value and facilitating exchange.

- Local currencies
    o They would underpin economic resilience at a regional level, straddling arbitrary national borders to reflect economic and social networks. A national network of currencies could replace the national currency to allow communities to trade with each other.
- P2P Networks
    o These community-based networks enable exchange between members. Prosper was an early P2P exchange for lending that enabled members to borrow from one another. Freecycle is another long-running P2P network that was set up to keep goods out of landfills by offering them to the community instead of throwing them out.
- LETS (Local Exchange Trading Systems) and Time banks
    o These are distinguished from local currencies by saying money is avoided by design here (but it can get fuzzy in practice). LETS and Time banks involve using and spending time credit — spend an hour helping and later receive an hour of help. LETS communal labor involve reciprocity, gift, or mutual aid; it is the labor that subject A performs for subject B, B for C. and C for A (circular reciprocity) or simply A for B (where karmic feel-good is the reward) (Lee et al., 2004; Collom et al., 2012; Ruzzene, 2015; De Angelis, 2017).
    o Groups use locally created units of value as currency which can be traded or bartered in exchange for goods or services. Most LETS groups range from 50 to 150 members, with a small core group who use the system as the basis of a lifestyle.

- o Transactions don't necessarily require a nominal exchange of units. For instance, members can repay other members who have performed for them a service by providing a service in return, as opposed to paying for the original service (Downey, 2021).
  - o Alongside the material benefits, idealistic and social elements also play a large role; that is, they are community-building tools that build social networks (Monetta.org, ND).

Community building

- Co-ops – Food co-ops are among the most common type. They are grocery stores owned by the people who shop there. Those who join have a voice in how they are operated. In the financial world, credit unions are essentially co-ops and they are also present in other sectors such as retail and insurance.

- Worker ownership – The most famous example is the Mondragon network of 120 worker cooperatives in the Basque region of Spain. It launched in 1956 and employs over 70,000 worker-owners. Mondragon employees own their company and make their own decisions and keep the profits (Hackl, 2020).

- Land trusts – In our context, they are used for conservation and enable groups to purchase, protect, and manage land that typically has natural resources, is a historical site, or maybe is used as a public recreational area.

- Urban or community gardens – Volunteer members of a community manage and maintain food and plant plots. Beyond the production of food, which can be for members or perhaps for donation to local food banks, they also provide other benefits such as beautification, encouraging social interaction, and community pride.

- Intentional or conscious eco-communities – Both of these types of communities can be organized around environmental or, in our case, *Circular Commons* concerns. Intentional communities tend to be residential and more about sharing life and resources — think commune. Whereas conscious communities tend to be more non-residential, with lots of programming, and less of the sharing of resources like rent, bills, land, etc. (Jamaluddin, 2021). The Global Ecovillage Network lists almost 500 self-identified eco-villages around the world from remote villages in

Sri Lanka to the popular Christiania commune in Copenhagen (Travel.Earth, 2020).

- Ecotats – These are local networks of autonomous settlements contained within an environmental region that are able to fulfill its community needs. Guiding these communities are use values that focus on social and ecological needs as opposed to capitalist exchange value. They are organized into sophisticated global-local networks that work with neighboring communities using compacts – agreed-upon guidelines around an issue, rather than contracts, which are legally enforced agreements – to help provide each other with whatever resources are needed (Nelson, 2022).

Financial

- Income topping
  - Pledging never to earn more than a certain amount of money in a year, with Eisenstein (2011) suggesting US$24,000.
- Negative interest
  - A credit system based on depreciating currency allows zero-interest loans. While loans must still be repaid, no longer must they be paid for. In that sense, money becomes free (Eisenstein, 2011, 209). It is essentially a tax on holding money, ensuring that the only way to maintain wealth is to keep investing it (Eisenstein, 2011).
- Progressive global tax on capital
  - This is Piketty's (2014) proposed redistributive mechanism from his massive work *Capital* that explored the systems causes of inequality. The global tax would be coupled with a very high level of financial transparency — a utopian idea, but could be approached step by step: continental, regional, etc.

Structures

- B-Corps
  - There are roughly 3,500 organizations globally that made it through the rigorous process of becoming B-Corps (Williams, 2022).
  - Danone's $6 billion North American division became the largest B-Corp in the world in 2018, defined by French law as requiring

Danone to both generate profits and benefit consumer health and the environment (Lamb, 2020). They've been recently surpassed by Natura (Brazilian group including Natura Cosméticos, Aesop, The Body Shop and Avon) as the current largest B-Corp at $7.9 billion (Aziz, 2022).

- Not-for-profits
  - The Post Growth Institute defines not-for-profit companies as follows: "100% of any profits these businesses make must be reinvested into the business or community — it really means not-for-private-profit. This structure could potentially transform corporations into vehicles for wealth distribution. Profits, instead of going to shareholders or the top management, would circulate back into the economy. The institute argues that not-for-profit companies are the ideal hybrid between innovative, but private profit-driven, businesses and socially focused, but charity dependent, non-profit foundations (Maclurcan, 2016).
- Leasing
  - Leasing, or performance contracts, instead of owning. A key circular concept is using rather than consuming, which involves sorting products into consumables and durables.

5.1.6 Personal

The *Circular Commons* concepts are mostly focused on what business needs to do, with some attention to government and consumer roles. Proponents are hopeful that citizens will demand that leaders will take more action regarding the environment. The values shift from modern to postmodern and integral provides hope that this could happen. Participation, community, collaboration, empowerment, and sustainability are key postmodern values, while commitment, connectivity and interdependence are integral values key to this guiding image. These value priorities could surely be organized in a way that promotes a *Circular Commons* future. As Scharmer (2013) put it, the shift from "me-to-we" thinking is required. While the long-term shifts in values suggest this is possible in 10-20 years, these values and "we" thinking seem far removed from the growing tribalism and social isolation that are prevalent today.

The concern for wellbeing of individuals is placed at the same level as the wellbeing of the planet (healthy people are more likely to want a health planet). Shaw and Waterstone (2020, 106) provide a very personal and local vision: "it's a question of knowing how to fight, to pick locks, to set broken bones, and treat sickness; how to build a pirate radio transmitter; how to set up street kitchens; how to aim straight; how to gather together scattered knowledge and set up wartime agronomics; understanding plankton biology, soil composition and studying the ways plants interact; to get to know possible uses for and connections with our immediate environment as well as the limits that can't be exceeded" (Shaw and Waterstone, 2020, 112).

There is a strong theme of more citizen involvement in community affairs and governance. Where today we have a small number of citizens involved in say homeowners' associations or neighborhood watches. For *Circular Commons* to work there will need to be much higher levels of participation. The commons are managed by the people at the local level. There is more time available for non-materialistic pursuits, since people are responsible for their community rather than their jobs, which seems to be a given in the *After Capitalism* future. Admittedly, this guiding image is less focused on describing the particular role of workers than *Non-Workers' Paradise* or even *Tech-Led Abundance*, but it is reasonable to assume something like UBI in place so that full-time work is not the norm. Re-orienting the economy to a *Circular Commons* model is assumed to be a key part of the activities or "work" of individuals.

5.1.7 Leadership

This is about mechanisms, enforcement, and power. How does all this get done? The role of government here is one of facilitation to enable local community citizens to participate in political decision-making. It seems that, in order to be successful, the commons approach is not just about resources and the environment but must also be part of a social and political transformation. It amounts to a kind of political philosophy with specific policy approaches. There is pretty strong consensus that leadership in a commons model is one that operates primarily at the local level using horizontal, bottom-up-driven decision-making rather than top-down, expert-driven decision-making.

Role of the state

Bollier (2014) and DeAngelis (2017) both believe that a commons-based approach can emerge alongside the existing system, and that the state has an important role in the transition. Eisenstein (2011, 187) suggests that the essential purpose of government is to serve as the trustee of the commons. This includes:

- a duty to prevent [further] enclosures of commons resources.
- chartering of commons (providing legal limitations on private property and setting up community management of the ecological commons).

The range of options or degree of intervention needed from the state depends on the severity of the context. If the environmental context in the future is better than expected, a steady state approach that would use a mix of government intervention and markets might be sufficient. If, however, as this work expects, the context is worse, a more radical degrowth approach would be needed. This in turn would suggest a strong intervention, such as creating new institutional mechanisms to shift from reliance on full-time paid work to some form of guaranteed income. Kallis et al. (2015) suggest that the state would need to take back control of the creation of new money from private banks (public money). There is no consensus yet on how to shift to bottom-up at this point, but the fact there is agreement on the target or direction provides some optimism that new participatory leadership models can be developed, tried, and implemented.

5.1.8 Pathway

Most likely, a massive social movement would be necessary to commonalize institutions and functions of public services (De Angelis 2017).

Environmentalists and their supporters are the core drivers of this image at present. Most of them would likely agree with the basic conclusion of this research that we cannot continue to grow the economy at current rates on a planet with finite resources – some might advocate steady state or even managed growth. Perhaps the key question is whether the shift to degrowth is chosen and gradual or is forced upon us more abruptly. The 13 concept authors agree that growth as we know it cannot continue. Alexander (2012) perhaps captured the essence of the collect view in suggesting there are two ways down:

- if we don't make good choices, it will be the harder way via overshoot and collapse (Meadows et al., 1972, 1993, 2004)
- if we do make good strategic choices, the softer way will be a more gradual long descent (Homer-Dixon, 2006).

There is also agreement that the sooner action is taken, the better, as it provides more flexibility. Delaying action narrows the range of options. The highlights of each author's proposed pathway, if offered, are in the 13 templates at the end of the chapter.

The ideas around pathways sorted into four sections:

- Pilots: ideas about how to develop local initiatives that could crystallize into larger-scale movements.
- Plans: probably closer to guiding principles than specific sequential steps, but they convey a sense of actions to take over time.
- Evolution or revolution: commentary on how the ideas sort on an evolution-revolution continuum.
- Capacity building: a summary of common ground on what needs to be done to move forward.

Pilots

Roughly half of the concept authors did not propose a specific plan or outline, as they saw it as out of the scope of the work. They generally proposed a set of organizing principles. They tended to focus on organizing at the local level by developing pilot projects, and ultimately sought to scale up these initial efforts into a larger movement.

In support of the scale-up idea, the research of Folke et al. (2021) suggests transformational change could eventually emerge from small-scale experimentation, innovation, and coalition-building. They found that small-scale processes can, under the right conditions, influence larger-scale systemic change. Clark (2020) has also identified several small-scale groups and movements under his eco-anarchist umbrella. He mentions the Zapatistas (referenced earlier), the Zadistes who used permanent occupation to defeat a proposed airport construction, and the Sarvodaya Movement (aka Gandhian Movement) in India that has established ashrams among other things. In Sri Lanka, for example, Sarvodaya has spread to more than 15,000 villages and has built more than 5,000 preschools, community health centers, and libraries, as well as establishing thousands of village banks and more than 100,000 small businesses — all without any government support (Flyer, 2022). They and others provide potential examples of transformational change. They are isolated examples, however, and not an integrated movement.

Specific pilot proposals, both from concept authors and others, include:

1. *From private to public investment.* Peter Victor (2008) in *Managing without Growth* suggested that changes to investment are the most influential factors in the transition to a sustainable economy. In the macroeconomic scenario that Victor developed for Canada as a case study, net business investment is reduced, accompanied by a shift in investment from private to public goods, implemented through changes in taxation and public spending (Mastini, 2017). Srnicek and Williams (2016) also noted that it has been collective investment, not private investment, that has been the primary driver of technological development. Indeed, a theme emerged in the research that despite our fascination with the efficiency and productivity of the private sector [see *privatization* section above], the public sector has been responsible for a great deal of innovation.

2. *Co-ops.* There seems to be a small movement toward cooperative economics. A 2019 Co-op IMPACT Conference brought together 400 cooperators from across the globe to give voice to the fact that cooperatives are well-positioned to grow in a rapidly changing economy (Reetz, 2019).

3. *Free public transit.* Luxembourg is among the first countries to pioneer fully free public transit. The move aims to help reduce inequality — - even though the tiny country is known for its wealth, poverty is increasing (Peters, 2020).

4. *Doughnut in action.* Amsterdam is the first major city to put the doughnut theory into action, including the so-called true-price initiative. The goal is to bring all 872,000 residents "inside the doughnut." One example is the true price initiative that spells out the cost of factors such as carbon footprint, the toll that farming takes on the land, and paying workers a fair wage. Acknowledging and paying these costs is designed to ensure that everyone has access to a good quality of life, but without putting more pressure on the planet than is sustainable (Nugent, 2021).

5. *The Buy Nothing Project.* This Gift economy concept challenges the consumerist mindset and reconnects neighbors. It involves no buying or selling, or even trading or bartering, but relies strictly on a Gift economy. The Buy Nothing Project has grown rapidly since then, reaching 6,000 groups in 44 countries (Martinko, 2021), but has recently fissured around efforts to "professionalize" the approach with a proprietary app leading some groups to break away (Chang, 2023).

Plans

Overall, there is not much activity at the national or international level with the commons. There are sporadic local examples, but the idea of shifting to a commons-based approach remains on the fringe.

There is some support for the circular aspect. While the US Federal Government does not have a plan, the circular economy is talked about at the state level, but it appears to be mostly as a buzzword. Looking just at packaging, the Sustainable Packaging Coalition identified over 132 bills in 27 US states introduced in the 2019/2020 or 2020 legislative session regarding just bags and films. They mostly proposed bag bans or bag fees, but only 15 bills in 11 states were signed into law (Reno, 2020). There is use of circular as a buzzword. For instance, examining California's "circular bills" reveals that they were mostly about recycling, which is the least desirable aspect of circular (Quinn, 2021).

The EU has taken a much more serious approach and has adopted a circular plan up to 2050 as part of its overall environmental and sustainability approach. The European Commission's CEAP (established in March 2020) is designed to reduce pressure on natural resources, help achieve its climate neutrality target, and create sustainable growth and jobs (European Commission, 2021). As one of the first major bodies of legislation and policy to promote a circular economy, it also provided one of the first blueprints for implementing circular economy policies across Europe and abroad. The CEAP mapped out 54 actions, as well as four legislative proposals on waste, containing targets for landfill, reuse, and recycling, to be met by 2030 and 2035, and introducing new obligations, such as the separate collection of municipal textiles and biowaste (Ellen MacArthur Foundation, 2020).

Eisenstein (2011) maps out a more radical approach that is arguably more like guiding principles than planning steps. They would require much challenging policy shifts from today's point-of-view:

- Negative-interest currency (to discourage accumulation)
- Elimination of economic rents, and compensation for depletion of the commons and the use of the subjects of economic rent as a currency backing
- Internalization of social and environmental costs
- Economic and monetary localization
- A social dividend
- Economic degrowth, noting there is much work to be done, but much of it does not generate an economic return.
- Gift culture and P2P economics

Jackson (2015) proposes a 12-point plan that focuses on three principal areas for building a sustainable economy:

- <u>Building a sustainable macro-economy</u>: Debt-driven materialistic consumption is deeply unsatisfactory as the basis for our macro-economy. The time is now ripe to develop a new macro-economics for sustainability that does not rely for its stability on relentless growth and expanding material throughput.
- <u>Protecting capabilities for flourishing</u>: The social logic that locks people into materialistic consumerism is extremely powerful, but detrimental ecologically and psychologically. A lasting prosperity can only be achieved by freeing people from this damaging dynamic and providing creative opportunities for people to flourish — within the ecological limits of the planet.
- <u>Respecting ecological limit</u>s: The material profligacy of consumer society is depleting natural resources and placing unsustainable burdens on the planet's ecosystems. There is an urgent need to establish clear resource and environmental limits on economic activity and develop policies to achieve them.

It may be disappointing not to have detailed plans, but this work is more oriented toward mapping out the destination – the guiding images – than the journey. The concept authors also see detailed plans as a separate piece of work.

Evolution or revolution

Despite increasingly dire warnings about climate change and carrying capacity, no real sense of urgency has developed. There seems to be no mainstream appetite for revolution regarding the environment. Hollo (2018) suggests that disconnection and atomization is to blame for the lack of urgency. There are some fringe groups or movements, but they are mostly small and disconnected at this point in time. Environmental anarchists, for instance, suggest building a new society at the local, grassroots level, where communities create self-governing, localized, participatory democracies.

It is hard to imagine how to mobilize the sophisticated global coordination that will be necessary to deal with climate change and carrying capacity in a revolutionary context. The connectedness of the challenge is so great that a deliberative, participatory, and coordinated approach is needed.

But perhaps there is a way to do both evolution and revolution? Gabriel (2017) believes that we are in for a "long ecological revolution, lasting for decades and even centuries, aimed at creation of society of substantive equality and ecological sustainability." But this movement needs to be revolutionary from the outset in opposing capitalism. It's an interesting idea — getting to evolution requires a revolution!

Capacity building

It was noted above in "Plans" that frankly there weren't many and they don't tackle the full scope of the *Circular Commons* image, i.e., some focus on circular but little on commons. At this early stage of *After Capitalism*, it is perhaps understandable that capacity-building ought to precede planning. There need to be people and organizations willing and capable of carrying out the plans. Six themes for capacity building were identified in the research, in a rough sequential flow:

1. *Starts with guiding principles*: there are some ideas on potentially beneficial changes.
2. *Starts on the periphery*: change always begins on the edge of the mainstream rather than the center.
3. *Get a meme in place*: a description of the concept that catches on and is passed along.
4. *Individuals get involved*: small group(s) of people begin to act on the concept.
5. *Crystallizing rather than scaling*: early on, there is a refining of the concept in practice.

6. *Gain political power*: with its purpose getting clearer, group(s) begin to work on gaining some political influence and begin making plans to scale further.

Below are examples of what is currently happening regarding each of the steps in capacity building. The first bullet describes activities regarding circular, and the second focuses on the commons.

1. Starts with guiding principles

- For the **Circular** aspect, the MacArthur Foundation has been important in bringing together and promoting ideas about the circular economy, including Stahel's (2019) closed-loop approach developed in the 1970s, McDonough and Braungart's (2010) cradle-to-cradle and *Upcycle* (2013), Janine Benyus's (2009) regenerative design, and Gunter Pauli's (2010) Blue Economy.

- For the **Commons** aspect, in 1985, the National Academy of Sciences sponsored a conference in Annapolis, Maryland, to discuss common property resource management, which kicked off interest in "common pool resources." Five years later Elinor Ostrom (1990) laid the intellectual foundation for rethinking a commons approach to resource management. A key contribution was refuting the popular "Tragedy of the Commons" notion put forth by Garrett Hardin.

2. Starts on the periphery

- With **Circular**, the early idea of McDonough's cradle-to-cradle achieved some recognition among the deeply committed but did not break through. The strong commitment by the MacArthur Foundation is an interesting exception to the rule that innovation starts on the periphery, as it is a well-known mainstream group and has somewhat successfully employed a strategy of recruiting high-profile organizations as sponsors. It has played a leading role in raising awareness about circular.

- The **Commons**, in contrast, has indeed remained on the periphery with low overall public awareness. It has lacked a powerful champion such as the MacArthur Foundation, although few new movements are able to find such a powerful mainstream ally.

3. Get a Meme in place
- As noted above, the **Circular** meme is more prominent than the **Commons**.

4. Individuals get involved
- The concepts are challenging at the individual level since they are both inherently group-oriented concepts

5. Crystallizing rather than scaling
- For **Circular**, there are pockets of activity globally. In the US, the Loop delivery service has piloted a circular "as-a-service" concept involving several large, branded consumer product companies. Several multinationals have adopted circular practices and principles. The MacArthur site has several case examples including Philips, Renault and Solvay, as well as pilot projects in cities across the globe such as Sao Paolo, Cape Town, and New York City, and examples in various sectors such as food, fashion, and plastics. At the country level, China has committed to circular principles in its most recent 5-year plan (Koty, 2021). The EU, noted above for adopting the most comprehensive approach, continues to update its plans, for instance, updating regulations on batteries and waste batteries in July 2023 (Ernst and Young, 2023).
- For **Commons**, De Angelis (2017) suggests that individuals start communing now, arguing that it is not necessary to wait for a political revolution or a new system, but to start bringing about the change now. There is a handful of eclectic movements emerging, such as the Solidarity Economy movement, the Transition Town movement, alterglobalization activists, water activists, the Landless Workers' Movement, La Via Campesina, the free software Wikipedians, the open-access publishing world, etc.

6. Gain political power
- Not happening yet.

5.1.9 Circular Commons Images Templates

Author	Umair Haque is a London-based consultant who has been a passionate advocate for post-capitalist economics through books and blogging frequently on the topic on *Medium* since 2018.
Time horizon	Unclear
Scope	Notes global scope of problems
Key drivers	Inequality, Automation, Stagnation
Key ideas	+ Business as usual hasn't been able to create value, returns, jobs, fulfillment, income, net worth, and trust over the last decade. + Business isn't as profitable as "Betterness," which is a new way of thinking about business; three decades of evidence suggest that betterness yields greater equity returns, asset returns, returns, and profitability. + The corporation is obsolete; B corps are a better fit. + Need for new systems of national accounts.
Ideal or guiding values	+ Make a paradigm shift from negative to positive or from being in business to being in betterness. + An economy isn't an end, but it's a means to the end of a good life.
Emotional, aesthetic, and spiritual aspects	Passionate appeal that we can do better.
Personal	The transition will hurt traditional corporations, but the "people" are being hurt by today's approach to business; Betterness seeks to create a more human future.
Pathway or plan	Has some guiding principles.

Author	The Ellen Macarthur Foundation was launched in 2010 to accelerate the transition to a circular economy and has been a key thought leader and champion for the concept.
Time horizon	Unclear
Scope	Global
Key drivers	Climate and carrying capacity
Key ideas	+ Today's goods are tomorrow's resources, forming a virtuous cycle that fosters prosperity in a world of finite resources by taking advantage of design for reuse principles. + Sorts products into consumables and durables: durables are designed for re-use via leasing rather than consumption models (use rather than consume); and consumables are increasingly made of biological materials; thus after use they can be returned to the earth. + From consumers to users: Getting products returned to the manufacturer at the end of the usage cycle requires a new customer relationship: 'consumers' become 'users' with leasing or performance contracts in place.
Ideal or guiding values	+ Is restorative or regenerative by intention and design + In the midst of a pervasive shift in consumer behavior; new generation of customers seem prepared to prefer access over ownership
Emotional, aesthetic, and spiritual aspects	Stewardship ethic
Personal	Mostly focused on what business needs to do, with some attention to government and consumer role.
Pathway or plan	The EU has adopted a circular plan up to 2030 and 2035.

Author	Bollier studies the commons and works to try to protect it.
Time horizon	Unclear
Scope	Local, bottom-up
Key drivers	Shifting values, Inequality, Climate and carrying capacity
Key ideas	Commons = the shared management of a resource by many. Shows how enclosure, commodification, and financializing of nature are the root of the resource problem. **Commons principles:** + commons- and rights-based ecological governance as a practical alternative to the state and market; + the Earth belongs to all; + state has a duty to prevent enclosures of commons and protect large-scale common-pool resources; + state chartering of commons; + legal limitations on private property as needed to ensure the long-term viability of ecological systems; and the human right to establish and maintain ecological commons.
Ideal or guiding values	+ Believes commons could be a vehicle for social and political emancipation and societal transformation. It amounts to a kind of political philosophy with specific policy approaches. + Commons must have clear boundaries so commoners can know who has rights to use a resource. The rules for appropriating a resource must take account of local conditions and include limits on what can be taken and how.
Emotional, aesthetic, and spiritual aspects	+ Only through commoning do we start to reintegrate ourselves with nature and with each other. + A commons requires that there be a community willing to act as a conscientious steward of a resource.

Personal	Hardin's "Tragedy of the Commons" has become a cautionary lesson about the impossibility of collective action. For Hardin, the best approach is "the institution of private property coupled with legal inheritance … and those who are biologically more fit to be the custodians of property and power should legally inherit more." But Bollier objects: "that is not a commons!"
Pathway or plan	+ Crystallizing rather than scaling + A top priority should be expanding the conversation about the commons. Next, get the cultural meme in circulation, and then ground it in actual practice. + Notes the rise of eclectic movements, e.g., Solidarity Economy movement, the Transition Town movement, alterglobalization activists, water activists, the Landless Workers' Movement, La Via Campesina, the free software Wikipedians, the open-access publishing world, etc.

Author	De Angelis lectures in Political Economy at Univ. of East London. His work covers commodity-fetishism, value theory, the political economy of globalization, and a critique of mainstream economics.
Time horizon	Unclear
Scope	Global; very local, autonomous approach
Key drivers	Shifting values
Key ideas	+ We can decide what a commons is. Examples are networks of supporting friends, community gardens, P2P networks; LETS systems or time banks (Ruzzene 2015; Collom et al. 2012; Lee et al. 2004). They are generally instituted as ways to organize and rationalize reciprocal labor in conditions of social fragmentation to overcome them. + In a commons, group members have the right to exclude nonmembers from using a resource. Open access regimes include the oceans and the atmosphere – long considered as having no limits on who is authorized to use a resource. + Capitalist development needs to create a dependency on the commodity form of social relations so that people become unable to escape the capitalist imposition of work.
Ideal or guiding values	Commons are social systems in which resources are pooled by a community who govern the resources to guarantee their sustainability and the reproduction of the community. People engage in communing (doing in commons that has a direct relation to the needs, desires and aspirations of the commoners).
Emotional, aesthetic, and spiritual aspects	A very theoretical work that ultimately suggests a highly local model in which people self-organize within current systems and expand from there.
Personal	Suggests people start communing now: "This priority of social (rather than political) revolution also implies that to bring about radical transformation we do not need to have a worked system to replace the old one before dreaming of or wishing its demise."
Pathway or plan	A massive social movement would be needed to commonalize institutions and functions of public services.

Imagining After Capitalism | 179

Author	Kallis is a professor at Barcelona's Institute of Environmental Science and Technology and has written four books on degrowth.
Time horizon	Unclear
Scope	Talks about the French origins of the concept. Notes a frequent criticism of degrowth is that it is applicable only to the overdeveloped economies of the Global North. The poorer countries of the Global South still need to grow; Degrowth in the North will liberate ecological space for growth in the South.
Key drivers	Shifting values, Climate and carrying capacity
Key ideas	+ Movement seeking to abolish economic growth as a social objective and favoring grassroots practices such as eco-communities, co-ops, local currencies, barter, commons, etc. + A degrowth, or décroissance, movement took off in France in 2002 and has spread to other parts of Europe since. + It suggests economic growth will eventually exhaust resources and calls for abolishing it as a social objective. + Degrowth ideas include new welfare institutions to decouple paid employment from growth, unconditional basic income, and for the State to take back the control of the creation of new money from private banks (public money). Admits there is no consensus on how to do this. + Advocates grassroots principles similar to communing and notes these grassroots practices share five features: 1. A shift from production for exchange to production for use. 2. Substitution of wage labor with voluntary activity, meaning a decommodification and de-professionalization of labor. 3. The circulation of goods is set in motion, at least partly by an exchange of reciprocal 'gifts' rather than in search of profit. 4. Unlike capitalist enterprise, they do not have a built-in dynamic to accumulate and expand. 5. They are outcomes of processes of commoning; they are new forms of commons.

Ideal or guiding values	+ Décroissance (French for degrowth), began as a movement of activists for whom sustainable development is an oxymoron. + Seek abolition of economic growth as a social objective.
Emotional, aesthetic, and spiritual aspects	The foundational theses of degrowth are that growth is uneconomic and unjust, that it is ecologically unsustainable and that it will never be enough; need to be more radical.
Personal	Sharing, simplicity, conviviality, care and the commons are primary significations of what this society might look like.
Pathway or plan	Very little on this: one could imagine a scenario under which political forces come democratically in power and enforce resource caps and social minima (e.g. a job guarantee for the unemployed), restricting the operation of capitalism.

Author	Kate Raworth is an economist at Oxford University's Environmental Change Institute. She explores the economic thinking needed to address the 21st century's social and ecological challenges.
Time horizon	Unclear
Scope	Global
Key drivers	Climate and carrying capacity
Key ideas	The doughnut depicts a social foundation of wellbeing that no-one should fall below and an ecological ceiling of planetary pressure that we should not go beyond. Economics should be reframed in terms of goals – what should the economy do – rather than its focus on explaining how it works. The doughnut suggests two primary goals by depicting a pair of concentric rings. + Below the inner ring—the social foundation—lie critical human deprivations such as hunger and illiteracy. + Beyond the outer ring—the ecological ceiling— lies critical planetary degradation such as climate change and biodiversity loss. Between those two rings is the Doughnut itself, the space where we can meet the needs of all within the means of the planet.
Ideal or guiding values	It is absolutely essential to have a compelling alternative frame if the old one is ever to be debunked.
Emotional, aesthetic, and spiritual aspects	The doughnut graphic has broad mass appeal.
Personal	Says that concern for the wellbeing of individuals ought to be at the same level of concern as wellbeing of the planet.
Pathway or plan	Not part of the scope; talks about evolution in how economics is taught.

Author	Scharmer is a Senior Lecturer in the MIT Sloan School of Management and co-founder of the Presencing Institute. He chairs the MIT IDEAS program for cross-sector innovation and introduced the concept of "presencing" (learning from the emerging future) in his books *Theory U* and *Presence*.
Time horizon	Unclear
Scope	Global
Key drivers	Shifting values
Key ideas	*[Does not position itself as "After Capitalism." Its evolutionary approach has a lot in common with conscious capitalism and H2 Collaborative Sharing Platforms; also shares H3 ideas like "eco" emphasis and commons-based approaches to property rights]* Eight disconnects between: 1. the financial and real economy 2. the growth imperative and the finite resources of the Earth 3. the Haves and the Have Nots 4. institutional leadership and people 5. gross domestic product (GDP) and well-being 6. governance and the voiceless in our systems 7. actual ownership forms and best societal use of property 8. technology and real societal needs + 1.0: The state-centric model: coordination through hierarchy and control in a single-sector society. [traditional] + 2.0: The free-market model: the rise of a second (private) sector and coordinated through the mechanisms of market and competition. [ego] + 3.0 The social-market model: the rise of a third (NGO) sector with negotiated coordination among interest groups [stakeholder] + 4.0: The co-creative ecosystem mode: the rise of a fourth sector that creates platforms and holds the space for cross-sector innovation that engages stakeholders from all sectors. [ecosystem]

Ideal or guiding values	The wellbeing of the whole is key to avoiding planetary disaster. The key is the needed shift in "consciousness" from ego-driven to eco. This shift in consciousness informs other needed changes, such as the main purpose of money 4.0 and capital 4.0 is to relink the creation of money with entrepreneurial intention in our communities – the function of money and financial mechanisms is to serve the real economy.
Emotional, aesthetic, and spiritual aspects	The current crisis of capitalism is frames of thought that conceive of nature, work, and capital as commodities.
Personal	Bad economics and bad politics result from defining one's self-interest too narrowly.
Pathway or plan	+ Any system shows up first at the periphery. + Shift the global field of entrepreneurship by creating a multiregional network of hubs that support the capacity of next-gen entrepreneurs to build intentional ecosystem economies that meet the challenges of our time.

Author	A network of socially responsible businesses; in 2019 BALLE transitioned to Common Future (www.commonfuture.co)
Time horizon	Unclear
Scope	Local
Key drivers	Climate and carrying capacity, Ineffective Left
Key ideas	*[Does not specifically target "After Capitalism", but acknowledges the current system is breaking down, and seeks to build a new economy based on local community networks]*
	Advocates a global system of human-scale, interconnected local level economies following these principles: 1. Act Local First: diversity of locally owned businesses. 2. Prioritize Equity: Build supportive services and infrastructure for the jobless and under-employed 3. Regenerate Soil & Nature: Apply holistic land management practices, embrace renewable energy and energy-efficient transit, divest from fossil fuels, and use business to restore ecosystems and reverse climate change. 4. Accelerate Collaboration: build shared infrastructure and technical assistance to advance collaboration. 5. Share Ownership: Move economic control from distant corporations to local communities, and choose democratic economic models like worker ownership, land trusts, and the protection of public assets. 6. Shift Capital: keeping more of their money in the community. 7. Co-Create Policy: Including all stakeholders 8. Build connection via purpose, community, awe, compassion.
Ideal or guiding values	Heavily focused on building local community business and entrepreneurship.
Emotional, aesthetic, and spiritual aspects	Function in harmony with local ecosystems, meet the basic needs of all people, support just and democratic societies, and foster joyful community life.
Personal	From "me" to "we" thinking.
Pathway or plan	Not specified

Author	Tim Jackson is an ecological economist and Professor of Sustainable Development and Director at the Centre for the Understanding of Sustainable Prosperity (CUSP) at the University of Surrey.
Time horizon	Unclear
Scope	Global, but more about the affluent consuming less
Key drivers	Inequality, Stagnation, Climate and carrying capacity
Key ideas	Strengthening ecologically and socially sustainable practices given the physical limits of the earth – a new macroeconomics for sustainability is not only essential, but possible. 12 Steps to a Sustainable Economy: Building a Sustainable Macro-Economy Debt-driven materialistic consumption is deeply unsatisfactory as the basis for our macro-economy. The time is now ripe to develop a new macro-economics for sustainability that does not rely for its stability on relentless growth and expanding material throughput. Four specific policy areas are identified to achieve this: 1. Developing macro-economic capability 2. Investing in public assets and infrastructures 3. Increasing financial and fiscal prudence 4. Reforming macro-economic accounting Protecting Capabilities for Flourishing The social logic that locks people into materialistic consumerism is extremely powerful, but detrimental ecologically and psychologically. A lasting prosperity can only be achieved by freeing people from this damaging dynamic and providing creative opportunities for people to flourish – within the ecological limits of the planet.

Key ideas	Five policy areas address this challenge: 1. Sharing the available work and improving the work-life balance 2. Tackling systemic inequality 3. Measuring capabilities and flourishing 4. Strengthening human and social capital 5. Reversing the culture of consumerism Respecting Ecological Limits The material profligacy of consumer society is depleting natural resources and placing unsustainable burdens on the planet's ecosystems. There is an urgent need to establish clear resource and environmental limits on economic activity and develop policies to achieve them. Three policy suggestions contribute to that task: 1. Imposing clearly defined resource/emissions caps 2. Implementing fiscal reform for sustainability 3. Promoting technology transfer and international ecosystem protection
Ideal or guiding values	Our myth of economic growth has us stuck in an "iron cage of consumerism," which is the self-reinforcing loop between the continual production of novelty by firms and the continuous consumption of novelty in households.
Emotional, aesthetic, and spiritual aspects	Questioning growth is deemed to be the act of lunatics, idealists, and revolutionaries. But question it we must.
Personal	Doesn't say much about individuals; suggests using brooms rather than leaf-blowers as an example.
Pathway or plan	See 12 steps in "Key Ideas" above.

Imagining After Capitalism | 187

Author	Charles Eisenstein writes about civilization, consciousness, money, and human cultural evolution. He sees himself as a steward and channel for the ideas of Sacred Economics.
Time horizon	Unclear
Scope	Local
Key drivers	Inequality, Stagnation
Key ideas	+ A gift economy based on shrinking the formal economy and shifting money away from being a store of value to a medium of exchange, including adopting negative interest to discourage rents.
	+ Social capital refers to relationships and skills or services that people once provided for themselves and each other in a gift economy, such as cooking, child care, healthcare, hospitality, entertainment, advice, growing food, making clothes, and building houses. Only one or two generations ago, many of these functions were far less commoditized.
	+ If we are merely paying for something once provided through self-sufficiency or the gift economy, then the logic of economic growth is faulty.
	+ For many categories of goods, marginal costs of production are now practically zero.
	+ Income topping (pledging not to earn more than $24,000 p.a).
	+ Money's divine property of abstraction (disconnection from the real world), reached its extreme in the early 21st century as the financial economy lost its mooring in the real economy.
	+ Gifts embody the key qualities of the sacredness; "Barter, in the strict sense of moneyless exchange, has never been a quantitatively important or dominant model or transaction in any past or present economic system about which we have hard information;" Such transactions should not be called barter but ritualized gift exchange.
	+ Because economic growth is almost always lower than the rate of interest, if debtors cannot, in aggregate, make interest payments from the new wealth they create, they must turn over more and more of their existing wealth to their creditors and/or pledge a growing proportion of their current and future income to debt service.

Ideal or guiding values	+ A revolution in money is needed, to transform its nature.
+ We live in a world of fundamental abundance, but have developed an economics based on scarcity.
+ The commodification process – for something to become an object of commerce, it must be made scarce first.
» Most goods/services meet needs that once met for free.
» Are people happier for having films not storytellers, MP3 players rather than gatherings around the piano?
+ Calls for economic degrowth; (Western economies have probably been in zero-growth for at least 20 years).
+ The crises of our time arise from "Separation" – the human/nature split, disintegration of community, the division of reality into material and spiritual. Separation is woven into our civilization; our attitude of human exceptionalism from the laws of nature is ending as well.
+ Negative interest – a tax on holding money, ensuring that the only way to maintain wealth is to invest it.
Emotional, aesthetic, and spiritual aspects	+ Money is a social construct that we can change
+ Monetization of social capital is the strip-mining of community
+ Be in large part a local economy
Personal	A gift is open-ended, creating an ongoing tie. Gifts embody the key qualities of sacredness.
Pathway or plan	+ Today's financial crisis arose because there is almost no social, cultural, natural, and spiritual capital left to monetize.
+ Unraveling: we will first experience persistent deflation, stagnation, and wealth polarization, followed by social unrest, hyperinflation, or currency collapse.
+ The next stage is one of co-creative partnership with Earth.
7 steps
1. Negative-interest currency
2. Eliminate economic rents and compensate for depletion of the commons
3. Internalize social and environmental costs
4. Economic and monetary localization
5. The social dividend
6. Economic degrowth. There is much necessary and beautiful work to be done—but much of it does not generate an economic return.
7. Gift culture and p2p economics

Imagining After Capitalism | 189

Author	Herman E. Daly was Professor Emeritus at the University of Maryland School of Public Policy, and a senior economist at the World Bank.
Time horizon	Unclear
Scope	The United States and other large, wealthy economies
Key drivers	Stagnation, Climate and carrying capacity
Key ideas	+ Seeks an economy with relatively stable size that leaves room for nature and gives high levels of human wellbeing without undermining the planet's life-support services. + Aims for stable population and stable consumption of energy and materials at sustainable levels. **Four basic rules or system principles:** 1. Maintain the health of ecosystems and the life-support services they provide. 2. Extract renewable resources like fish and timber at a rate no faster than they can be regenerated. 3. Consume non-renewable resources like fossil fuels and minerals at a rate no faster than they can be replaced by the discovery of renewable substitutes. 4. Deposit wastes in the environment no faster than they can be safely assimilated.
Ideal or guiding values	The global economy has grown too large. The industrial economy (like a child) has reached adolescence – a time of great change and challenge, fraught with confusion and crisis. Like all adolescents, the economy must stop growing in size, and refocus on growth in mental, moral, and spiritual capacity.
Emotional, aesthetic, and spiritual aspects	The steady state economy is dynamic and changes/develops over time, but remains balanced with the natural environment. It is something different from both capitalism and socialism, using a mix of government intervention and markets.
Personal	Citizens should exercise as much freedom as possible without impinging on the freedom of others.
Pathway/plan	Unclear

Author	Samuel Alexander is co-director of the Simplicity Institute, and a Lecturer at the Office for Environmental Programs, University of Melbourne. He is author of thirteen books on the themes of degrowth and simplicity.
Time horizon	Unclear
Scope	Typically associated with developing economies focused on meeting mostly local needs with mostly local resources, this updated view considers it within the context of the developed world, arguing that is where it is most needed.
Key drivers	Stagnation, Climate and carrying capacity
Key ideas	+ A degrowth approach aims for a world in which everyone's basic needs are modestly but sufficiently met, in an ecologically sustainable, highly localized, and socially equitable manner. + Using the Amish as a rough touchstone or benchmark may not be so far from the truth.
Ideal or guiding values	+ The growth paradigm has no future. + An acceptance that just enough is plenty. + The full implications of our predicament are typically grossly underestimated. + We are already well into overshoot.
Emotional, aesthetic, and spiritual aspects	Instead of using our increased productivity for more leisure time, we've used it to keep buying more stuff. It isn't working. Perhaps the simple life is a quite sensible notion?
Personal	Human beings would realize that they were free from the demands of continuous economic activity and could therefore dedicate more of their energies to non-materialistic pursuits.
Pathway or plan	Growth as we know it cannot continue, and there are two ways down: the smart way via strategic choice, and the hard way via overshoot and collapse.

Author	Fioramonti is Professor of Political Economy at the University of Pretoria, where he directs the Centre for the Study of Governance Innovation. His research covers alternative economic paradigms, governance of the commons, global political innovations, and new forms of supranational regionalism.
Time horizon	Unclear
Scope	Local
Key drivers	Shifting values, Stagnation
Key ideas	+ Argues for shifting away from GDP to more holistic measures. The problem with GDP is that growing trees does not add to economic growth, but cutting and selling them off does. + GDP should be replaced by a "dashboard" integrating the key dimensions of human and ecological wellbeing. + Proprietorship will continue to have its place, but the role of public, collective, and shared ownership will increase significantly. + A network economy that scales horizontally will thrive in a climate-compatible economic system. The localization and blending of production and consumption will result in a better circular system, with less waste and negative externalities. + Local currencies would underpin prosperity and economic resilience at a regional level, straddling arbitrary national borders to reflect economic and social networks. A national network of currencies could replace the national currency to allow communities to trade with each other.
Ideal or guiding values	We must redesign our social organization, starting with a restructuring of the economy that will trigger profound changes in both political institutions and society-at-large.
Emotional, aesthetic, and spiritual aspects	The wellbeing economy is a vision that unites local currencies and B-corps and many other streams of governance innovation into a coherent narrative, placing fundamental change within reach.
Personal	The separation of production and consumption roles leaves "consumers" on the receiving end of the growth process.
Pathway or plan	Not clear

Chapter 6 NON-WORKERS' PARADISE

Non-Workers' Paradise plays on the Socialist idea of a worker's paradise, because in the After Capitalism world we are not working in paid jobs as a means of sustenance.

> "The goal of the future is full unemployment, so we can play."
> Arthur C. Clarke

Non-Workers' Paradise At-A-Glance

In this image, the world has moved beyond the exchange of wage-labor for market access as a means of sustenance. A hallmark of this image is that the needs of the economy have been subjugated to the needs of society. One's job is no longer the defining characteristic that determines status in society and ability to access goods and services.

Post-work is at the core of this image. The reader's indulgence is begged for using the admittedly problematic term of paradise, but it does highlight the shift from work to post-work. Post-work is also not without some baggage as it might suggest people are lying around doing nothing. Indeed, it will take a lot of work to get to a post-work future. There is no magic wand. There is no switch to flip. Individuals have to make this image happen — not wait for it. The post-work future still has plenty of work to do, or activities that need to be undertaken, just not in the form of full-time jobs that are vital to one's survival.

The challenge aside, the momentum is here. The workweek has been shrinking gradually. For most of the workforce, it has been shrinking for a long time. The Great Resignation, Quiet Quitting and Lying Flat, while their pace will eventually slow, highlight an emerging sensibility that there is more to life than work — a significant conceptual shift.

There are 9 AC Concepts comprising this image. The idea of a post-work society is the most central one here, but it also represents an outcome in how people relate to one another in the future. The purpose, succinctly stated, is reducing inequality to create a more just and fair society. The key aspects of Non-Workers' Paradise are underlined, followed by a brief description of supporting community values, economics, and governance.

1. <u>Prioritizing society over economy</u>: Capitalism puts the economy and work first, and everything social second. This image flips that and refocuses life so that the economy supports social life. Thanks to the abundance of wealth brought about by advances in technology and automation, the role of work in the form of exchanging labor for wages is relegated to a background role in society. Income from jobs is no longer needed for individuals to access society's wealth.

2. <u>Reducing inequality via redistribution</u>: The most inflammatory issue focused on by this image is reducing the huge inequality gap. This means rethinking the distribution of wealth. UBI, sovereign wealth funds, and employee stock ownership funds are among the tools to enable this.

3. <u>Adopting [some form of] UBI</u>: UBI is a concept that is generating much discussion and is in the spirit of this image. At the least, it provides a starting point to build from — universal basic services, for instance is an idea emerging from it. UBI is first implemented by the state, and then delegated to a more local scale — utilizing the new abundance of wealth to ensure all people are provided with a basic stipend. As time goes on, communities manage things themselves or simply offer UBI in the context of their own localized currencies.

4. <u>Confronting the laziness lie</u>: A major concern, reflecting how strong the work ethic has been ingrained through capitalism, is that without work, people will lose purpose. Research suggests that this may be true for some, but certainly not all. "Paradise" is redefined. Instead of the idea of not having to do anything, it becomes the freedom to do what makes one happy and/or contributes to the collective good.

5. <u>The left gets it together</u>: It is not unthinkable that the left reexamines and modifies its approach to the future. It moves away from "reaction" and instead actively proposes a pragmatic vision of how to move towards a better society.

6. <u>Tech acceleration is a key enabler</u>: Post-work still requires the creation of wealth and the ability to get tasks and activities done. Tech acceleration enables a wealth bounty that can be distributed more fairly.

7. <u>Organizing via local and direct [democracy]</u>: As with Circular Commons, there is an emphasis on mobilizing at the local level and using more direct approaches to decision-making. People no longer see themselves as consumers, but as users of goods for productive local activity. The former guiding principle of supply chain management — not holding excess

inventories, just-in-time logistics to promote efficiency, getting the lowest possible cost through economies of scale and deregulation — is exchanged for a resilient system that is guided by dispersion and diversification so any one disruption cannot upset an entire line of products. The technical approaches are available, but the political approach will likely require a great deal of time and effort.

Supporting community values. The Mean Green (See Section 2.3.1) turn of a significant part of the left eventually lets go of its paternalistic folk politics approach. In general, the left takes a more hands-off approach to differences in social views, demonizes conservatives less, and takes more time developing its own agenda rather than just reacting — typically in indignation — to the right. It recognizes the divisiveness inherent in assuming one knows what's best for others and goes back to the core principle of tolerance. The integrals lead the way in finding approaches that enable left and right to make some small progress on issues after decades of stalemate. More effective organizing techniques are developed; these shift the focus to structural issues that affect people of all political orientations. The left-right culture wars subside, and compromise becomes possible.

Economics. The Non-Workers' Paradise confronts the question: Do we want to be an economy or society? The modern worldview and capitalism align with economy — this image aligns with society. The mindset shift is such that economics is no longer seen as a game in which a few win and most lose. The redesign of the economy seeks to achieve a more balanced outcome that reduces the extremes and aims toward a satisfactory middle ... with the economy reoriented to being in service to society rather than the other way around.

Governance. Democratic engagement is bolstered by introducing co-ops, free public transit, worker ownership of production, land trusts, collective pooling of resources, promoting community gardens, the introduction of Local Exchange Trading Systems, and moving away from the constrictions of the long-accepted homo economicus model. Localities are strengthened by emphasizing various aspects of cooperation, such as by establishing cooperative economic development, worker cooperatives, community land trusts. More democratic financing models, such as negative income tax, are important as well. A useful operating principle is to emphasize multisectoral approaches, which is critical in connecting the many local activities, such as moving capital or finance to communities needing it.

The *Non-Workers' Paradise* puts the post-work future on the table. This image requires a big shift in the minds of the workers – from advocating for good jobs to advocating for their elimination. This could be especially difficult for labor unions, who have fought hard for better jobs and benefits for workers. In effect a post-work future means the end of labor unions, which is likely to be a difficult position for them to adopt. Most workers are not in labor unions, of course, and are left to decide on their own. The Great Resignation, quiet quitting, lying flat and the like suggest that fundamental questions are being raised about the role of work in one's life.

This image is closest to the historical class struggle envisioned by Marx. The class nature is less clearly defined than it once might have been, but the inequality driver suggests a huge and growing gap between the haves and have-nots that is fundamental to this image. There is clearly a divide whether it is framed in class terms or not.

The accelerant for the post-work fire is automation. There is little doubt that more jobs can be, and are very likely to be, automated. Unless provision is made for those displaced, there will understandably be fierce resistance to this approach. Automation could be wielded as a club to keep worker demands toned down with an omnipresent threat of automating the job out of existence. The flip side explored in this image is what happens if the opposite tack is taken. Provision is made for those displaced, and automating jobs begins to be seen as a positive. The equation is simple: if automation enables the production of the same amount of wealth that human workers were producing, then there is sufficient wealth to cover the displaced. Of course, the politics of this strategic shift would be quite challenging!

Unlike *Circular Commons*, in which none of the concepts specified a time horizon, there were two here that both suggested mid-century as a rough estimate. This fits with my estimated timeframe of 2040-2050.

The 9 concepts that inspired the *Non-Workers' Paradise* are listed with the author and a brief description here.

- ***Alter-Worlds***, Shaw and Waterstone. Leverage movements of de-commodified and autonomous territories (e.g. Zapatistas) springing up outside or on the margins of the system.
- ***Communism***, Peter Frase. A vision of communism illustrated by four scenarios based on uncertainties of scarcity/abundance and inequality, with automation as a predetermined.
- ***Economic Democracy***, David Schweickart. A socialist approach with market and democratic features centered on three key ideas of

worker self-management, a market for enterprises, and social control of investment.

- ***FALC Fully Automated Luxury Communism***, Aaron Bastani. Advocates a shift towards worker-owned production, a state-financed transition to renewable energy and universal services aided by technological progress and placed beyond commodity exchange and profit.
- ***Pluralist Commonwealth***, Gar Alperovitz. Evolutionary reconstruction redistributes productive assets, based on (1) democratization of wealth (2) community as a guiding theme (3) decentralization and (4) substantial democratic planning to achieve economic, democracy-building and ecological goals.
- ***Post-capitalism***, Paul Mason/Srnicek and Williams. Makes the case for *Neoliberal Capitalism* declining and the need to design a transition and create a "new hegemony" vision of an abundance future.
- ***Precariat***, Guy Standing. Describes a social class rather than an economic system per se.
- ***Solidarity***, Solidarity Economy Initiative. Social justice movement among lower-income people of color seeking to go beyond socialism and communism by shifting consciousness, building [political] power, and creating economic alternatives.
- ***Utopia for Realists***, Rutger Bregman. Suggests that reduction of work first has to be reinstated as a political ideal. Makes the case for universal basic income and the need for a massive redistribution of wealth.

This section is organized as follows:

- <u>Driver outcomes</u>: how do the drivers project forward in each image?
- <u>Challenges</u>: the central problems that the image focuses on
- <u>Purposes</u>: the key motivation for developing the image; what it's trying to achieve
- <u>Principles</u>: guidelines followed in working towards the image
- <u>Tools</u>: mechanisms or activities for enabling or realizing the image
- <u>Personal</u>: the role of "regular" in this image
- <u>Leadership</u>: the role of leaders in this image
- <u>Pathway</u>: high-level take on how to get to the image from the present.

6.1.1 Driver outcomes

The two dominant drivers are Inequality and Ineffective Left. Inequality is the high-profile public issue driving a perception that capitalism is not working, or rather is only working for those at the top. It serves as a rallying cry for change. Supporters of reducing inequality point out that the structure of capitalism by design will produce inequality. There is also some blaming of the rich for being greedy, but this is not the dominant storyline – at least not yet.

As was pointed out above, the view here is that it has more to do with the structure or system of capitalism than the people. The problem of focusing on the greedy or "bad" people is that it creates a view that the system can be reformed if people simply behave better. Systems thinking, however, suggests that it is the structure that is the problem and changing the people won't fix the problem.

Some of the *Non-Workers' Paradise* concepts saw great potential for technology acceleration and automation in creating the opportunity to reduce the need for work, which is at the center of this post-work future. Those drivers are also very important to enabling this guiding image, albeit in more of a secondary role given its social and political emphasis. Table 6.1 shows the projections of the drivers in *Non-Workers' Paradise*.

Table 6.1 Driver outcomes in *Non-Workers Paradise*

DRIVER	OUTCOME IN *NON-WORKERS PARADISE*
Shifting values	Traditional
Technology acceleration	Pace of tech managed
Inequality	Reduced via UBI
Jobs & automation	Automation balanced with human needs
Stagnation	Not viewed as problem; move to UBI
Climate & carrying capacity	Improves but secondary to social issues
Ineffective Left	Significant shift is effective mobilization

The story of the driver outcomes is centered on work, workers, and the political struggle for social justice. There is a shift from a worker's rights approach to a focus on building a just, post-work society. The political process is key here, both within and outside the established system. The left moves away from reactive mode and builds its own story and gets to work on the very difficult challenge of taking on the status quo. An important shift is that the left is able to adjust and develop narratives and an approach that galvanizes support. The small and local approach is effectively coordinated to mobilize change on the regional, national, and even global scale.

A key aspect of the new narrative of the left is embracing technology as an enabling tool for the post-work society. Rather than resisting automation and technology, the left sees that the productivity and wealth it produces is distributed in a just way. The shift might be described as from fighting for workers' rights to citizens' rights.

6.1.2 Challenges and responses

Post-work is the key challenge of this guiding image. Inequality provides the motivation for post-work and abundance may be an enabler, but questions about the role of work and political participation will need to be addressed.

Inequality is the key driver of post-work. Its sharpest focus is on jobs and work where what the capitalists get and what the workers get most vividly highlights inequality. While some supporters seek to maintain the centrality of work, the view here is that the focus is better placed on moving beyond it. But the role of work in daily life suggests that such a shift won't be easy, and it will require a strong political movement to succeed. The four challenges of the *Non-Workers' Paradise* are broken down as follows:

- Inequality and distribution of wealth: The systemic inequality produced by capitalism has come into the spotlight with the working class and supporters as likely focal points to mobilize against it.
- Abundance and the need to work: The potential for accelerating technology to provide an abundance of wealth raises the possibility of work becoming less important or unnecessary.
- Role of work: Any change to work will face difficult challenges due to the multiple roles that work plays in our identity and the structure it provides to daily life, along with its role as the primary wealth distribution mechanism.
- Political participation: This image focuses most sharply on the role of people in shaping their future, similar to the commons aspect of *Circular Commons*.

Inequality and the distribution of wealth

Figure 6.1 Post-work

Bregman (2017) is among the many calling for a massive redistribution of wealth. Supporters of capitalism will often cite how capitalism has been the greatest wealth creation system in history. True, but compared to what? Most of human history was based on subsistence and it is since the Industrial Revolution that growth even began to happen. Capitalism has been the primary system in the growth era, except for brief and limited attempts at socialism and communism. Socialism and communism aimed at the wealth distribution problem, but those systems have problems of their own. There are perhaps 3-5 communist countries left and perhaps two dozen countries that are socialist to some degree. The two largest examples, the former Soviet Union and China have swung in almost the opposite direction. Although China maintains the fiction that it is communist, it could be more accurately described as an authoritarian capitalist state. The few places it exists are in countries that are fairly undeveloped, such as North Korea, Vietnam, and Cuba. These countries hadn't developed enough to enable redistribution to work. Development theory would suggests that individuals and countries need to pass through the full development "spiral" first. The values driver explained above draws on Spiral Dynamics which suggests that development proceeds through stages and that skipping or neglecting stages has a pathological effect. In this case, trying to leapfrog from a traditional stage of development to a more advanced one seems to have stunted their growth. Think in terms of the numerous failed attempts to impose democracy on less developed countries — they were simply not yet mature enough developmentally speaking to properly handle it (granted, one might make the same argument against some mature nations).

Capitalism is the first system that directly confronts the question of significant surplus wealth. In short, the systems structure of capitalism is that the surplus goes to those providing the capital, which is a very small percentage of those at the top — the 0.1% in today's parlance. Another common argument is that capitalism creates a rising tide that lifts all boats. If you replace "all" with "most," true again. The problem is that it lifts some boats much more than others. Piketty's (2014) exhaustive *Capital* study chronicled how that accumulation goes to the "renters" (i.e., capitalists) and how that is an endemic feature of the system. My view is that attempts to reform capitalism can mitigate or reduce inequality, but not fix it. The bottom line is that supporters of the *Non-Workers' Paradise* are no longer willing to accept the "rising tide" argument.

Responses

Many, like Mason (2015), suggest that there is plenty of opportunity to do better than the current market approach for distributing goods, and to do better than the current finance system for allocating capital. Lanier (2013) preaches about the need to beware of the power and unprecedented fortunes accumulating to those owning the "siren servers" (playing on the sirens from the Odyssey), which are big computer server networks and platforms that are powerful enough to manipulate a market space by gathering data from the network, often without having to pay for it, i.e., Amazon, Apple, and Google.

So, what could redistribution look like? Let's start with Piketty's (2014) calculation that if global output and the income to which it gives rise were equally divided, each individual in the world would have an income of about €760/$912 per month. Keep in mind that the global poverty line set by the World Bank is roughly $57 per month.

There literally is enough abundance already for everyone in the world to live a reasonably comfortable life. It would require a massive redistribution of resources. It is a choice to keep a system that promotes inequality as a feature. It is not as simple as transferring money from some bank accounts to others. A lot of work would need to be done to bring standards of living in underdeveloped areas up to the global average. Without the necessary infrastructure and support systems, living standards could easily fall back once the initial redistribution stipend is gone. Recipients would need ongoing help to maintain their gains.

In a post-work world, many wonder what people will do, particularly in affluent countries. One possibility is helping the rest of the world develop and maintain a better standard of living. To give a simple example, imagine a Global Development Corps along the lines of the Peace Corps. Sure, one can point out that historical attempts from the more developed countries to help the less developed have been plagued with problems, but that is not a sufficient basis to conclude that it cannot work.

Abundance and the need to work

Automation is already increasingly supplanting cheap labor (Frase, 2016). This was a point we debated in our book *2025: Scenarios of US and Global Society as Reshaped by Science and Technology* back in 1995, where we foresaw that automation would eventually out-compete cheap labor (Coates et al., 1996). Mayer-Schonberger and Ramge (2018, 86) suggest that "we will be able to direct a machine learning system to do the boring stuff and reserve those decisions that give us the most joy and pleasure for ourselves." But one could imagine the reverse being equally plausible — humans focused on minutiae while machines make the important decisions.

If society were to decide to make work reduction a priority, work hours could gradually be reduced in line with increases in productivity, so that people could gradually work less and less (Frase, 2016). Already, many municipalities and several countries — including Spain, Japan, and New Zealand — are piloting four-day workweeks (Brin, 2021). A recent shortened workweek experiment conducted in a wide range of enterprises in Iceland yielded perhaps the most promising results thus far. It was left up to individual workers to restructure their own shortened work schedule. Productivity either increased or remained constant, while worker satisfaction and health vastly improved. The findings were so overwhelmingly positive that 86% of workplaces in Iceland have now instituted these changes (Haridy, 2021).

Most *Non-Workers' Paradise* concepts are projecting a future where paid full-time jobs are not necessary. It is important to emphasize that there is still work to be done, but it is no longer organized around jobs, employers, and employees. A key reason that jobs are [eventually] not seen as necessary is as a result of significant advances in technology. It links to the *Tech-Led Abundance* guiding image, which suggests people will not need to work because of the wealth produced by technology. The Fully Automated Luxury Communism (FALC) concept directly describes a society in which work is eliminated, scarcity is replaced by abundance, and where labor and leisure blend into one another. Mason (2015) observes that utopian communities failed due to scarcity. What's different this time is that a shift from scarcity to abundance is a significant development in the history of humanity.

The key challenge for this guiding image is how to distribute that wealth. Capitalism uses jobs as the primary distribution mechanism — one's share of society's wealth is decided by the assigned value from the job one has, i.e. a lawyer's job is assigned more value than that of a security guard.

Responses

The key to success here is in managing the very legitimate worker concerns that they will be automated out of a job. How do we tell the 3.6 million American truck-drivers, for example, that their jobs will simply vanish in the automated age? In the short term, labor advocates are likely to push to protect jobs from automation. When, or how, does that switch over to support for the elimination of jobs? The strategy will have to involve some sort of UBI rather than fighting to keep jobs. Jobs can and should be automated, but only with a plan in place to compensate or retrain the displaced. As will be shown below, the centrality of jobs and work to individuals and society is strong.

Role of work

It will not be easy to replace work – a big understatement! It plays three essential roles in daily life, as depicted in Figure 6.2:

| Figure 6.2 Key roles of jobs

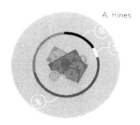

Jobs are central to identity

Jobs structure daily life

Jobs are the primary source of income

Imagining After Capitalism | 203

Jobs are central to identity

When you are introduced to someone, how long is it before you let them know what you do for work? And how soon do you ask: "So, what do you do?" Social protocols aside, how would you describe yourself to yourself? I suspect most readers, myself included, have our work at or near the top of the list.

Even if we don't like our jobs, they still serve as sources of identity and social worth. Unemployment carries a powerful social stigma. Historically, the data shows that a shift from being unemployed to being retired brings about immediate and dramatic increases in happiness (Frase, 2016). "Internalized capitalism" is a term that has emerged to highlight the idea that our self-worth is directly linked to our productivity — our value is not as human beings, but as human doings who add productive value to the economy (Dastigar, 2021).

However, an Australian study showed unambiguously that the psychosocial quality of bad jobs is worse than unemployment. It found that those moving into poor-quality jobs showed a significant worsening in their mental health compared to those who remained unemployed (Bevan, 2014).

The Great Resignation, Quiet Quitting, and Laying Flat (the Chinese version of "quiet quitting) suggest that the centrality of work to our identity is lessening (Carnegie, 2022). My own research has suggested a long-term slow decline in the importance of work, which fits with the shift to postmodern and integral values (Hines, 2011).

Responses

This shift away from work as the all-encompassing source of our identity is already underway, especially among younger people. In terms of where to put effort, perhaps the highest leverage point is in persuading the older generation, who indeed worked hard their whole life, to see that hard work as enabling a better life for future generations. Instead, there is a tendency toward inter-generational conflict where the older workers see the younger as soft. One can imagine those still in the "work as identity" paradigm not wanting to stop working and not really developing alternatives. The most effective effort might be aimed at providing new and useful ways for those folks to make a meaningful contribution outside of the traditional world of work.

Changing how we think of and describe ourselves is not going to be a simple task. A post-work future strikes right at who we are.

Jobs provide structure to daily life

For almost a century, the bulk of work life has been based around a Monday-Friday, 9-5 schedule. The rest of life is organized around work. We have meals before and after work, kids go to school during the day, and adults in the evening after work. Religious activities are typically held on weekends. And so on. If we no longer need to go to work, how would we arrange our daily life? An even bigger question is what would we do with this big block of time?

In part because not working is seen as too radical, some labor supporters favor reform and the right-to-work. Schweickart (2011) observes that a right-to-work has long been a basic tenet of socialism. Every able-bodied person who wants to work should be able to find decent employment. The International Labour Organization (2019), for instance, is still advocating for the right-to-work and better working conditions — such as lifelong learning and reskilling — rather than not working.

Historically speaking the 9-5 world is just a brief instant of the human experience, but it seems like it's the only way it's ever been. It has been changing, and concepts such as the Gig economy have raised awareness of the change. The pandemic accelerated the long-term trend toward virtual work, which is upending the 9-5 schedule.

Responses

Like the subtle shifts in identify away from work, this one is also slowly changing already. The pandemic gave a turbo-boost to virtual work, and though there has been a counter-reaction to order people back to the office, the genie is out of the bottle. We have experienced that virtual work is a legitimate approach and it enables flexibility. The biggest challenge for many people is that virtual work and non-traditional schedules put more burden on the individual to structure their daily life. Most of our education systems, however, are still based on the old industrial model of everyone moving from class to class signaled by bells and following a rigorous schedule. It hardly prepares one to organize one's own life. Nonetheless, this is a great opportunity, not only in organizing one's daily schedule, but in teaching personal responsibility for one's future. In my realm of foresight, there is increasing attention to personal futures planning, which adapts the tools and techniques of organizational planning to individuals.

Jobs as an income distribution problem

Jobs serve as the primary mechanism by which the economy distributes wealth. The paradigm of the existing economic order is focused on full employment. I vividly recall the quizzical and dismissive looks and the eye rolls when I suggested "full unemployment" ought to be our goal earlier in my career. The good news, though, is that just in the last few years, ideas such as UBI that were previously taboo, are increasingly being discussed. The number of pilots has increased globally from a few dozen small ones (Samuel, 2020) to nearly 200 according to the Stanford Basic Income Network (ND). The city of Chelsea, Massachusetts launched the USA's largest guaranteed income project, shifting its relief efforts from municipal-run food distribution sites to simply sending money to thousands of residents (DeCosta, 2021). Los Angeles is contemplating a UBI program, in which it would join its neighbors Stockton, Oakland, and San Francisco (Canon, 2021). And lest we forget, former US President Richard Nixon proposed a version of basic income back in the early 1970s. Globally, several countries have launched trials, including Brazil, Canada, Finland, Iran, Kenya, Namibia, South Korea, and the UK. India recently launched the largest pilot project yet attempted (World Population Review, 2023; Ramirez, 2023).

The whole concept of a 9 to 5 job for life was a historical quirk.
(Susan Lund, McKinsey & Co)

In 1900, 45% of people in the United States were self-employed (Slaughter et al., 2016, 12). The "workism" idea of humans being wired to work has not applied for most of human history, where work was typically seen as a means to an end, not an end in itself (Beckett, 2018). Today, of course, it seems normal and that it's always been that way, and for many the suggestion of alternatives raises the boogeymen of socialism and communism or the fear that the lazy will abuse their free time. Jackson (2021) notes that some work is for care and sustenance, some is for creation and creative expression, and ultimately maintains the security and durability of the human world for world-building. He maintains that both work itself and the world it creates are vital to healthy psychological and social functioning.

Responses

As noted above, a key mindset shift needed here is to flip the goal of full employment to full unemployment. That shift in target could enable a gradual approach over time that would be easier for societies to accommodate. The average workweek has been declining overall on its own for decades. That change can be accelerated by policy choices such as the four-day workweek, UBI, and the strategic use of automation.

Political participation

The ideas comprising *Non-Workers' Paradise* have their roots in the class struggle adopted by the far left, which is stronger in Europe and weak in the US. The far left has taken on some of the historically labor-centric approach — again stronger in Europe than in the US. The "danger" with this guiding image is that it is framed as a revival of either socialism or communism. Supporters of capitalism would likely welcome such a framing. Both socialism and communism are backward-looking "used futures"— to borrow Inayatullah's (2008) wonderful conception in which he asks whether an image is really yours or whether it is unconsciously borrowed from someone else. Socialism and communism indeed are used and loaded down with a ton of baggage given their challenging historical implementations. Both ideologies are more palatable outside the US but are deadly within it. Regrettably the debate is already moving in this direction towards social and communism as the alternatives to capitalism.

A Google trends search finds socialism spiking during the 2020 US presidential campaign. Lol and Jimenez (2017, 5) point out that "… what we need is a long-term vision of transformation that is not stuck in old paradigms of either socialist revolution or endless capitalism." It appears that the US may be the most anti-communist country given its long participation in the Cold War. It is difficult to get a read on global views on communism. In several countries, including Indonesia, Iran, Turkey, and the Ukraine, one can still be arrested for displaying communist symbols or spreading communist literature (Saed, 2021).

The Mean Green Meme, introduced in Section 2.3.1, is another aspect of the ineffective left driver. The Mean Greens lean left and to some degree can be viewed as a response to the left's ineffectiveness. They do value participation, which is an important aspect of the *Non-Workers' Paradise*, but they often fall into the hubris of their view being the correct one and creating an us-and-them dynamic. Participation is only valued from those with the correct views. This stance discourages the participation they value and turns it into confrontation and stalemate.

The left in power in the US today, rather than seeking to heal the divisions of the last four years, has charged ahead in a tone-deaf fashion with an agenda antagonistic to the right. Although the left in power is not the group that will support the *Non-Workers' Paradise*, it reflects the moral superiority tendencies that are deadly to coalition-building.

Responses

Srnicek and Williams (2016) are, in my view, spot-on in suggesting that any leftist universal view must be one that integrates difference rather than erasing it. The Shift Values driver toward postmodern and integral values noted above suggests a trend to greater emphasis on choice and participation. The voting apathy in the US somewhat obscures participation that largely takes place around single-issue politics. So, there is some evidence participation is there, and the trend suggests it ought to grow, but it remains to be seen.

It is fair to ask what kind of political participation is needed. Hahnel's (2022) wonderful participatory economy book lays out detailed plans for a democratic approach to building political and economic planning based primarily on worker's councils. This would be a massive shift in approach to go from today's top-down expert-led approach to planning to a bottom-up participatory approach. It will likely invoke the specter of socialism as well. Nonetheless, it provides a useful blueprint and one can imagine more and more small-scale examples emerging that will take these ideas from the theoretical to the practical realm.

6.1.3 Purposes

The purpose of reducing inequality is to create a more just and fair society. My view is that in the long term this can be accomplished by reducing and eventually eliminating the need for formal work and the need to have a job in order to gain access to society's wealth. Two assumptions are hindering the move to this purpose:

- The first assumption is that resources are scarce and that work is, put simply, vital. The economy won't function or not enough wealth can be produced without work.
- The second assumption is that if people did not work, they would lose purpose and drift into all sorts of bad habits.

Let's look at how these might be addressed and overcome.

1. Rethink scarcity to abundance ... and redistribution.

Capitalism in particular, and economics in general, have been based on the idea that resources are scarce, and a system is needed to allocate them fairly.

It is easy to point to the very real and horrible amount of poverty in the world and believe that income/resources/wealth are scarce.

But is scarcity still true? Or do we, right now, produce enough to provide an income for everyone to live at a fairly comfortable level — if we distributed wealth equally? As mentioned above, Piketty (2014, 63) suggested a global income of about €760/$912 per month is possible. The *Limits to Growth* team, in their thirty-year update suggested eight billion people could be supported at the level of lower-income nations of present-day Europe (Meadows et al., 2004). More recently, a KPMG study confirmed the basic conclusions of the "Limits" model (Ahmed, 2021).

The opportunity is to first make the policy commitment to a more equitable distribution of resources. Then comes the very difficult question of how to do it. Hahnel (2023) suggests a participatory economic model that sets economic reward commensurate with effort, sacrifice, and need. A key enabling principle is that decision-making input, or power, is in proportion to the degree one is affected by economic choices. While there is much more to their proposed approach, in short, people's income is based on the efforts and sacrifices they make – as judged by their peers. It should be noted that Hahnel sees Worker's Councils as a key mechanism, which may seem ironic as an example of post-work, but the nature of work proposed in his approach is post-capitalist.

2. <u>Rethink jobs and work to post-work.</u>

The replacement of work opens plenty of options for a different purpose in life. Bastani (2019) points out that our labor could become a route to self-development rather than a means of survival. A post-work world is not one of idleness; rather, it is a world in which people are no longer bound to their jobs, but free to create their own lives (Srnicek and Williams, 2016).

As I have talked about a post-work future and *After Capitalism* over the years, the question of "what we do with all that free time" inevitably comes up. Rifkin (1994, 235) suggested almost thirty years ago that "redefining the role of the individual in a society absent of mass formal work is, perhaps, the seminal issue of the coming age" (Rifkin, 1994, 235).

But what is really going on here? Eisenstein (2011), points out that the necessities of life have been given over to specialists, leaving us with nothing meaningful to do (outside our own area of expertise) but to entertain ourselves. This is currently embodied in the as-a-service trend, in which practically anything can be outsourced to a service provider. We even suggested parenting-as-a-service as part of a client project!

The other aspect is the "laziness lie," which has three central tenets: (McKeever, 2021)

- our worth is our productivity > this is taking the Protestant worth ethic too far
- we cannot trust our own feelings and limits > this is taking the modern values achievement ethic too far
- there is always more we could be doing > this is epitomized by the "Rise and Grinders" who seem to have made a virtue out of misery.

An example of post-work comes from Israel where a significant percentage of ultra-orthodox Jewish men do not work but spend their lives studying holy scriptures and performing religious rituals. Their wives often work, and the government provides them with generous subsidies. While they are poor, surveys report that they have higher levels of life-satisfaction than any other section of Israeli society (Harari, 2017b).

Plenty of things would still need to be done even it wasn't a job per se. But more free time for sure. The big fear might be captured facetiously as people lying around, getting drunk, and watching TV. Some would choose that path. But most are likely to find more productive uses of their time. The text box suggests ten things we could do if we didn't have to work (Hines, 2019).

Ten things we could do if we did not have to work

- Learning for the sake of learning
- Parenting, more time raising children
- Participating in political and civic affairs
- Helping the less fortunate locally/ and globally
- Exercising, in light of the growing obesity epidemic
- Connecting to family/ and friends outside social media
- Reinvigorating our interest in space exploration
- Restoring and enhancing the environment
- Travelling to experience other cultures
- Hobbying, reading, music, cooking, surfing, etc.

6.1.4 Principles

Three key principles guide the *Non-Workers' Paradise*:

1. Equity
2. Redistribution
3. Elimination of work and jobs

1. <u>Equity</u>

The initial framing of this principle was equality. The idea was it would be more direct to reframe inequality to equality. But it is not as straightforward as it perhaps ought to be. It is not as if capitalism comes out and explicitly or enthusiastically touts inequality as a feature, benefit, or goal. Rather there are complex explanations or justifications for why this outcome is necessary. One can imagine touting equality as a feature, benefit, or goal. It is a strong fit with emerging postmodern and integral values as well. Nonetheless, equality would have some explaining to do as well. Does it mean everyone gets exactly the same? If not, how are differences accounted for? Hahnel (2022) in the Purposes section above suggested equitable distribution based on one's effort, sacrifice, and need. It seems that equity is thus more appropriate than equality.

Equality also conjures up what we might call the four horsemen — Marxism, socialism, communism, and class. In the US these are ideas that scare people. Even a relatively simple idea such as universal health care has struggled to find a foothold in the US. The US is behind the curve here, as 72 countries do have some form of universal health care (World Population Review, 2023). Thus, the two major parties have steered clear of suggestions that might conjure up the four horsemen. And it is left to the fringe. In 2006, the US Green Party launched the GND Task Force, which aimed to provide sustainable green energy infrastructure, and achieve zero carbon, but also included a solution to economic inequality (Delaney 2021). That said, the severity of inequality has been highlighted and awareness is high. Former fringe politician Bernie Sanders almost won the Democratic nomination in 2016 on a platform of universal health care. It may be that the gravity of the situation is enough to overcome the historical opposition to this issue.

2. <u>Redistribution</u>

The only way to get to a more equitable society is by restructuring the system for distributing wealth and income. The authors of the *Non-Workers' Paradise* concepts generally favor doing this as a choice because it is the right thing to do. But there is an argument to be made that automation will force this choice by creating massive technology-based unemployment. Standing (2018) points out that contrary to conventional wisdom, the case for UBI does not rest on the assumption that robots and artificial intelligence will cause mass unemployment. Rather, the main arguments are ethical and relate to social justice, individual freedom, and the need for basic security.

There are significant issues to address in redistribution: (Srnicek and Williams, 2016)

- How does one measure value without labor?
- What are the likely effects of profits falling?
- How do we distribute goods and services efficiently in the absence of market prices?

Responses to each of these questions are already emerging, but not at the scale needed for an *After Capitalism* future. The struggles with assigning value have been noted, in particular the need to create scarcity in order to assign value. The reframing from scarcity to abundance is a first step in setting the context for redistribution. While this work does not get into the specific mechanics of economic redesign, it does point out that the stagnation driver and support for degrowth both suggest that profits falling is actually aligned with an *After Capitalism* future. Distribution without a pricing mechanism is indeed a challenge, but pricing mechanisms are already breaking down and creating the need for a new approach to distribution/redistribution.

3. <u>Post-work</u>

There are two key questions about post-work: should we and can we? This guiding image answers yes to both. But many people of course will not agree. Projecting forward, it is possible to imagine that the objections above can be addressed and will lessen over time.

Should we?

You won't break my soul. Release your anger, release your mind, release your job, release the time.
(Break my Soul, Renaissance, Beyoncé)

The "should we" has a lot to do with the points above about work's central role in our identity, daily life structure, and economy. Those points have been addressed above, but let's succinctly summarize them again here. In short, it's already happening:

- <u>Identity</u>: The Great Resignation was just one indicator that maybe work is not as central to who we are as it has historically been.

- <u>Daily life</u>: Gigging, along with globalized and virtual work, is already making the 9-5 a quaint memory for many.

- <u>Economy</u>: Automation and AI are increasingly important factors in productivity.

Work provides stability and comfort. Interestingly, if you ask most people if they want their job, they will probably say no. Sure, some people really do enjoy their work. Those who don't, don't really want the job per se, but the security it provides. There is also the non-issue of what to do with our time that we explored above. The question for the future is whether that security can be provided, such that people feel comfortable letting go of their crappy or bullshit jobs (Graeber, 2018). As futurists know all too well, change is difficult — the comfort of known misery is often preferable to the unknown.

Can we? Again, it's already happening.

- <u>Less reliance on job income</u>: The Shift Commission found less of our income is coming from work, and more is coming from other sources, such as dividends, investment income, and government programs like Social Security and disability insurance. Today, only half of personal income comes from wages and salaries, down from almost two-thirds in the 1960s (Slaughter et al., 2016).

- <u>Less reliance on regular, full-time work</u>: The Gig economy is being driven by employers seeking to cut costs and avoid benefits, and employees seeking greater flexibility and freedom.

- <u>Less match of skills and requirements</u>: Eberstadt's (2016) *Men without* Work provides lots of useful data on why many men in the US have essentially given up on finding work, noting that since the early 1950s the work rate for adult men has declined by 18%.

The economy is generally becoming more productive (avoiding the problems with GDP here). Bastani (2019) points out that a challenge of capitalism is that increased productivity doesn't lead to more free time but simply the production of more goods and services. Rather than working less, people consume more, which perpetuates the capitalist system.

Finally, there is still plenty of important work to be done albeit without jobs. Eisenstein (2011, 274) notes "there are forests to replant, sick people to care for, an entire planet to be healed."

6.1.5 Tools

The list of potential tools looks mostly familiar. The idea of a Universal Basic Income (UBI) has been around but it has got a lot of recent attention, including being a platform of US longshot political candidate Andrew Yang.

Universal basic income (or services)

The Basic Income Earth Network defines UBI as "a periodic cash payment unconditionally delivered to all on an individual basis, without means test or work requirement." The key points are that the payment is basic, unconditional, and universal. Basic means the payment is sufficient to cover the essentials of life (Dunlop, 2017). Calls for a UBI have been increasing, including as part of the "Green New Deal" introduced by Rep. Alexandria Ocasio-Cortez, D-N.Y., and supported by at least 40 members of Congress (Brown, 2018).

There are many small-scale experiments or pilots going on in the US and around the world:

- US President Johnson's National Commission on Guaranteed Income in 1967 was unanimous in support of it, but the report was largely ignored (Rifkin, 1994, 261).

- Canada has had a long flirtation with the idea of a GAI (Guaranteed Annual Income). Between 1968 and 1980, five field experiments were conducted in North America, primarily to investigate the impact of a GAI on the labor market. One of these experiments, MINCOME, was conducted in the province of Manitoba between 1974 and 1979. It was carried out more or less as intended, but the data was not analyzed. A MacDonald Commission made a case for GAI in 1986, but it was dropped. Forget (2011) revisited the data and found that a GAI implemented broadly in society may improve health and social outcomes at the community level.

- In a three-year pilot funded by the provincial government, about 4,000 people in Ontario were getting monthly stipends to boost them to at least 75% of the poverty line. That translates to a minimum annual income of CAN$17,000 (about US$13,000) for single people and CAN$24,000 for married couples (Bergstein, 2018).

- Panera's nonprofit arm launched a new experiment: It opened a café in St. Louis that looked exactly like the company's other restaurants, but customers could pay what they wanted for the items on the menu, or not pay at all. Conscious capitalism — a philosophy that some business leaders subscribe to — suggests that consumers will do good if given the opportunity. But that wasn't borne out at the time and the experiment was abandoned (Peters, 2018).

- Using oil revenue proceeds, the Alaska Permanent Fund has paid equal yearly dividends to every resident, including children, ranging from about $1,000 to over $3,000. (Bear in mind that a family of four collects four same-sized dividends.) While this isn't enough to live on, it nicely supplements Alaskans' other earnings. And paying such dividends regularly for more than thirty years has bolstered the state's economy, reduced poverty, and made Alaska one of the least unequal states in America (Barnes, 2019).

- Workers at Microsoft Japan got a four-day work week, a three-day weekend — and got their normal, five-day paycheck. The result, the company says, was a productivity boost of 40% (Chappell, 2019).

There have been many studies of the potential impact of UBI, with most anticipating a positive impact:

- A Roosevelt Institute study projects that if adults are given $1,000 every month, the US economy could grow by 12.56% after an eight-year implementation — translating to total growth of $2.48 trillion (Galeon, 2017). While this addressed the concern that UBI would slow the economy, ironically the growth is at odds with the basic premise of degrowth supported by this work.

- UCL's Institute for Global Prosperity suggests universal basic services (instead of UBI) including access to mobile and internet, housing, food, and transport would add about 2% to GDP per annum (Painter, 2017).

- A Canadian group proposes a comprehensive basic income known as a Recovery UBI that would provide a CAN$500 monthly payment to all adults. It increases to guarantee each individual an income of $2,000/month ($3,000/couple, $1,500/additional adult in the family).

- Yanis Varoufakis suggests a "universal dividend" approach, arguing that wealth is not created individually, then appropriated through the tax system by the state, but rather that wealth is generated collectively, and then privatized — thus, it is a distribution of a dividend (Parkins, 2017).

- Studies have generally provided evidence that free money works. The prestigious medical journal *Lancet*: "When the poor receive no-strings cash they actually tend to work harder" (Bregman, 2017).
- A synthesis in *Harvard Political Review* found "encouraging results of UBI pilots ranging from Finland to Brazil to Stockton, CA" (Ruiz, 2021).
- UBI Works has put together 8 ways to pay for a Recovery UBI, drawn from a list of $874bn in funding proposals from right across the political spectrum. They show that a basic income can be paid for without raising personal income taxes, without eliminating existing needs-based social programs, and without adding to the national debt (UBI Works, 2021).

ESOPs (Employee Stock Ownership Plans)

- ESOPs are a way for owners to perpetuate a company they have built and are proud of. They are essentially retirement plans created to reward and incentivize employees' best interests. Because they have an ownership stake in at least part of the business, employees have increased motivation to help the company prosper. They can cash out when they leave the company or retire. There are over 6,000 companies with ESOPs in the USA, according to the National Center for Employee Ownership. The ESOPs have assets that total nearly $1.4 trillion. The plans cover approximately 10.6 million active workers and 14.2 million participants overall (Swenson, 2020).

Co-management

- Systems for sharing voting rights within firms have existed in Germanic and Nordic Europe since the late 1940s. Workers' representatives hold half the seats on boards of directors in German companies and a third of the seats in Sweden (including small businesses in the Swedish case), regardless of whether they own any capital. Though shareholders initially fought these changes tooth and nail, the new rules have now been in force for more than half a century and enjoy widespread public approval. All available evidence shows that co-management has been a great success (Sledge, 2020b).

Negative income tax

Brynjolfsson and McAfee (2016) in their very balanced treatment of the future of automation, came out in favor of a negative income tax. It provides people with a percentage of the difference between their income and an income cutoff at which they would start paying income tax. For instance, if the income cutoff was set at $40,000, and the negative income tax percentage was 50%, someone who made $20,000 would receive $10,000 from the government. This structure is designed so that people who work will always make more than people who don't, which would ideally incentivize people to work. It is different from UBI, in which everyone regardless of income level, receives the same amount of money. The US uses an earned income tax credit, which functions similarly (Linke, 2018).

Autonomous zones

Autonomous zones are typically temporary protest camps. Perhaps the most famous historical example is the Paris Commune in 1871 when left-wing Parisians expelled the French Army from the city. A prominent US example was Occupy Wall Street's 2011 encampment in Manhattan (Marcus, 2020). Most recently, the CHAZ and later CHOP autonomous zone was formed in the wake of George Floyd's killing, after Seattle Police vacated the nearby East Precinct building following clashes. The protesters created a sustained occupation-style protest in the area, working with city personnel to block off street traffic in a six-block radius around the precinct (Burns, 2020).

Sovereign wealth funds

A sovereign wealth fund is a state-owned pool of money that is invested in various financial assets. The money typically comes from a nation's budgetary surplus. When a nation has excess money, it uses a sovereign wealth fund as a way to funnel it into investments rather than simply keeping it in the central bank or channeling it back into the economy. It could be used as a mechanism for redistributing wealth. The first sovereign wealth fund was the Kuwait Investment Authority, established in 1953, and then there was a lull until Abu Dhabi began one in 1976, Singapore in 1981 and Norway in 1990. They started to pick up and there are now more than 91 sovereign wealth funds worth over $8 trillion (Wilson, 2022).

Other

The list could be longer. Some tools described below were also mentioned in the tools section of Circular Commons: Worker's councils (ownership), community gardens, intentional communities (communes), and LETs.

6.1.6 Personal

There is more attention to the personal level here compared to the other two guiding images. While the conceptualization of the image is top-down, as Polak (1971) suggested they typically are, the action emphasis is on bottom-up grassroots organizing and movements.

The roots of classic far left thinking are often present in citing the necessity of sufficient class consciousness. Without getting into whether that consciousness be class-based or not, there is a need for citizens to come together collectively. Standing (2014) described the precariat, the contemporary version of the historical proletariat, as a class-in-the-making that is still developing. There is also a tendency toward what might be called romantic struggle ideas that fit with the folk politics, in which participants feel good about what they are doing at the local level, but don't create significant change.

A next step to watch for is whether or when individuals start joining movements organized around a revolutionary consciousness. The *Solidarity Economy* is an example of such a movement. It is a social justice movement based on three pillars: (Lol and Jimenez, 2017)

- shifting consciousness
- building [political] power
- creating economic alternatives (prototypes, experiments, etc.).

There is also a role for individuals in participatory politics, such as meeting in popular assemblies. Hahnel (2022, 67) advocates for greater citizen participation in matters affecting them, making the observation that "how we regulate our exchanges and coordinate our disparate economic activities influences what kind of people we become." He observes that our economic system has created a society in which people have become alienated and thus proposes a "participatory economy" approach for addressing it.

6.1.7 Leadership

A big leadership challenge is that currently the left has no effective story to counter capitalism. Srnicek and Williams (2016) suggest that the problem is folk-political thinking, described in the ineffective left driver, which is content to remain at (and even privileges) the transient, the small-scale, the unmediated, and the particular. They lament that the left once excelled at building enticing visions, but that that skill has deteriorated. Nonetheless, over the next twenty to thirty years, it is quite plausible that the left will find a direction and voice. The AC Concepts center around the local, participatory and more democratic. The challenge is how to organize and lead such arrangements.

There may be the elements of a story in something like "power to the people." Hahnel (2022) talks about works and consumers councils as fundamental units of economic and political governance. It is not clear how the leadership would work within them and in coordinating them, but this kind of arrangement seems to be the consensus as a starting point. They could be viewed as the guardians of the transition to the post-work future. The state would be a mechanism to enable the grassroots politics of power to the people, but here too a lot of details are left to be worked out.

Some ideas of this relationship between bottom-up empowerment and guidance provided by the state, include:

- Re-localization: Schweikart (2002) talks about the social control of investment. Funds for new investment are generated by a capital assets tax and are returned to the economy through a network of public investment banks. Bastani (2019) suggests re-localization of economies through progressive procurement and municipal protectionism and the introduction of a set of universal basic services (UBS). He also favors socializing finance and creating a network of local and regional banks.

- Worker self-management: Each productive enterprise is controlled democratically by its workers.

- Worker-owned production: Alperovitz (2013) suggests moving ownership beyond just workers to the community as a whole. This includes older people, stay-at-home spouses, children, and the infirm. His Pluralist Commonwealth concept advocates changing the basic institutions of ownership of the economy, so that the broad public, rather than a narrow band of individuals (i.e. the 0.1%), increasingly owns more and more of the nation's productive assets. He advocates the traditional radical principle that the ownership of capital should be subject to democratic control.
  o The concept of economic democracy shifts a firm's decision-making process away from a board of directors towards the broader base of people whom those decisions directly affect (Akbuluta and Adaman, 2020).

- Direct democracy: Srnicek and Williams (2016) suggest a consensus decision-making, prefigurative politics (reflect the future society being sought), an emphasis on direct action, and an intention to revive deliberative democracy.
    o The Liquid Democracy model has people voting directly on issues, or delegating their vote to representatives who have more specialized knowledge or are more informed (Schiener, 2015).

6.1.8 Pathway

As with *Circular Commons*, there are few detailed plans for achieving a *Non-Workers' Paradise*. Of course, it is challenging to develop plans without a vision to aim at. With this guiding image, even more than with Circular Commons, there is much more focus on fixing the problems of the present than leapfrogging into what the future could be. There were not any specific plans identified for this image, but some pilots, guiding principles, and suggestions for capacity building.

A key emphasis for this guiding image to succeed will be shifting from today's emphasis on better jobs and working conditions to focusing on a post-work future. There are developments favoring the emergence of the post-work future, such as ICT as a force eroding capitalism. ICT is already messing with pricing and market mechanisms and reducing the need for work. Mason (2015) suggests that ICT is challenging how capitalism works as follows:

- Information goods are corroding the market's ability to form prices correctly.
- The spontaneous rise of collaborative products: goods services and organizations that no longer respond to dictates of the market, e.g. Wikipedia.
- ICT, far from creating a new and stable form of capitalism, is dissolving it, corroding market mechanisms, eroding property rights and destroying the relationship between wages, work, and profit.
- ICT has reduced the need for work.
- With info-capitalism, a monopoly is the only way an industry can run (Mason, 2015).
    o We are headed for zero-price goods, unmeasurable work, an exponential takeoff in productivity, and extensive automation. For instance, a zero-carbon energy system produces machines,

products, and services with zero marginal costs, and the reduction of necessary labor time as close to zero (Mason, 2015).

The erosion of market mechanisms weakens capitalism and in turn weakens the effectiveness of jobs as the primary way for people to get access to goods ands and services. For instance, less reliable market and pricing mechanisms make it harder to assign a value to labor. At the same time, automation will reduce the need for work. As it becomes more difficult to value labor, and as fewer people are needed to work, the use of jobs as the resource distribution mechanism will become increasingly anachronistic.

Crisis, of course, is a potential stimulus or catalyst to change. Srnicek and Williams (2016) suggest the buildup could look something like this:

- The precarity or instability of the working class will intensify due to surplus global labor supply.
- Jobless recoveries will become more frequent and longer.
- Slum populations in developing countries will continue to grow due to the automation of low-skilled service work and will be exacerbated by premature deindustrialization.
- Urban marginality will grow as low-skilled, low-wage jobs are automated.
- The continuing transformation of higher education into job training will be hastened in a desperate attempt to increase the supply of high-skilled workers.
- Growth will remain slow and make the expansion of replacement jobs unlikely.
- Those without jobs are increasingly subjected to coercive controls.

The view above sees the pathway as a negative one in which eventually change arises due to a collapse or near-collapse. There is also the possibility of choosing to manage the transition to post-work, albeit the less likely path.

Pilots and plans

The most well-known model of how an approach to work could be different is the Mondragon Cooperative in Spain. Futurist Joel Barker (1996) has long cited it in his work as a useful model that flips the traditional relation of capital first, labor second, by putting labor needs as the priority. He cites the following observations that provide evidence for an alternative to the current capitalist paradigm:

- Worker democracy and ownership is a real and viable alternative to the stockholder paradigm.
- Education plus community vision plus a bank that is committed to job formation instead of capital formation can create a long-term community job base.
- There is another way to create entrepreneurial wealth.
- Workers themselves can reinvent their work if the right kind of support is available.
- The role of a bank can be profoundly positive and supportive for communities if it has the right paradigm.
- Self-capitalization, in which people raise their own capital, can be a powerful tool.
- The power of a shared vision cannot be overestimated.

There were plans identified for this guiding image. There are guides to capacity building, which is a necessary precursor to developing and implementing plans. Two capacity building examples are provided below in "Capacity building."

Evolution or revolution

In our discussion of the decay of the *Neoliberal Capitalism* Baseline in Chapter Three the case was made that reform was unlikely to work, as it is too weak, and that the capitalist system is no longer sustainable. Thus, the choices here are between evolution and revolution.

An evolutionary path appeals to those preferring a less confrontational approach. It suggests there are tangible ways that one can start working toward this new future vision now. Progress can be made by working on the margins or outside the system today, and then creating economic alternatives (prototypes, experiments, etc.).

A key feature would be something like a UBI. As that comes on, workers will be less willing to accept poor working conditions. Alongside that, the wage for desirable work eventually falls to zero, because people are willing to do it for free as they have UBI to fulfil their basic needs (Frase, 2016).

Revolutionary concepts are often precipitated by crisis or collapse and usually but not always accompanied by violence. One idea is that the word 'revolution' is too tainted by history to describe what is required. Transformation might be a more useful concept (Standing, 2014).

Mason (2015) suggests that the transformation can happen from within the existing systems and does not require a violent overthrow. He describes similar types of steps to the two laid out above: model first, act later. He mentions a wiki-state, in which the state is like the staff of Wikipedia, to nurture the new economic forms to the point where they take off and operate organically. He also includes expanding collaborative work, suppressing or socializing monopolies, letting market forces disappear, socializing the financial system, paying everyone a basic income, and unleashing the communications network.

Capacity building

There are some examples of what a pathway might look like, but they are still at the stage of capacity building rather than the implementation of plans. Several works explored how to build capacity and what it might look like. Two examples are provided here. The first from the Solidarity Movement is organized as a sequence of steps to build capacity, while the second, Alperovitz's idea of Evolutionary Reconstruction, does not necessarily follow a specific order.

First, the **Solidarity Movement** suggests a transformative approach to change would include: (Lol and Jimenez, 2017)

- Start with vision: A long-term vision for an alternative to capitalism is necessary, because if you don't know where you're going, any road will take you there.

- Build on existing work to strengthen local: Support the growing number of groups that are already experimenting with cooperative economic development, such as worker cooperatives, community land trusts, and democratic financing models to develop a more expansive approach to building local control, wealth, and power.

- Build broader coalitions with multisectoral organizing: These might include alliances with the small business sector, progressive capital and finance providers, and the progressive faith community.

- Build independent political power: Develop political tools that move beyond voter engagement to build independent political power towards a vision of self-governance.

- Encourage healing: A transformative movement must also help our communities heal from the trauma of institutional and cultural persecution.

- Build organizational capacity: Too many groups are barely hanging on. An infrastructure is needed to fortify more stable and sustainable organizations.

Second, **Evolutionary Reconstruction** proposed by Alperovitz (2013) favors a nonviolent transformation of the political economy that unfolds systematically over time. The key principles include:

- Democratization of wealth: The decline of labor unions means relying on other institutions such as co-ops, land trusts, municipal enterprises, and other national financial, health, and manufacturing forms challenging dominant ideologies.

- Community, both locally and in general, as a guiding theme: Emphasizes practical forms of community ownership in systemic design, vision, and theory, such as a central institution that is a community-wide, neighborhood-encompassing non-profit corporation, with a board that includes representatives of both the worker cooperatives and of key community institutions.

- Decentralization in general: The principle of subsidiarity — keeping decision-making at the lowest feasible level, and only referring to higher levels when absolutely necessary — is a guiding principle of the emerging model.

- Democratic planning: Planning to stabilize the local "market" and its anchor institutions (non-profit hospitals and universities) to be robust enough to encourage and accommodate outside competitors.

6.1.9 Non-Workers' Paradise Image Templates

Author	Ian Shaw is senior lecturer in human geography at the University of Glasgow and author of *Predator Empire*. Marv Waterstone is professor emeritus in the School of Geography and Development at the Univ of Arizona.
Time horizon	Not clear
Scope	Local scale on the global scene
Key drivers	Inequality, Ineffective Left
Key ideas	Shift from work at increasingly meaningless jobs to work directed at resourcing Alter-Worlds. Talks about autonomous zones, Workers' Councils, community gardens, free schools, pirate radio stations, squats, collectives, communes, LETs, etc. These offer refuge and prefigure new post-capitalist politics. A key example is the Zapatista movement in Mexico. Brings in Polanyi's three communal forces that capital destroyed, using their restoration as part of the solution: + Reciprocity, a territorially bound principle of give-and-take or obligation. + Redistribution, the sharing and exchange of goods between people, as with potlatch. + Householding or autarky, producing for one's own needs.
Ideal or guiding values	No one approach – lots of them! Much to be learned from movements appearing outside or at the edge of the
Emotional, aesthetic, and spiritual aspects	In some ways, this makes it refreshing as it suggests very tangible ways that one can start working toward this new future vision now.
Personal	A personal and local vision suggesting that progress can be made by working on the margins or outside the
Pathway or plan	"It's a question of knowing how to fight, to pick locks, to set broken bones and treat sickness; how to build a pirate radio transmitter; how to set up street kitchens; how to aim straight; how to gather together scattered knowledge and set up wartime agronomics; understand plankton biology; soil composition; study the ways plants interact…"

Author	Schweickart is a leading theorist of economic democracy with primary research interests in Marxism and various questions at the intersection of philosophy and economics.
Time horizon	Not clear
Scope	Could be viable in just one country
Key drivers	Inequality, Ineffective Left
Key ideas	A socialist approach with market and democratic features centered on three key concepts: + *Worker self-management*: Each productive enterprise is controlled democratically by its workers. + *The market*: These enterprises interact with one another and with consumers in an environment largely free of government price controls. Raw materials, instruments of production, and consumer goods are all bought and sold at prices largely determined by the forces of supply and demand. + *Social control of investment*: Funds for new investment are generated by a capital assets tax and are returned to the economy through a network of public investment banks.
Ideal or guiding values	"We must confront the claim that there is no alternative [to capitalism] —by proposing one."
Emotional, aesthetic, and spiritual aspects	+ Perhaps seen as less radical or jolting than some others - it is a successor system that preserves the efficiency strengths of a market economy while extending democracy to the workplace and to the structures of investment. + It is beyond dispute that the Mondragon "experiment" has been economically successful.
Personal	A genuine "right to work" has long been a basic tenet of socialism. Every able-bodied person who wants to work should be able to find decent employment.
Pathway or plan	It could be considered an H2 transition concept, as "some capitalism would be permitted in any realistic version of Economic Democracy — or at least some wage labor."

Author	Dr Aaron Bastani is Co-founder and Senior Editor at Novara Media. His research interests including new media, social movements, and political economy.
Time horizon	Between rising populations, climate change, a dearth of fresh water and stretched bio-capacity, just avoiding widespread famine by mid-century would be an astonishing achievement.
Scope	The Global North must reduce its CO_2 emissions by 8% p.a. from 2020-2030. Then, in 2030, the Global South will embark on the same journey at the same rate. If successful that will mean a full, global transition to renewable energy by 2040.
Key drivers	Technology acceleration, Inequality, Automation, Stagnation, Climate and carrying capacity, Ineffective Left
Key ideas	+ Advocates a shift towards worker-owned production, a state-financed transition to renewable energy and universal services -- aided by tech progress and beyond commodity exchange and profit. + FALC seeks to describe a society in which work is eliminated, scarcity replaced by abundance and where labor and leisure blend into one another. Our labor – how we mix our cognitive and physical efforts with the world – becomes a route to self-development. + The program for FALC includes: "re-localization of economies through progressive procurement and municipal protectionism; socializing finance and creating a network of local and regional banks and, finally, the introduction of a set of universal basic services. + The intention is to create a society where work is eliminated, scarcity replaced by abundance and where labor and leisure blend into one another.

Ideal or guiding values	Challenges two key assumptions of capitalism: + that scarcity will always exist + that goods will not be produced if their marginal cost is zero. There is more than enough technology for everyone on Earth to live healthy, happy, and fulfilling lives. What stands in the way isn't the inevitable scarcity of nature, but the artificial scarcity of market rationing and ensuring that everything is produced for profit.
Emotional, aesthetic, and spiritual aspects	+ Recognizes that it is easier to imagine the end of the world than the end of capitalism. + The most pressing crisis of all is an absence of collective imagination.
Personal	The Great Recession exposed that neoliberal capitalism is socialism for the rich and market capitalism for the rest.
Pathway or plan	Five such crises, which at times overlap. + *climate change* and the consequences of global warming; + *resource scarcity* – particularly for energy, minerals and fresh water; + *societal aging*, as life expectancy increases and birth rates concurrently fall; + [inequality] a growing surplus of global poor who form an ever-larger 'unnecessariat'; and, + a *new machine age*.

Author	Alperovitz is Professor of Political Economy at the University of Maryland and is a Founding Principal of The Democracy Collaborative. He was a Legislative Director in the US House of Representatives and the US Senate and a Special Assistant in the Department of State.
Time horizon	Not clear
Scope	+ A central emphasis is the reconstruction of communities – and the nation as a community – from the ground up. + Subsidiarity, keeping decision-making at the lowest feasible level, and only elevating to higher levels when absolutely necessary.
Key drivers	Inequality, Ineffective Left
Key ideas	*Evolutionary reconstruction redistributes productive assets*, based on: 1. democratization of wealth 2. community as a guiding theme 3. decentralization 4. substantial democratic planning to achieve economic, democracy-building and ecological goal. + Advocates changing the basic institutions of ownership of the economy, so that the broad public, rather than a narrow band of individuals (i.e., the "one percent"), increasingly owns more and more of the nation's productive assets. + The various institutions briefly highlighted above – from co-ops to land trusts, as well as municipal enterprises, national financial, health, and manufacturing forms – all challenge dominant ideologies.

Imagining After Capitalism | 229

Ideal or guiding values	This is a systemic model, developed and refined over the last forty years. It attempts to resolve theoretical and practical problems associated with both traditional corporate capitalism and traditional state socialism.
Emotional, aesthetic, and spiritual aspects	Shift in the ownership of wealth would slowly move the nation as a whole toward greater equality. Among other things the changes would also help finance a reduction in the workweek so as to permit greater amounts of free time, thereby bolstering both individual liberty and democratic participation.
Personal	The basic idea is that citizens meet in popular assemblies throughout the city to deliberate about how the city budget should be spent.
Pathway or plan	Three pathways: + Reform suggests changes or improvements to the existing [capitalist] system. + Revolutionary concepts are often precipitated by crisis or collapse and usually but not always accompanied by violence. + Alperovitz favors evolutionary reconstruction, a systemic institutional step-by-step nonviolent transformation of the political economy that unfolds over time.

Author	Mason is a journalist, writer, filmmaker and public speaker. He sees crisis ahead but also sees that we have the capacity to deal with it.
Time horizon	Cites that climate change, aging, and population growth kick in around 2050 and it will be chaos if a sustainable economic order isn't in place.
Scope	Global, but mostly aimed at affluent countries
Key drivers	Technology acceleration, Automation

Key ideas	+ Neoliberal capitalism is declining and the need to design the transition with ICT being a key driver to abundance.
	+ Mason suggests three impacts of new technology driving toward postcapitalism:
	  » Infotech has reduced the need for work.
	  » Information goods are corroding the market's ability to form prices correctly.
	  » The spontaneous rise of collaborative product: goods services and organizations that no longer respond to dictates of the market, e.g. Wikipedia.
	
	Top goals
	+ rapidly reduce carbon emissions.
	+ stabilize and socialize the financial system.
	+ prioritize information-rich technologies toward solving major social challenges.
	+ gear technology towards the reduction of necessary work to promote transition towards an automated economy … eventually work becomes voluntary.
	
	It is increasingly evident that information goods conflict fundamentally with market mechanisms.

Ideal or guiding values	+ Free market capitalism is a clear and powerful idea, while the forces opposing it looked like they were defending something old, worse, and incoherent. + Utopian communities failed due to scarcity ... the advance from scarcity to abundance is a significant development in the history of humanity.
Emotional, aesthetic, and spiritual aspects	+ The main contradiction today is between the possibility of free abundant goods and information and a system of monopolies, banks, and governments trying to keep things private, scarce, and commercial. Everything comes down to the struggle between the network and the hierarchy ... between old ... and what comes next. + For infocapitalism to survive it would have to push the market into sectors where it hasn't been before, creating new forms of person-to-person micro-services, paid for using micro-payments.
Personal	Talks a lot about how neoliberal capitalism destroyed unions and workers' ability to fight back against capitalists.
Pathway or plan	First we need an open, accurate and comprehensive computer simulation of current economic reality: + model first, act later + the wiki-state + expand collaborative work + suppress or socialize monopolies + let market forces disappear + socialize the financial system + pay everyone a basic income + basic income initially comes from taxation...allows people to build an income in the non-market economy.

Author	Srnicek and Williams are lecturers at City University, London. They study, and write on, the future of work and capitalism.
Time horizon	Not clear
Scope	Criticism of the Left's focus on the 'folk' as the locus of the small-scale, the authentic, the traditional and the natural.
Key drivers	Technology acceleration, Automation, Ineffective Left
Key ideas	The "folk politics" approach of the left is ineffective. There is a need to systematically create a vision or "new hegemony" of the future: 1. A rejection of all forms of domination 2. An adherence to direct democracy and/ or consensus decision-making 3. A commitment to prefigurative politics 4. An emphasis on direct action + Requires some combination of reducing duplicate programs, raising taxes on the rich, inheritance taxes, consumption taxes, carbon taxes, cutting spending on the military, cutting industry and agriculture subsidies, and cracking down on tax evasion. + In order to install a new hegemonic order, at least three things will be required: a mass populist movement, a healthy ecosystem of organizations; and an analysis of points of leverage.
Ideal or guiding values	+ The problem is that folk-political thinking is content to remain at (and even privileges) that level – of the transient, the small-scale, the unmediated and the particular. + A skill that the left once excelled at – building enticing visions for a better world – has deteriorated. + For any leftist universal – it must be one that integrates difference rather than erasing it.

Imagining After Capitalism | 233

Emotional, aesthetic, and spiritual aspects	+ They believe a post-work society is not only achievable, given the material conditions, but also viable and desirable. + Resistance ... it is a defensive and reactive gesture, rather than an active movement.
Personal	A post-work world is not a world of idleness; rather, it is a world in which people are no longer bound to their jobs, but free to create their own lives.
Pathway or plan	When that crisis occurs, the actions that are taken depend on the ideas that are lying around: 1. The precarity of the developed economies' working class will intensify due to the surplus global labor supply (resulting from both globalization and automation). 2. Jobless recoveries will continue to deepen and lengthen, predominantly affecting those whose jobs can be automated at the time. 3. Slum populations will continue to grow due to the automation of low-skilled service work, and will be exacerbated by premature deindustrialization. 4. Urban marginality in the developed economies will grow in size as low-skilled, low-wage jobs are automated. 5. The transformation of higher education into job training will be hastened in a desperate attempt to increase the supply of high-skilled workers. 6. Growth will remain slow and make the expansion of replacement jobs unlikely. 7. The changes to workfare, immigration controls and mass incarceration will deepen as those without jobs are increasingly subjected to coercive controls.

Author	Standing is a Professor of Development Studies at the School of Oriental and African Studies, University of London, and a co-founder of the Basic Income Earth Network.
Time horizon	Unclear
Scope	Global
Key drivers	Inequality, Ineffective Left
Key ideas	+ Globalization, starting in the 1980s, has generated a class structure, superimposed on earlier structures, comprising an elite, a salariat, proficians, an old 'core' working class (proletariat), a precariat, the unemployed and a lumpen-precariat (or 'underclass'). + The precariat consists of people living through insecure jobs interspersed with periods of unemployment or labor-force withdrawal (misnamed as 'economic inactivity') and living insecurely. + The idea of 'social income' aims to capture all forms of income that people can receive – own-account production, income from producing or selling to the market, money wages, enterprise non-wage benefits, community benefits, state benefits, and income from financial and other assets. *The Precariat Charter* » Article 1: Redefine work as productive and reproductive activity » Article 2: Reform labor statistics » Article 3: Make recruitment practices brief encounters » Article 4: Regulate flexible labor » Article 5: Promote associational freedom » Articles 6-10: Reconstruct occupational communities » Articles 11-15: Stop class-based migration policy » Article 16: Ensure due process for all » Article 17: Remove poverty traps and precarity traps » Article 18: Make a bonfire of benefit assessment tests

Key ideas (cont.)	» *Article 19: Stop demonizing the disabled* » *Article 20: Stop workfare now!* » *Article 21: Regulate payday loans and student loans* » *Article 22: Institute a right to financial knowledge and advice* » *Article 23: Decommodify education* » *Article 24: Make a bonfire of subsidies* » *Article 25: Move towards a universal basic income* » *Article 26: Share capital via sovereign wealth funds* » *Article 27: Revive the commons* » *Article 28: Revive deliberative democracy* » *Article 29: Re-marginalize charities*
Ideal or guiding values	+ The main arguments for a universal basic income are ethical and relate to social justice, individual freedom and the need for basic security (not the necessity from automation). + Today it would be better to think of citizenship as a continuum, with many people having a more limited range of rights than others.
Emotional, aesthetic, and spiritual aspects	We should define the 'right to work' as the right to pursue an occupation of one's choice, where occupation comprises a combination of work, labor, leisure and recuperation that corresponds to one's abilities and aspirations.
Personal	Precariat is a class-in-the-making that must become enough of a class-for-itself in order to seek ways of abolishing itself.
Pathway or plan	The word 'revolution' is too tainted by history to describe what is required. The word 'reform' is too tainted by the neo-liberal use of it, and is too weak. The essence is captured by the concept of 'transformation'.

Author	The Solidarity Economy Initiative (SEI) was founded in 2015 as a joint project of seven local and national philanthropic organizations. SEI launched with a 3-year pilot commitment of grants and technical assistance to leading grassroots organizations from across the state.
Time horizon	Unclear
Scope	Local
Key drivers	Inequality
Key ideas	This is a social justice movement among lower-income people of color seeking to go beyond socialism and communism by shifting consciousness, building [political] power, and creating economic alternatives. Their recommendations include: + See solidarity economy holistically, as a transformative social movement. + Join up the building of alternatives with resist and reform efforts. + Be willing to innovate and be prepared to fail forward. + Take an ecosystem approach to building and scaling up. + Support core organizing and incubation infrastructure. + Inspire and connect initiatives so that we can learn from one another and scale up. + Build the solidarity finance sector, with funders and investors who see themselves as part of, and not apart from, the movement.
Ideal or guiding values	Based on three pillars: + shifting consciousness + building [political] power + creating economic alternatives (prototypes, experiments, etc.)

Emotional, aesthetic, and spiritual aspects	Solidarity economy is more than just cooperatives. It is a social justice movement seeking to transform political and economic systems and our worldview
Personal	Grassroots movements coming together and people taking control of their lives.
Pathway or plan	Transformative approach to change: + *Long Term Vision for Alternatives to Capitalism.* This vision is necessary, because "if you don't know where you're going, any road will take you there." + *Cooperative Economic Development.* A growing number of groups are experimenting with this. + *Worker cooperatives*, community land trusts and democratic financing models to express a more expansive approach to building local control, wealth and power. We can build on these already existing elements of solidarity economy. + *Multisectoral Organizing.* While Massachusetts' organizing sector engages hundreds of thousands of residents as voters, workers, and residents, there is an opportunity to build broader coalitions capable of challenging consolidated corporate power. These include alliances with the small business sector, progressive capital and finance providers, and the progressive faith community. + *Political Power-Building Innovation.* We need political tools that move beyond voter engagement to build independent political power towards a vision of self-governance.
Pathway or plan	+ *Healing and Transformative Leadership.* A transformative movement must also help our communities heal from the trauma of institutional and cultural persecution. This is inextricably linked to our ability to fight for our collective freedom. + *Organizational Capacity Building.* Member- led, nonprofit base-building organizations are essential to a transformative movement, but too many of our groups are barely hanging on. We need to fortify the infrastructure for more stable and sustainable organizations.

Author	Rutger Bregman is a historian who has published books on history, philosophy and economics.
Time horizon	Not clear
Scope	Global
Key drivers	Inequality, Ineffective Left
Key ideas	Suggests that reduction of work first has to be reinstated as a political ideal. Makes the case for universal basic income and the need for a massive redistribution of wealth.
Ideal or guiding values	+ We need a new lodestar, a new map of the world. In our terms, a guiding image of the future. + Notes the effectiveness of the neoliberal movement in getting its message across, and by contrast, how poorly the left has done: "The left seems to have forgotten the art of politics. They've got no story to tell, nor even any language to convey it in."
Emotional, aesthetic, and spiritual aspects	+ "Imagine just how much progress we've missed out on because thousands of bright minds have frittered away their time dreaming up hyper complex financial products that are ultimately only destructive." + The goal of the future is full unemployment, so we can play — Arthur C. Clarke
Personal	Studies from all over the world offer proof positive that free money works. The prestigious medical journal the *Lancet* summed up their findings: When the poor receive no-strings cash they tend to work harder.
Pathway or plan	+ There's only one choice left, and that's redistribution. + Notes that utopias are initially attacked on three grounds: » futility (it's not possible) » danger (the risks are too great), » and perversity (it will degenerate into dystopia) And once they are implemented, they come to be seen as "utterly commonplace."

Imagining After Capitalism | 239

Chapter 7 – TECH-LED ABUNDANCE

Tech-Led Abundance sees technological progress driving and leading to an abundance of wealth that fixes the core distribution problem of capitalism.

Tech-Led Abundance At-A-Glance

There is no doubt a strong case to be made that technology has provided great benefits. It is the engine driving the growth central to capitalism. Of the three images, it is the one that fits capitalism best and, in that regard, it may be challenging for it to replace capitalism. While there may be some resistance among supporters to leaving capitalism behind, the image of abundance here is so great that it crushes capitalism even if it doesn't necessarily want to!

While this image is composed of just six AC Concepts, the smallest number of the three images, the immense popularity of most of them shows that they have already resonated with wider audiences. The Singularity, Abundance, and Homo Deus have already broken through to the mainstream and earned some esteem among both experts and the public. The purpose is to create a bountiful abundance that solves the world's pressing problems through sophisticated new technologies.

The key aspects of *Tech-Led Abundance* are underlined, followed by a brief description of supporting community values, economics, and governance.

1. <u>Focusing sharply on tech</u>: This image is the most sharply focused on one driver and one solution, namely technology. There is an almost religious faith in the continued amazing progress of technology in key application areas such as renewable energy, automation enabling a post-work future, and even suggesting a remaking of humanity itself by human-machine integration.

2. <u>Moving from a scarcity to an abundance mindset</u>: Technology is the key enabler of a shift in economic assumptions away from scarcity — a fundamental guiding assumption of capitalism — and toward abundance. The critical point is that capitalism is a system that in essence encourages growth to improve the conditions of scarcity. It then allocates those scarce resources in a way that inevitably leads to inequality. If you take away scarcity, then what do you need capitalism for?

3. <u>Automating work</u>: Automation likely starts by replacing cheap, labor-intensive work that brought little satisfaction to anyone and relegates those tasks to AI-guided machines to do the dirty work. Improvement in AI will be key here as it grows to be capable of analyzing data from multiple sources, making decisions, and taking physical actions with little or no human input. AI should eventually be able to perform a wide range of tasks — ultimately surpassing the intelligence of humans.

4. <u>Partnering between people and machines</u>: The relationship between people and machines functions as a partnership. In this image more responsibility is given to the machines. To keep up, people may begin to modify themselves to become more machine-like, using various augmentation methods and enhancement approaches including wearables, implants, smart prosthetics as well as using biological means of genetic engineering via CRISPR and stem cells.

5. <u>Taking calculated risks with geoengineering & species modification</u>: While the more enthusiastic and dogmatic supporters minimize the potential for risks, others are more willing to point them out. The various geoengineering proposals for addressing climate change, for example, have huge upsides and downsides, as do AI and augmentation technologies that could threaten the essence of the human species itself.

6. <u>Acknowledging zero marginal cost makes pricing obsolete</u>: A key factor enabling abundance is that digital technology offers the ability to reproduce copies at near zero cost, which disrupts conventional capitalist economics and opens the door for alternative conceptions. Copying and 3D printing are likely to become preeminent, eliminating many of the functions that globalized markets used to perform. One can envision systems for sharing cars, homes, clothes, or most anything through online platforms and cooperatives to ensure that everyone has access to needed goods.

7. <u>Incentivizing entrepreneurs</u>: This image acknowledges that the human element is essential to the development of the technology. Entrepreneurs need to be properly incentivized to develop the needed technologies, which is in line with how capitalism functions.

Supporting community values. The key values question for this image is how the bounty from *Tech-Led Abundance* will be distributed. How do we distribute wealth without jobs? The concepts don't say much on this, but rather assume that the abundance is so great that it will take care of itself, but one might be inclined to want to pin down this distribution question more directly. It requires an evolution of values away from the modern values emphasizing "to the victor goes the spoils" toward postmodern values with more concern for the collective and community good.

Economics. The continuation of tech acceleration suggests the bounty to deliver abundance will be there. Today, there are daily headlines of amazing breakthroughs or potential ones. Even if "change is slower than we think" (Hines, 2020b), with our 20-30-year timeframe there should be spectacular advances. To take one small example, the cost reductions and efficiency gains in solar technology are astounding. They have happened despite a powerful entrenched industry working against them, and very sporadic support. If society made a major commitment to renewables and was able to overcome inertia and sunk interests, progress would be even greater.

Governance. This image would suggest that intelligent technology can be used to address the distribution challenge. Big breakthroughs in the realm of computer-simulated models enable a more measured approach to economic planning, with people heavily involved in planning and distribution at the local level. Antiquated supply-demand models will fade away with a shift towards using complex algorithms and simulations to determine what resources are needed and where they should be directed. Human oversight is key to guiding the decision-making processes.

The three guiding images are connected, of course. Fully Automated Luxury Communism (FALC), for instance, was put in *Non-Workers' Paradise* but could easily fit here as well. Bastani (2019) sees technology acceleration as a key enabler of the FALC concept. He talks about the great potential for renewable energy, asteroid mining, AI, and low-cost genetic engineering. Indeed, his vision sees scarcity replaced by "abundance." FALC is not the communism of the early twentieth century!

That said, *Tech-Led Abundance* is the narrowest or most focused of the three guiding images. It is centrally focused on technology as the answer and does not spend as much time exploring other aspects of an economic, social, and political system. Diamandis's (2012) title says it all: *Abundance: The Future Is Better Than You Think*. He is a true believer in the idea that technology will solve our problems. He believes that, by 2035, we will be able to provide goods and services, once reserved for the wealthy few, to any and all who need them. He believes that exponential technology is the key and critiques our "local and linear brains" that are blind to the amazing possibilities ahead.

Many futurists are likely to say "not so fast" and note that technological capacity development has outstripped the supporting values and cultural development to properly manage it. That is, humanity's ability to wisely use that technology is under-developed. The modern values driving this guiding image of technological progress indeed have supported a growth imperative that has created the climate and carrying capacity problems. Can the system that has created the problem also solve it? Nonetheless, it is a positive, hopeful, and plausible vision.

The image is not just about solving current problems. It explores the longer-term question of the relationship between people and machines. A basic question is: how do people keep up with this technology? Homo Deus, Superintelligence, Transhumanism and Singularity raise the possibility of a new species of humans. It could be that people blend or merge with it, and perhaps end up so different as to constitute a new species.

These concept authors were more willing to suggest a potential time horizon than concept authors of the other two images. The sweet spot was within a generation or a couple of decades, which at the time of writing nets out at 2035 to 2040.

The *Tech-Led Abundance* concepts are listed with the author and are described here:

- *Abundance*, Peter Diamandis. Technological progress is such that, within a generation, we will be able to provide goods and services, once reserved for the wealthy few, to any and all who need them.
- *Homo Deus*, Yuval Harari. Biology and robotics enabling the upgrading of humans into new species via three paths: biological engineering, cyborg engineering, the engineering of non-organic beings.
- *Singularity*, Ray Kurzweil. Exponential technological change leads to machine intelligence surpassing humans and eventually no clear distinction between humans and machines.
- *Superintelligence*, Nick Bostrom. Explores paths to beyond-human superintelligence, the strategic choices available to it, and what we could do to shape the initial conditions.
- *Transhumanism*, Max More. Transhumanism is an intellectual and cultural movement that seeks to fundamentally improve the human condition through applied reason and technology development to eliminate aging and to greatly enhance human intellectual, physical, and psychological capacities.
- *Zero Marginal Cost*, Jeremy Rifkin. Massive economies of scale provided by digitization push the cost of reproducing information to zero, thus enabling abundance, or an empathic civilization.

This section is organized as follows:

- Driver outcomes: how do the drivers project forward in each image?
- Challenges: the central problems that the image focuses on
- Purposes: the key motivation for developing the image; what it's trying to achieve
- Principles: guidelines followed in working towards the image
- Tools: mechanisms or activities for enabling or realizing the image
- Personal: the role of "regular" in this image
- Leadership: the role of leaders in this image
- Pathway: high-level take on how to get to the image from the present.

7.1.1 Driver outcomes

Technology acceleration and automation are the key drivers of this guiding image. Kurzweil has long been an advocate of the great potential for exponential technology. He has made a career out of understanding the rate of exponential technological growth and accurately predicting many innovations based on that. His Singularity concept at its foundation predicts the point at which computing power will surpass that of the human brain and thus exceed its capabilities. When tied in with advances in other technologies, such as robotics, genetics, and nanotechnology, the changes are so vast that they create a technology singularity whose outcome is impossible to imagine.

Table 7.1 Driver outcomes in *Tech-Led Abundance*

DRIVER	OUTCOME IN *TECH-LED ABUNDANCE*
Shifting values	Modern
Technology acceleration	Rapid & successful; general AI
Inequality	Mostly reduced
Jobs & automation	Strong role for automation
Stagnation	Abundant wealth via automation
Climate & carrying capacity	Tech fixes succeed
Ineffective Left	Not a big factor

Automation is perhaps the more publicly discussed driver, with the key issue currently framed as its potential for creating job loss. This framing sees job loss as a threat, and in the current capitalist system, rightly so. But in the long term, and in a different system, one could see job loss as a positive. In essence, it is quite plausible to imagine people letting go of jobs if the payoffs were accounted for, as was outlined in the previous guiding image.

The story of the driver outcomes here is obviously technology. The promised technology bounty comes to fruition. It produces and facilitates a redistribution of wealth that creates a more just society. It provides solutions to mitigate the worst effects of climate change and carrying capacity issues. As it deals with unavoidable impacts over the next few decades, it also begins to develop preventative and restorative approaches that provide even greater hope for the future.

Perhaps the most underrated aspect of this image, if it is to succeed, is that it requires significant progress in the people and political aspects. It is people who ultimately decide what to invest in and apply – technology does not emerge in a vacuum. The wise guidance of technology development, application, and oversight is critical to the success of this image.

Figure 7.1 *Tech-Led Abundance* concepts

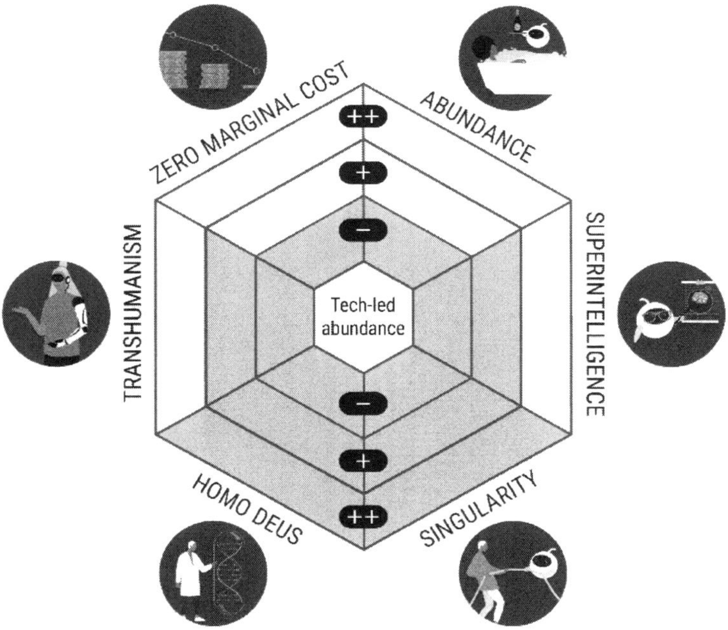

7.1.2 Challenges and responses

The six *Tech-Led Abundance* concepts vary in how radical or far-reaching their projections are, as depicted in Figure 7.1. The first challenge, Zero Marginal Cost, explains a key reason that accelerating tech change is making a big impact on the economy, which is by destroying price mechanisms. The second, Abundance, is the central concept suggesting the outcome of radically increased output and wealth. The other four are grouped into a third major challenge, in which the aclerating technology goes a step beyond and suggests long-term impacts that could affect the future of the species itself.

The challenges below are arranged from those coming from the weaker to the stronger concepts.

<u>Zero marginal cost erodes pricing mechanisms</u>

A key problem for capitalism is how to make money in a world moving toward zero marginal cost. Zero marginal cost reminds us of Stewart Brand's 1984 quip: "Information wants to be free." A little less well known follow-up is that he also noted that it wants to be expensive, which represents all the convoluted efforts to protect IP and other creative ways to monetize the reproduction of information. Lanier (2013) also observed that when copying is easy there is almost no intrinsic scarcity. Scarcity needs to be invented or market value will collapse. Of course, *After Capitalism* embraces the idea that markets could collapse amidst the production of plenty!

The Zero Marginal Cost concept recognizes the massive economies of scale provided by digitization and essentially pushes the cost of reproducing information to zero or near zero. Rifkin (2014) goes beyond just information to essentially free energy via renewables and free goods via 3D printing. As the costs drop towards zero, society could reorganize around self-sufficient communities. This concept has a lot in common with commons and post-work concepts in the other two guiding images.

The pricing mechanism is central to assigning value. Value typically increases with actual or perceived scarcity. As this mechanism breaks down, there are increasing efforts to create scarcity. As noted above in the challenges to growth mechanism of *Circular Commons*, capitalism historically brings in new things to monetize and create scarcity to keep creating perceived value and keep the growth engine going.

While supporters of *Tech-Led Abundance* extol its potential to revolutionize standards of living, they are typically within the capitalist frame. There is a tendency to support if not aggrandize the tech entrepreneurs as the heroes that are going to save us. The entrepreneurs deserve the money they get, and it is assumed the largesse will spread and benefit all.

Responses

Zero Marginal Cost presents something of a dilemma. On the one hand, it suggests that scarcity no longer matches the conditions and that we are moving towards abundance. On the other, the distortion of price mechanism is not good for business or capitalism. Capitalists argue that if incentive to innovate is harmed, there will be no motivation to produce goods and services. It is a similar argument to the Laziness Lie in *Non-Workers' Paradise* — people would lie around doing nothing without proper incentives. The good news is that the cost of production is coming down. Because we are so embedded in the current system, positive developments like lower costs of production are seen as a threat. We don't recognize how odd that really is!

This development provides support for the case that we can afford to live in the *After Capitalism* world. It is often argued that this is a utopic idea that lacks a firm basis in the harsh world of business, but in reality the trend is in this direction.

From scarcity to abundance

The promise of this guiding image is that accelerating technology will continue to grow exponentially, and it will eventually reach a point of almost unimaginable productivity that in turn creates unprecedented wealth. Proponents believe that technology-led progress is going to help humanity to rein in famine, plague and war, tackle longevity, and even increase happiness.

It will raise questions about the need for, or role of, human workers. Indeed, several *Non-Workers' Paradise* concepts note that the gains in productivity and wealth pave the way for a post-work future. One can make a case that it is already here. It was pointed out earlier that there is already enough wealth produced for everyone on Earth to live a reasonably comfortable life *if* it were distributed equally. *Tech-Led Abundance* is much more interested in rewarding the tech entrepreneurs than in distributing the bounty more equitably. For instance: "A new technology with massive value for society should make the people who invent it wealthy and will concentrate power in their hands. That's how capitalism works" (Hines, 2023). This is what *After Capitalism* is up against!

Responses

There is still a strong perception that scarcity is a prevailing condition, although the growing awareness of inequality is denting that perception. It is a big mindset shift, and futurists know these shifts are not easily accomplished. The goal is two-fold: (1) raise awareness of the actual concrete evidence for abundance that is already here and should continue to emerge, and (2) shine the spotlight on the potential for inequality so that abundance doesn't end up in the hands of just a few entrepreneurs.

Transhumanism: Is tech the savior?

Vita-More (2018) captures the strong tech-driven nature of transhumanism in suggesting that 'haves' and 'have nots' may not be an issue we will have to deal with in the future, because we'll be in a post-scarcity or abundance scenario. The implication is that the solution to global poverty is not in redistribution, but in technological growth. Proponents of *Tech-Led Abundance* often talk about it as a big global vision and criticize failure to see it as a failure of imagination.

The primary critique of *Tech-Led Abundance* is that tech-fix does not pay enough attention to the rest of the contextual STEEP factors: the social, economic, environmental, and political. All too often, amazing tech possibilities either do not come to fruition or take much longer than expected, due to these other factors, such as consumer acceptance, affordability, environmental impact, regulatory regime, and lack of a supporting infrastructure.

It is useful to keep in mind the arguments of the *Limits to Growth* authors, who have repeatedly addressed and rejected the suggestion that technology will be the magic bullet that solves the growth challenge. They suggest that technology can help solve problems for sure, but "technology market responses are themselves delayed and imperfect … they take time, they demand capital, they require materials and energy flow … if those are the only changes, the model tends to generate scenarios of collapse" (Hines, 2005).

Responses

An important principle here is to avoid getting into a black-and-white argument where tech is either all good or all bad. This may be challenging for some who are skeptical about technology and may favor more natural approaches to the future in the case of supporters of

Circular Commons. It may also be challenging for supporters of *Non-Workers' Paradise* who are more inclined to protect workers' rights than to move to post-work.

If one is labelled as an opponent, it probably suggests lapsing into the us-them perspective. Rather, the goal is to bring balanced perspectives to discussions about technologies. Note the benefits, but also note the contextual factors that so often get overlooked when a new technology is being hyped. The potential for technology to play a useful role in both *Circular Commons* and *Non-Workers' Paradise* is huge and it is worth staying involved and participating in the discussion and ongoing development.

A new species?

> *In seeking bliss and immortality, humans are in fact trying to upgrade themselves into gods.* (Harari 2017a, 43)

A big challenge from accelerating technology is the possibility that it actually achieves one of the ultimate imagined ends, whether it's a singularity, the merging of human and machine, or literally the creation of a new species. Kurzweil's by now well-known Singularity concept sees life on the other side of the rise of superintelligent technology as unimaginable. He and others, such as the Transhumanists, foresee that people will choose to, or be forced to, augment themselves in order to keep up with technological advances — in effect a merger of human and machine. Transhumanists envision a post-human future in which people no longer suffer from disease, aging, and inevitable death in a wide range of possible future environments, including space colonization and the creation of rich virtual worlds. They see the unique status of human beings being superseded and that humans are part of a spectrum of biological organisms and possible non-biological species of the future (More, 2013).

Perhaps the most challenging future is one of machine superintelligence that far surpasses human abilities. Proponents suggest that the beneficial impacts include not only abundance but also could reduce many other existential risks, e.g. asteroid impacts, super volcanoes, and natural pandemics. Harari suggested the notion of *Homo Deus* in his popular book with that title. He sees technological progress leading to such profound change that Homo Sapiens is upgraded into a new species.

These extraordinary possibilities are likely to boggle the mind of those not paying attention. To speak of augmentation, human/machine mergers, superintelligent machines, and a new human species — is going to seem like the realm of science fiction. But it is indeed in front of us to consider.

Responses

This development is still at an early enough stage that the key need is to raise awareness and start discussing what this potential means. In my practice, I have been introducing this idea as a Horizon Three "weak signal" to bring it into the conversation, but for many it is almost unthinkable – yet the potential in a 20-30 year time horizon is unquestionably real.

7.1.3 Purposes

Tech-Led Abundance suggests that accelerating technological capabilities will produce economic abundance that will in turn improve a range of other issues from the environment to health to work. Technology will be aimed at addressing and solving these key problems. The productivity rise enables increases in wealth that in turn can be used to address inequality. Diamandis (2012) talks about providing wealth for the "bottom billion" to become the "rising billion."

The principal enabling mechanism suggested is to provide tech entrepreneurs the incentives to address and solve the key problems just mentioned. It is a fair argument that abundance could help enable *Circular Commons* and the *Non-Workers' Paradise*. There is more discussion of that later — tech advances making work less necessary — but there is some discussion of how accelerating technology could aid the environmental focus of *Circular Commons*, e.g. advances in renewable energy, or materials sciences advances facilitating longer-lived products or product re-use. Rifkin (2014) even talks about a "global collaborative commons."

1. <u>Rethink the role of AI and data from a dominant to a supportive role</u>

The production, collection, and analysis of data is at the heart of abundance, with AI the key tool for using it. Harari (2017a) sees reliance on data as mutating into a religion that claims to determine right and wrong. He suggests that human decision-making is being ceded to the data. As ICT gets smarter, it will control more and more of the decision-making. The Houston Foresight program developed a scenario on the future of work to

2050 in which humans are learning to be back in charge after "pulling the plug" on self-aware AI (Hines et al., 2017).

While the *Tech-Led Abundance* concepts focus heavily on digital technologies, they also included biological data. ICT and associated technologies — predictive analytics, AI, machine learning — are at the core, but there is discussion of how to integrate with other technologies, such as biotech, nanotech, and robotics.

The potential ceding of decision-making to AI/data is a choice. It could be viewed by leaders as a way to make better decisions and thus be pursued as a deliberate strategy. Or it could be more gradual and less intentional and simply result from using new AI as its capabilities improve without thinking through the long-term implications of growing more dependent on it.

My view is that AI/data should be primarily viewed as a tool in a support role. That is, humans are always in charge or in the decision-making loop. This will likely run into opposition as it will be seen as slowing down progress, which would be true. Keeping humans in the loop will slow down the application of AI/data, thus it is an important choice and purpose.

2. Rethink scarcity to abundance and embrace the revolutionary possibilities

Diamandis (2012) sees the applications like dominos, as one challenge after another falls or is met. Kurzweil (2005) suggests a key milestone on this pathway is when machines achieve and surpass humans in the ability to design and engineer technology.

Kurzweil (2005) suggests three overlapping revolutions of genetics, nanotech and robotics:

- Genetics includes cloning for life-extension purposes; it could also be a possible solution to world hunger by creating meat by cloning animal muscle tissue in a factory.

- Nanofactories with negligible energy requirements; Drexler estimates that molecular manufacturing will be an energy generator…using typical organic feedstock and assuming oxidation of surplus hydrogen.

- Robotics, or strong AI is comparable in importance to the advent of biology itself.

Rifkin (2014) suggests that as the costs of goods drop towards zero, society can reorganize around self-sufficient communities. He calls this an

Empathic Civilization, where globally connected networked collectives share communal resources in an empathic fashion.

The purpose here is similar to the one above regarding AI/data, to keep technology in its proper place as a supportive role guided by human strategic choice. At the same time, a trap to avoid is becoming anti-technology and missing out on the possibilities it enables.

3. <u>Rethink the relationship between people and technology and confront revolutionary possibilities of species modification</u>

The big changes suggested by these *Tech-Led Abundance* concepts are focused more on changes to the species than the economy. As noted above, they are not specifically aimed at replacing capitalism. The abundance could be managed by capitalism. The main long-term focus of the authors is more on the relationship of humans to machines, and most see a future where that relationship is dramatically altered. There is a viewpoint that technology should be applied to improve the species:

- Transhumanism suggests the possibilities of a post-human new species. It seeks to transcend the human form via science and technology but does explicitly suggest a need for this to be guided by life-promoting principles and values (More, 2013).

- Kurzweil (2005) notes that exponential technological change leads to machine intelligence surpassing humans and eventually no clear distinction between humans and machines. The integration of this intelligence with people results in a world that is still human but transcends our biological roots.

- Superintelligence suggests a future where AI overtakes humanity in its capabilities; there is the potential for solving human problems, but the risk of losing control of our destiny to AI (Bostrom, 2014).

- On the cautionary side, dataism threatens to do to Homo Sapiens what Homo Sapiens has done to all other animals. Harari (2017) warns that superintelligent technology could treat humans this way and that people may end up in zoos.

The idea of species modification can be terrifying to the extent that people will not want to talk about it. It can also be dismissed today as "science fiction." But it is not science fiction anymore and in our 20–30-year timeframe, this possibility will become increasingly viable. It is beyond the scope of this work to suggest an answer to how to handle the new species question, but it is in scope to insist that it be discussed.

7.1.4 Principles

Three key principles guide *Tech-Led Abundance*:

1. Optimism ... with a touch of caution
2. Pivotal role of data
3. Augmenting humans

1. <u>Optimism ... with a touch of caution</u>

There is generally a buoyant optimism among supporters of *Tech-Led Abundance*, but concern among opponents. The extremely powerful technologies are something of a double-edged sword. They provide revolutionary potential for good but also potential for harm. Diamandis (2012) is perhaps the most optimistic. He cites abundance as a tale of good news and criticizes the doubters who "cling to bad news like a comfort blanket." He points out how by using almost any metric currently available, quality of life has improved more in the past century than ever before. Rifkin's (2014) optimistic view talks about a collaborative commons — similar to the image of *Circular Commons* developed in this book — in which the distinction between producers and consumers blurs. He foresees people plugging into the fledgling IoT and making and sharing their own information, entertainment, green energy, and 3D-printed products at near zero marginal cost, while also sharing cars, homes, clothes and other items via social media sites, rentals, redistribution clubs, and cooperatives.

Bostrom and More, while generally optimistic about greater use of tech, acknowledge the risks and that there are no guarantees. Harari also raises warnings about over-reliance on data and technology.

Overall, *Tech-Led Abundance* is bullish about the future. There is a can-do attitude that technology can solve the problems ahead. Supporters of this guiding image tend to be far more optimistic about the future than supporters of other images.

2. <u>Pivotal role of data</u>

The *Tech-Led Abundance* concepts strongly support a growing reliance on data as the fuel of the technology revolution. Access to data is the key input technologies need to be effective. Access to personal health data, for example, could revolutionize public health enabling more customized treatments, predictive capabilities, and prevention. More data about the environment will enable technological solutions to resource and climate problems. Better data and algorithms could help tackle the complex problem of wealth redistribution. Privacy questions are acknowledged, but the benefits of using the data are generally seen as outweighing the costs.

Harari is a strong exception. He sees that people are increasingly shifting their decision-making onto "the data" which in essence is shifting it to technology. He sees it mutating into a religion that claims to determine right and wrong. The supreme value of this new religion is 'information flow' (Harari, 2017a, 380). He sees a danger of algorithms pushing people out of the job market, leading to wealth being concentrated in the hands of those owning the all-powerful algorithms (Harari, 2017a, 322-3).

3. <u>Augmenting humans</u>

Augmentation includes biological as well as digital enhancement. Transhumanism believes that augmentation can fundamentally improve the human condition by enhancing intellectual, physical, and psychological capacities. Augmentation can also be part of eliminating aging. Transhumanists see the human form as limiting, and that science and technology can transcend its limitations. The possibility of extending longevity, as well as the idea of possibly uploading human consciousness to the digital realm, is central to the Singularity concept. Kurzweil (2005) estimates that the upload of consciousness will be possible by the 2030s.

The talk about augmentation in the longer-term focuses on how it is as a way for people to keep up with technology. The Singularity concept popularized the idea of exponential technological change that leads to machine intelligence surpassing humans. The principle here is that accelerating technological change eventually ends up remaking the human species. As technology becomes more powerful, the only means of keeping up is to begin augmenting ourselves via technological means. It's a reminder of the aphorism 'if you can't beat 'em, join 'em'. Kurzweil suggests that there will be no clear distinction between human and machine, and no distinction between physical and virtual reality, with more of our experiences taking place in virtual environments (Kurzweil, 2005).

The new species concept is generally seen as a good thing, as a transcendence of our limited human form. The merger of biology and technology results in a world that is still human but transcends our biological roots (Kurzweil, 2005). Harari (2017a, 351) suggests our reliance is such that humans have completed their cosmic task and should now pass the torch on to entirely new kinds of entities.

There is some caution about tech progress. Bostrom notes that the potential of superintelligence, where machine capabilities reach a point far surpassing human capabilities, could come upon us quickly and thus people should be thinking now about how to prepare for or shape that possibility.

How will the more conservative elements of society adapt to these changes? Will there be strong resistance, or will they see the vast potential for betterment of the human condition? It is certainly reasonable to suspect that a new anti-technology lobby may arise, or perhaps an anti-Transhumanist or anti-Singularity movement or party could emerge to protest the rising tide of technological change.

7.1.5 Tools

The most significant tools for this guiding image are technological, but there is some mention of the social, economic, and governmental context.

Technology

Technology is seen as the resource-liberating mechanism. In particular, digital technologies with transformative potential include IoT, AI, ER (extended reality), Big Data, Predictive Analytics, etc. Two additional related tools here not covered in Chapter 2 include:

- Computer simulation: New forms of computer simulation could rejuvenate economic planning and give us the ability to direct economies rationally in unprecedented ways (Srnicek and Williams, 2016).

- Cryptocurrencies: What role, for instance, could non-state cryptocurrencies have? (Srnicek and Williams, 2016).

A second cluster of tech tools identified in Chapter 2 is the emerging wave of bio, nano, robo and augmentation. The conversation about potentially reinventing the human species was discussed in Principles 3 and 4 above.

A third cluster of tech tools covers a wide range of miscellaneous categories, but each with significant long-term potential, such as:

- Solar energy: Few resources are truly scarce; they're mainly inaccessible, according to Diamandis (2012).

- Space: breakthrough potential of space to provide off-world materials and other economic benefits.
- Cloning could also be a possible solution to world hunger by cloning animal muscle tissue in a factory for meat (Kurzweil, 2005).
- Nanotechnology-based manufacturing devices in the 2020s will be capable of creating almost any physical product from inexpensive raw materials and information (Kurzweil, 2005).
- Geoengineering or planetary engineering: Bill Gates advocates tech-led geoengineering approaches for dealing with climate change, such as spraying aerosols into the sky to dim the light from the sun, in his book on avoiding climate disaster (Leguichard, 2021).

The incorporation of these avant-garde technologies could very well face opposition among a hesitant public: most notably, geoengineering, which involves mass human intervention in natural systems, such as using connected systems of climate-controlling satellites. This fear has already reached mainstream recognition. For instance, the 2017 film *Geostorm* looks at potential disasters if a planet-wide climate-controlling system were to be compromised by rogue actors. Though geoengineering technology is still in its infancy, there is already some awareness of the potential downsides.

Providing a supportive business context

The tools here focus on how to provide the best incentives for motivating innovation and entrepreneurship. Diamandis is the strongest advocate of the belief in the entrepreneur and the power of the human mind. His advocacy harkens back to the arguments of famous contrarian Julian Simon who argued against fears of over-population triggered by *Limits to Growth* in the 1970s by suggesting that more people equals more minds equals more potential for breakthrough developments (Simon, 1981).

An example of how to develop the needed talent was the establishment of Singularity University by Diamandis and Kurzweil in 2008 to offer a program and courses to understand how technology could be used to tackle global challenges. It is now a benefit corporation known as Singularity Group that has expanded its mission to focusing on the implications and potential impact of these technologies for people and planet. A wide range of people go through the programs, including CEOs, entrepreneurs, investors, teachers, or policymakers. They say the call to action is the same:

leverage technology to help "create companies, change companies and change communities" (Singularity Group, 2022).

An example of how to stimulate innovation is the X PRIZE Foundation, which is a nonprofit that funds projects specifically dedicated to bringing about radical breakthroughs. The projects must be for the benefit of humanity and participants compete for a significant monetary prize. Diamandis (2012) sees big value in the clear and measurable goals that these incentive competitions provide.

The economic or business context can provide tools to encourage technology-driven innovation. Srnicek and Williams (2016) mention open-source design and copyleft creativity. Harari suggests the move to reliance on data as the new economic engine is largely complete, but it is worth considering how that could be slowed, stopped, or even reversed by greater privacy protections.

Perhaps the most important point is that the *Tech-Led Abundance* concepts are generally fine with capitalism. The competition ethos that accompanies capitalism aligns with the views that entrepreneurial approaches are the best way to problem-solve.

7.1.6 Personal

Relatively scant attention is given to the role of the individuals by the proponents of *Tech-Led Abundance*, other than the entrepreneurs creating the technologies that will provide the abundances. The entrepreneurs are to be well compensated for their efforts. The rest are assumed to passively accept the abundance and be happy with the progress that it brings. Given the promise that people, perhaps now post-humans, would no longer suffer from disease, aging, and inevitable death, perhaps this is a reasonable bargain?

7.1.7 Leadership

The *Tech-Led Abundance* AC Concepts favor the entrepreneurs, wealthy technophilanthropists, and titans of business as the leaders of the abundance future. Think of *Atlas Shrugged* in which the industrials prevail (Rand, 1957). The challenge with the *Tech-Led Abundance* image in terms of *After Capitalism* is that current supporters are generally just fine with capitalism to provide the supportive context, although there is a recognition that the technology acceleration and resulting abundance will reach a point where the old capitalist structures no longer make sense. Kurzweil describes a point in his Singularity in which the context has changed so much that it is unrecognizable. It might be fair to question this on the grounds that as the Singularity nears, it will come into sharper focus. Bostrom suggests superintelligent AI could soar past human capability. The transhumanists and Harari talk about a new species. Taken together, it seems that technology itself is assumed to provide the leadership of the future. Self-aware AI or fully augmented "people" become the leaders. In effect we have the current structure running up against a significantly transformed future context.

There is much work to be done here in terms of managing or guiding technology development at the core of this image. But there are positive signs. For instance, a recent agreement among 18 countries, including the USA, Britain, Germany, Estonia, Australia, Chile, Israel, Nigeria and Singapore, provides non-binding guidelines and recommendations on monitoring AI systems for abuse. It is the latest in a series of initiatives by governments round the world to shape the development of AI, although they generally lack enforcement capability (Satter and Bartz, 2023).

On the one hand, it seems that the view is that once everything is free and abundant, all the problems are solved, and there is not a need for leadership. One might question this assumption that it will be relatively straightforward to manage an abundance — there is already a degree of abundance and we have not done a very good job of managing it so far. It is noteworthy that the transhumanists formed a new political party, the US Transhumanist Party, in October 2014 (Istvan, 2016). The movement is rooted in the US but is spreading globally, including in the UK and the West and even Africa, with projects in Ethiopia and South Africa (Chace, 2023).

On the other hand, there is some concern about what a technology-led world might mean for humans. Harari sees that if intelligent machines treat us like we have treated less-intelligent species, we might be in trouble. Bostrom explores the potential for either a slow or fast takeoff of superintelligence, which could lead to a situation in which humans are dependent on it. He does suggest some ways that we might control this development. Frankly, my sense from reviewing these proceed-with-caution ideas is that they will have very little appeal and it will most likely be full speed ahead, unless there are some clear and obvious signals of a danger ahead. The hope is a proactive approach – and there is some evidence for this emerging, albeit weak. The reality may be reactive, but there is a leadership vacuum here to be filled if this image is to be a viable "positive" guiding image in a post-capitalist future and not an extrapolation of the current system forward.

7.1.8 Pathway

Entrepreneurs and their supporters are central to this image. The key is to provide capital support for entrepreneurial innovators to create the products, services, and solutions that will lead to a future of abundance. Diamandis (2012) sees a series of grand challenges ahead that are connected. He uses the metaphor of a row of dominoes, in which toppling one domino, by meeting one challenge, facilitates toppling the next, and so on.

Pilots

The best example of pilots supporting this guiding image is Diamandis' XPRIZE foundation. According to its website, XPRIZE designs competitions aimed at "achieving audacious yet achievable goals, launching and awarding competitions across various industries to accelerate crucial innovation." It began the competitions in 2004 and has completed 30 since then. It most recently launched the three largest incentive prize competitions in history with prizes of $100 million or more for each. One is about challenges with carbon removal, one is on extending lifespans, and the third is on water scarcity.

More recently, Open AI and its Chat GPT products have created a buzz about the long-term potential of AI. Open AI CEO Sam Altman foresees AI generating enough wealth to enable UBI. He suggested that in a decade AI could generate enough wealth to pay each US adult $13,500 a year (Shead, 2021).

Plans

No specific plans were found. There are sets of principles or projections that provide a sense of the road ahead.

Price Waterhouse Cooper (PwC) identifies three waves of automation between now and the mid-2030s (Hawksworth et al., 2018):

- Algorithm wave through the early 2020s that involves automating structured data analysis and simple digital tasks, such as credit scoring.
- Augmentation wave through the late 2020s that involves automation of repeatable tasks and exchanging information, as well as further developments of aerial drones, robots in warehouses and semi-autonomous vehicles.

- Autonomy wave by the mid-2030s in which AI will be able to analyze data from multiple sources, make decisions, and take physical actions with little or no human input.

Kurzweil sees a pathway driven by continuing technological acceleration with two key landmarks: (Reedy, 2017)

- 2029 is the consistent date I have predicted for when an AI will pass a valid Turing test and therefore achieve human levels of intelligence.
- 2045 for the 'Singularity' which is when we will multiply our effective intelligence a billion-fold by merging with the intelligence we have created.

The Transhumanists offer a balanced view of the path ahead. They are generally optimistic about the prospects for using technology to improve the human condition. But they do not believe progress is inevitable and acknowledge the potential dangers and downsides (More, 2013).

Bostrom (2014) sets out a simple but useful path for the future of AI, using three levels of intelligence:

- Level 1 Task intelligence, in which AI outperforms people in a single task. We are currently here.
- Level 2 General intelligence, in which AI is as intelligent as people in a wide range of tasks. This may be decades away…. Or closer.
- Level 3, Superintelligence, in which AI is orders of magnitude more intelligent than people across-the-board.

He describes three different ways that we might get to Level 3:

- The AI/machine-learning approach is not the only way, but the leading contender.
- The whole-brain emulation approach in which we basically simulate and transcend the brain structure.
- The biotech approach using stem cells and embryos.

Evolution or revolution

The projections noted above in "Plans" follow a wave or stage trajectory, which is more evolutionary than revolutionary. The developments are largely tied to advances in computing power, which has been following Moore's Law of doubling every 18 months to two years for more than four decades. That said, some of the concept authors mention the possibility of an inflection point that could suggest an acceleration that is more revolutionary.

Kurzweil's (2005) singularity is reached gradually, but there is an inflection point when human and machine intelligence merge, after which he believes life on the other side is impossible to anticipate. He believes human life "will be irreversibly transformed as humans will transcend the "limitations of our biological bodies and brains."

Bostrom (2014) also suggested an evolutionary staged approach toward superintelligence, but warns of an alarming possibility that AI's transition from level 2 general intelligence to level 3 superintelligence could happen very quickly. That initial superintelligence might be in a position to dominate humanity, the planet, and shape the future of intelligent life. He reassures us that there is no reason to suspect it would be malicious. Indeed, superintelligence could be a tremendous boon that helps solves major problems and facilitates abundance.

Capacity building

There is strong consensus that the best way to develop the capacity to enable *Tech-Led Abundance* is developing and funding entrepreneurs. The most obvious place where investment is desired is venture capital. Diamandis, with his XPRIZE foundation, believes that prize competitions could be a useful tool as well. They favor a private sector approach to innovation with government's chief role seen as providing funding and essentially not interfering.

7.1.9 Tech-Led Abundance Image Templates

Author	Diamandis is an engineer, physician, and entrepreneur; founder/chairman of XPRIZE Foundation and Singularity University.
Time horizon	2035/ "within a generation"
Scope	Ranges from the top to the bottom of the pyramid, including the poorest, who are finally plugging into the global economy.
Key drivers	Technology acceleration, Automation
Key ideas	Technological progress is such that within a generation, we will be able to provide goods and services, once reserved for the wealthy few, to all who need them. + Technology is a resource-liberating mechanism. It can convert what was once scarce to abundant. + Our challenges are not isolated but stacked like dominoes. Topple one, by meeting a challenge, others will follow suit. **Pyramid of abundance:** + the bottom is focused on food, water, shelter, survival. + the middle is the catalyst for further growth, such as abundant energy, ample educational opportunities, and access to ubiquitous communications and information. + the highest is for freedom and health – the two core prerequisites that let an individual contribute to society.
Ideal or guiding values	Abundance is a global vision built on the backbone of exponential change, but our local and linear brains tend to be blind to the possibilities.
Emotional, aesthetic, and spiritual aspects	+ It is very positive and criticizes negativity: "It's almost as if people cling to bad news like a comfort blanket." + The greatest tool we have is the human mind. + Quality of life improved more in 20th century than ever before.
Personal	Tends to glorify wealthy technophilanthropists who use their money to solve global, abundance-related challenges.
Pathway or plan	XPRIZE is a tool that is part of the pathway to abundance. It harnesses motivators using incentive prizes to tackle big challenges confronting humanity.

Author	Harari is a Lecturer at the Dept of History in the Hebrew University of Jerusalem. In 2019 he co-founded Sapienship as a social impact company with projects in the fields of entertainment and education.
Time horizon	Not clear
Scope	Not clear
Key drivers	Shifting values, Technology acceleration, Automation
Key ideas	Biology and robotics enable the upgrading of humans into a new species via 3 paths: biological engineering, cyborg engineering and the engineering of non-organic beings. + Relationships between humans and animals is best model for future relations between superhumans and humans. + Techno-religions are of 2 types: techno-humanism and data religion. Data religion argues that humans have completed their cosmic task and should now pass the torch on to entirely new kinds of entities. + Dataism declares that the universe consists of data flows, and the value of any phenomenon or entity is determined by its contribution to data processing. + Like capitalism, began as a neutral scientific theory, but is mutating into a religion that claims to determine right and wrong. The supreme value of this religion is information flow. + Dataism thereby threatens to do to Homo sapiens what Homo sapiens has done to all other animals.
Ideal or guiding values	The mantra of economic growth underlying capitalism has moved into the realm of making ethical judgements and religion. The Scientific Revolution gave birth to humanist religions, in which humans replaced gods.
Emotional, aesthetic, and spiritual	Changes ahead mean Homo Sapiens is effectively upgrading into a new species, which Harari calls Homo Deus.
Personal	The most important question in 21st-century economics may well be what to do with all the superfluous people.
Pathway or plan	Technology-led progress is helping humanity "rein in" famine, plague, and war. We will tackle longevity and even happiness. Changes ahead challenge what it means to be human.

Author	Kurzweil is an inventor, thinker, futurist, and Director of Engineering at Google since 2012. He claims a 30-year track record of accurate predictions related to ICT.
Time horizon	2045; computers will match human levels of intelligence by the year 2029
Scope	Global
Key drivers	Technology acceleration
Key ideas	+ Exponential technological change leads to machine intelligence surpassing humans and eventually to no clear distinction between humans and machines. + The Singularity is "a future period during which the pace of technological change will be so rapid, its impact so deep, that human life will be irreversibly transformed." + The Law of Accelerating Returns suggests technology is growing exponentially. He estimates that supercomputers will reach human brain capacity in the 2010s … and be able to upload our consciousness by the 2030s. + The first half of the 21st century will be characterized by three overlapping revolutions: GNR, genetics, nanotech and robotics.
Ideal or guiding values	The pace of change of our human-created technology is accelerating and its powers are expanding at an exponential pace.
Emotional, aesthetic, and spiritual aspects	The vision essentially suggests new species with the promise of immortality with the human-machine merger, but of course there are mixed views on the desirability of this.
Personal	There will be no clear distinction between human and machine, and no distinction between physical and virtual reality.
Pathway or plan	Based on law of accelerating returns – exponentially increasing tech capabilities.

Author	Swedish-born philosopher at the Oxford University known for his work on existential risk, the anthropic principle, human enhancement ethics, superintelligence risks, and the reversal test.
Time horizon	Likely to happen this century, but we don't know for sure; two decades is a sweet spot for prognosticators of radical change.
Scope	Global
Key drivers	Technology acceleration
Key ideas	Explores paths to beyond-human superintelligence, the strategic choices available, and how we could shape the initial conditions. **Three levels of intelligence:** + 1st, task intelligence: AI outperforms people in a single task. We are currently here. + 2nd, general intelligence: AI is as intelligent as people in a wide range of tasks. This may be decades away, or closer. + 3rd, superintelligence: AI is orders of magnitude more intelligent than people across-the-board. The next phase from general to superintelligence could go very quickly – we ought to prepare now for how to deal with it.
Ideal or guiding values	The introduction of machine superintelligence would create a substantial existential risk, but would reduce other existential risks, e.g. asteroid impacts, supervolcanoes, and natural pandemics, as superintelligence could deploy countermeasures.
Emotional, aesthetic, and spiritual aspects	While mostly a warning about negative possibilities, he also notes that "The human species as a whole could thus become rich beyond the dreams of Avarice."
Personal	Superintelligence suggests that as the gorilla is more dependent on people for its survival, so could humans be more dependent on superintelligence.
Pathway or plan	Different paths to superintelligence: + the AI/machine-learning approach is the leading contender. + also suggests whole-brain emulation (we basically simulate and transcend the brain structure). + a vastly more rapid biotech route, using stem cells & embryos.

Imagining After Capitalism | 265

Author	More is a philosopher and futurist who writes, speaks, and consults on emerging technologies. He was the president and CEO of the Alcor Life Extension Foundation from 2010 to 2020.
Time horizon	Not clear
Scope	Not clear
Key drivers	Technology acceleration
Key ideas	+ An intellectual and cultural movement that seeks to radically improve the human condition through applied reason and technology development to eliminate aging and enhance human intellectual, physical, and psychological capacities. + It seeks the continuation and acceleration of the evolution of intelligent life beyond its human form and human limitations by means of science and technology, guided by life-promoting principles and values.
Ideal or guiding values	While firmly committed to improving the human condition and generally optimistic about our prospects for doing so, Transhumanism does not entail any belief in the inevitability of progress nor in a future free of dangers and downsides.
Emotional, aesthetic, and spiritual aspects	Envisions a post-human future in which people no longer suffer from disease, aging, and inevitable death in a wide range of possible future environments, including space colonization and the creation of rich virtual worlds. The unique status of human beings is superseded by an understanding that we are part of a spectrum of biological organisms and possible non-biological species of the future.
Personal	+ Emphasis on progress (its possibility and desirability, not its inevitability) and taking charge of creating better futures. + Posthuman beings would no longer face disease, aging, and inevitable death (but are likely to face other challenges).
Pathway or plan	Not stated

Author	Rifkin is an economic and social theorist, writer, speaker, political advisor, and activist. He claims his vision of a sustainable, post carbon economic era has been endorsed by the European Union and United Nations and embraced by world leaders.
Time horizon	Not clear
Scope	Seems to be focused primarily on affluent countries
Key drivers	Technology acceleration
Key ideas	+ Massive economies of scale provided by digitization push the cost of reproducing information to zero – enabling abundance. + A big shift from the industrial goods producing economy, where each new unit – e.g. cars – is still costly to produce. He goes beyond just information, to essentially free energy via renewables and free goods via 3D printing. As the costs drop towards zero, society can reorganize around self-sufficient communities. He calls this an Emphatic Civilization, where globally connected, networked collectives share communal resources in an emphatic fashion.
Ideal or guiding values	The emerging Internet of Things is speeding us to an era of nearly free goods and services.
Emotional, aesthetic, and spiritual aspects	The metamorphosis of consumption from vice to virtue is one of the most important yet least examined phenomena of the twentieth century (Rifkin, 1994).
Personal	Redefining the role of the individual in a society without mass formal work is, perhaps, the seminal issue of the coming age.
Pathway or plan	+ Plummeting marginal costs are spawning a hybrid economy—part capitalist market and part Collaborative Commons. + Hundreds of millions of people are already transferring parts of their economic lives to the global Collaborative Commons. + Prosumers are plugging into the fledgling IoT and making and sharing their own information, entertainment, green energy, and 3D-printed products at near zero marginal cost. + They are also sharing cars, homes, clothes etc. via social media sites, rentals, redistribution clubs, and cooperatives at low or near zero marginal cost.

7.2 Comparing the images

Table 7.2 Comparing the images

ASPECT OF DAILY LIFE	CIRCULAR COMMONS	NON-WORKERS PARADISE	TECH-LED ABUNDANCE
Living	People go back to nature and increasingly grow their own food and simplify lifestyles using a circular approach	Emphasis on spreading the post-work future to all nations requires a significant amount of development work	People live in a balanced relationship with machines and are increasingly part machines themselves
Working	A lot of the work is aimed at restoring nature and resetting economy on circular approaches	People no longer need formal jobs but still contribute to the common good by carrying out activities negotiated by the collective	Done by robots and automation
Learning	A lot of emphasis on nature as well has how to make a commons approach work	A lot of emphasis on political education	Learning as a leisure pursuit
Playing	Going back outdoors	Plenty of time for leisure	Gaming & VR
Connecting	Technology is vital and heavily used, but in the background	Town halls and community organizing brought together by tech	Metaverse
Participating	Local and direct	Local and direct	Electronic voting

If we thought of the three guiding images as runners in a horse race, *Tech-Led Abundance* is the fastest out of the gate and has the early lead, with *Circular Commons* a fair distance behind, and the *Non-Worker's Paradise* bringing up the rear. Each of the guiding images is present today to some very small degree; that is, they are at a low level of maturity today, but as we move into the future, they ought to become more mature over time, if the analysis is accurate.

Tech-Led Abundance may be a fast starter that runs low on fuel as we move further into the future. It is the least coherent of the three guiding images in that there are few cross-cutting plans, programs, proposals, or conceptual glue to keep the ideas together. There is also not a central problem per se or even a target, which is different than the other two images -- *Circular Commons* and climate and carry capacity/growth and *Non-Workers' Paradise* and inequality/post-work. There are myriad independent ideas emerging from individuals and organizations that are effectively competing with one another. It is certainly plausible that governments, or the entrepreneurs themselves, could organize and seek to build a more coherent program, but that would require a shift away from the competitive values at the heart of this image.

Circular Commons is in second place at the moment, but it may be well-positioned for a late surge. There is a mixed bag today in terms of strong awareness of the central challenge of climate change and carrying capacity, but there is not much consensus about what to do regarding the root cause of growth. Degrowth, which is advocated here, has only recently emerged from the fringes as a topic approaching the mainstream. This horse gains some ground in the middle of the race, as the circular ideas already in circulation and needing to be tested out start coming to fruition. The late burst at the clubhouse turn comes from the commons piece. The perhaps optimistic view here is that the growing urgency of the issue eventually creates enough support to embrace the more radical aspect of a commons approach to resource management.

Non-Workers' Paradise is perhaps the least mature in the present. It suffers from its key sponsor being the ineffective left. It's also been noted that this ineffectiveness can be remedied, and perhaps rather quickly. We might imagine this horse briefly surging ahead of *Circular Commons* and challenging *Tech-Lech Abundance* in the middle of the race, only to fall back a bit near the end. The inequality driver is firmly on the agenda today, but as with climate and growth in *Circular Commons*, agreement around the problem — inequality — is not matched by agreement around the solution — post-work (and redistribution). As AI and automation gain steam, as economic stagnation becomes more and more apparent, and as the results roll in from UBI trials and related activities, one could imagine a big surge of interest in designing a post-work future. But this surge will run into the complicated process of wealth redistribution, which may slow it down for the stretch run.

A second way to compare the guiding images is in terms of what it would be like to live in each one. It is hoped that the one-pagers at the beginning of each image help to create a mental picture of each image. The detailed descriptions after the one-pagers are designed to reinforce that mental picture. It is a lot of information to process! Table 7.2 below may help clarify the distinctions between the three by comparing how "daily life" might be different in each. The six aspects of daily life are taken from previous work on the future of student life (Hines, 2017a) that was in turn based upon the Bureau of Labor Statistics (2022) *American Time Use Survey*.

The "living" column highlights the key difference in emphasis between the three images: the environment, post-work, and our relationship with technology. The focus on work is pretty distinct. The differences in learning are not particularly large; in all three images learning takes on a more important role particularly in the sense of pursuing one's interest. Play may see a stark contrast in which *Circular Commons'* emphasis on reintegrating with nature may sharply differ from the likely emphasis on the metaverse in *Tech-Led Abundance*. This same contrast may show up in connecting as well in different degrees of emphasis on physical versus virtual. Finally, participating, which is more precisely defined as participating in civic life, is likely similar to learning in that each image suggests more direct participation in political matters. Could these distinctions feature more heavily in the discussion of the guiding images themselves?

Chapter 8 – IMPLICATIONS

…as a capitalist, I believe it's time to say out loud what we all know to be true: Capitalism, as we know it, is dead. — Marc Benioff, CEO, Salesforce

Let's recap the main arguments of the book:

1. Changes underway — captured as seven drivers — are undermining the *Neoliberal Capitalism* Baseline.

2. The Three Horizons framework frames "the journey" to Transformation.

3. There is currently a vacuum — a lack of positive guiding images of the future and a danger that we'll turn to used futures that will derail the development of new images and systems.

4. There is a surge of interest in alternatives to capitalism, which this research has synthesized into three potential guiding images.

5. There is a plausible case for these three guiding images.

6. It will take a long time to make the three horizons journey: 2040-2050 is the best guess.

7. It will take long because a mindset/values/worldview change is needed.

The *After Capitalism* work started with a simple catalog identifying potential new economic concepts, sparked by an interest in thinking about the long-term economic future. As the number of AC Concepts mounted, it became evident that there might be a way to cluster them into a smaller set of *After Capitalism* images. Many of the AC Concepts were transitionary in nature, describing how to reform or evolve capitalism. This observation led to the introduction of the Three Horizons framework, which includes a second horizon of Transition in addition to its first horizon Baseline and third horizon of Transformation. The Three Horizons framework enabled a sorting of the growing body of research into H1 signals of change, H2 transition concepts, and the H3 guiding images. At that point, a book structure was sketched out and a scanning library was set up to complement the many AC Concepts — eventually pruned to the 52 included here. The key deliverables of the work became the development of proposed Polakian guiding images of the future — *Circular Commons*, *Non-Workers' Paradise*, and *Tech-Led Abundance* —

described in Chapters 5, 6, and 7. The Collapse versions of each were sketched out as well to paint a balanced picture. And the H2 transition concepts were fleshed out in Chapter Four to help envision the pathway.

Now, in this chapter, the implications are presented in five sections. The first three cover the past, present, and future. The past highlights what might be learned from the history of capitalism. The present compares the seven key drivers, which are already present today, and looks at how they might evolve differently and lead to different futures. The future section provides insights into the role of utopias in exploring the future, noting in particular that what may seem utopic in the present may be almost mundane in the futures.

The fourth section frames the vital but challenging question of whether the transition to *After Capitalism* can happen in just one country or must it be global. Some ideas on the timing of the pathway to the guiding images conclude the chapter.

8.1   Past: As prologue?

Heilbroner (1996) did some interesting research that identified a prevailing view or attitude of the future from the past. The scope was limited to people in the affluent Western nations. He did not identify specific images. Nonetheless, it is instructive and may provide some clues for our own investigation. He divided history/human existence into four time periods:

- <u>The distant past</u>, from the beginning of *Homo sapiens* 150,000 years ago to "yesterday".
- <u>Yesterday</u>, which he puts at roughly 250 years ago (Note: *roughly* arrival of the industrial revolution and capitalism).
- <u>Today</u>, it was written in 1995.
- The future.

I added a column on values based on my work on the future of values published in *ConsumerShift* (Hines, 2011).

He notes that the visions of the distant past, while varied in form, had the common element of saying little about changes in people's material condition, and focused on the rewards or punishments of the next life. The view of the future is one of resignation to one's fate. As I've noted in my research on values, my shorthand for the traditional values prevalent here is "follow the rules." One's job is to stay in one's prescribed role and not rock the boat. There is a tight fit between resignation and traditional follow-the-rules values.

Table 8.1 Views of the future from the past

TIME PERIOD	VIEW OF THE FUTURE (HEILBRONER)	VALUES (MY ADD)
The distant past, 150,000 years ago to "yesterday"	Resignation	Traditional – follow the rules
Yesterday, 250 years ago (arrival of industrial revolution and capitalism)	Hopefulness	Modern – grow and achieve
Today (it was 1995)	Apprehension	Postmodern – what's it all mean?
The future	___?___	Integral – make a difference

The visions of yesterday are characterized by "the rise and flourishing of capitalism." In this period "the future now enters into human consciousness as a great beckoning prospect ... re: improving the human condition ... and we begin to look to the human future with confidence." The vision of the future shifts from the next life to this one. There is hope that if we work hard, we can change our role or position. In values terms, this mirrors the rise of modern values — in short "achieve." It's no longer about passive acceptance of one's birthright or assigned role, but about more actively shaping one's destiny. The tradeoff in a competitive situation is that while some win, others will lose. And the capitalist system structure produces a small number of big winners and a large number of losers. Again, a strong fit between hopefulness and achievement values.

The transition from "yesterday" to "today" leads to another shift in visions to "a new degree of pessimism," which Heilbroner dubbed apprehension. He notes that science begins to supplant religion, which was the central visionary element of the past. We also begin to see "the seismic pressure exerted by the accumulation of capital." He refers to how Marx acknowledges the tremendous dynamism and growth resulting from capitalism but cautions that it is like "a sorcerer who is no longer able to control the powers of the nether world whom he has called up by his spells."

He observes that "since its postwar reconstruction boom, capitalism has evidenced serious malfunctions in every nation." He characterizes the visions as apprehensive. There is less certainty about capitalism being the right approach. This aligns with the postmodern values of a "search for meaning." The postmodernist, having achieved material success, still has an empty feeling (borne out by the data), and tries to figure out what can really make them happy. There is a strong fit between apprehension and the postmodern search for meaning.

Heilbroner's assumption when he talks about tomorrow — he was writing in 1995 — is that "it is likely that capitalism will be the principal form of socioeconomic organization during the twenty-first century … because no blueprint exists for a viable successor." At the same time, he acknowledges that "capitalism will not last forever … its internal dynamics are too powerful." It is revealing to see leading thinkers twenty-five years ago making the point we are still wrestling with today — capitalism is decaying, but there is no clear alternative. The tomorrow vision is rather mundane:

- A secure terrestrial base for life (preserve the environment)
- Preserving the human community against its war-like proclivities (avoid cataclysmic conflict)
- Respect for human nature and give culture and education the centrality they demand (respect one another).

He admits it's not much but asks his critics "if they have anything better." The need here is for effective action by producing a functional alternative, which fits with the make-a-difference ethos of integral values.

8.2   Present: Comparing drivers across the scenarios

Table 8.2 provides an at-a-glance view of how the seven drivers play out in the Baseline, the New Equilibrium scenario of *Collaborative Sharing Platforms* and the Transformation guiding images [note: to keep it simple, the Collapse scenarios and the other two New Equilibrium scenarios are not included]. Our experience is that in most domains a relatively small number of major drivers is central to the future of any domain and it is unlikely that a significant driver will come out of nowhere or "blindside" us. If the scanning is tracking H3, it will identify weak signals that could possibly develop fast — but fast progress from H3 is very rare. Signals typically take time to develop and strengthen. The caveat about knowing the key drivers is that we don't know how the specific timing or interactions will play out.

Table 8.2 suggests some different ways the drivers could play out using the archetype technique, which sorts the potential outcomes of the drivers into the various archetypes or typical patterns of change. The drivers are organized by STEEP category to ensure that the coverage is balanced across the domain, albeit with a slightly stronger focus given to the economic emphasis of *After Capitalism*.

The values outcomes in the Transformation guiding images are a significant difference. Table 8.2 notes which images will most appeal to the types, but it is important to note that the attraction may be a negative one, at least to start with. They may not like the new guiding images that challenge existing approaches, but they are likely to be engaged by it.

Table 8.2 Comparing drivers across selected scenarios

STEEP CATEGORY	DRIVER	NEOLIBERAL CAPITALISM (BASELINE)	COLLABORATIVE SHARING PLATFORMS (NEW EQUI)	CIRCULAR COMMONS (TRANS 1)
Social	Shifting values	Modern	Modern-Postmodern	Postmodern
Tech	Technology acceleration	Tech for profit	Tech enables CSP	Tech as a key support tool
Economic	Inequality	Worsens	Slight improvement	Reduced via sharing
Economic	Automation	Increases w/ few restrictions	Increases w/ few restrictions	Intentional and selective automation
Economic	Stagnation	Continues but hid by the numbers	Continues to be hid by numbers	New metrics
Environmental	Climate & carrying capacity	Continued decline	Slight improvement	Key focus of new order
Political	*Ineffective Left*	*Continued ineffective*	*Begins to organize*	Supportive

Imagining After Capitalism | 275

Table 8.2 Comparing drivers across selected scenarios

STEEP CATEGORY	NON-WORKERS PARADISE (TRANS 2)	TECH-LED ABUNDANCE (TRANS 3)	MIRRORS OF TRANSFORMATION (COLLAPSE)
Social	Traditional	Modern	Mirror the positive transformations
Tech	Pace of tech managed	Rapid and successful; General AI	AI takes over
Economic	Reduced via UBI	Mostly reduced	Severe
Economic	Automation balanced with human needs	Strong role for automation	Unemployment a severe issue
Economic	Move to UBI	Abundant wealth via automation	Downward spiral
Environmental	Improves but secondary to social issues	Tech fixes succeed	Ecosystem collapse
Political	Effectively mobilized	Not a big factor	Class war

The *Non-Workers' Paradise* image is centered on traditional values. It addresses the centuries-old struggle around class warfare. The idea is that the motivation for this guiding image will appeal to traditional values holders who see this question as a vital one. They may prefer to keep things the way they are and feel challenged by the new guiding image, but it is the image most likely to get their attention.

The motivation for those drawn to *Tech-Led Abundance* is competition. The belief is in creating the conditions that enable competition and to see that the best tech entrepreneurs win. They will most likely prefer to keep the current capitalist approach but will see this image as most attractive of the new ones, even if they reject it at first.

The primary motivation for the *Circular Commons* will come from the postmoderns with their strong environmental values. They may feel their current efforts around sustainability are quite sufficient and not see the need for the more radical Circular Commons image … at first.

In all three images, there is also support from Integrals, who will have grown from their small numbers of 3-5% today to perhaps 15-20% by 2040/2050 when the guiding images are becoming prevalent. It is important to note that the integrals could embrace any of the three, depending on their functional view of which looks most likely to succeed. Arguably their support is the most important since they are the type most inclined to action.

8.3   Future: Utopia not impossible

Bregman (2017) cites the work of economist Albert Hirschman in noting that utopias are initially attacked on three grounds:

- futility (it's not possible)
- danger (the risks are too great)
- and perversity (it will degenerate into dystopia).

And once implemented, it comes to be seen as "utterly commonplace." Indeed, the Neoliberal movement, an idea once dismissed as radical and marginal, came to rule the world in less than 50 years! (Bregman, 2017).

I think these are useful criteria, so let's see how the guiding images fare on the utopia scale. The criteria apply, or have all applied at some point, to

Figure 8.1 Key tests for the guiding images

	CIRCULAR COMMONS	NON-WORKERS PARADISE	TECH-LED ABUNDANCE
Futility (it's not possibe)	X		
Danger (risks are too great)			X
Perversity (it will degenerate into dystopia)		X	

each. Perhaps it is more useful to compare where the guiding images are in relation to one another.

- Of the three, the *Circular Commons* image is perhaps the least developed, and if presented to a representative audience, would probably generate the most skepticism. The circular aspect has some "brand recognition" and I think most would see that as not futile, but the commons part would likely be a different story. A great deal of resistance is likely here, especially if that effort gets branded as a new version of communism, which is quite plausible.

- The *Non-Workers' Paradise* has passed the futility point. The discussion around UBI, even though it is far from representing agreement, has at least entered "polite society." The fact that Andrew Wang ran for the Democratic Presidential nomination on the UBI platform is pretty amazing, given that a decade ago this idea would have been dismissed as madness. As discussed in the previous chapter however, there is a great fear that if people don't have jobs, they won't know what to do with themselves. We debunked that idea, but it will likely be brought up if progress is made toward this guiding image.

- *Tech-Led Abundance* is an interesting case. We futures thinkers are perhaps more aware of both the potential and the potential danger of this one than the public at large. The public has a vague fear of a Terminator-like future, but this is not based on any deep thinking. Judging by the present, there is some anxiety about the danger of AI, but it is basically full speed ahead.

8.4 The Global Question

Communism wrested with the global question in its own day, namely must the revolution be global, or could it be accomplished in one country? In the former Soviet Union, Trotsky was the advocate for it being international and Stalin the champion for socialism in one country. And we know what happened. The world would probably have turned out differently if Trotsky had won, but of course we cannot know for sure. As an undergraduate history and political science major, I preferred Trotsky and his support for the larger global principle but could see why Stalin's pragmatic approach prevailed. *After Capitalism* faces a similar conundrum. Here, too, I prefer the global route, but I can see the enormous challenge of doing that and being left with the choice of trying it in one country. Indeed, the legacy of capitalism and its modern values sees economics as a competitive game pitting nations against one another for a larger share of the pie, which is hardly conducive to global sharing.

Can a nation with UBI exist in a world with extreme global poverty? The developed world's track record of helping the developing world does not instill confidence. There is a similarly poor track record in getting global cooperation on any issue. It will likely be necessary to rethink development assistance. Perhaps the work left to do — referencing the question of what to do in the post-work *Non-Workers' Paradise* — is bringing the bottom of the pyramid/rest of the world up to a common level?

- Using Kauffman's (2021, 116), systems rule No. 16: "If you can't make people self-sufficient, your aid does more harm than good." This usually comes up in discussing problems of poverty or hunger, where temporary relief often postpones the disaster at the cost of making it much worse when it comes. It is not really an argument against helping, but an argument against half-way measures. Gandhi said the same thing in a more positive way: "If you give me a fish, I eat for a day; if you teach me to fish, I eat for a lifetime."

- Piketty (2014, 70) notes "the possible convergence of output per head does not imply convergence of income per head. After the wealthy countries have invested in their poorer neighbors, they may continue to own them indefinitely, and indeed their share of ownership may grow to massive proportions, so that the per capita national income of the wealthy countries remains permanently greater than that of the poorer countries, which must continue to pay to foreigners a substantial share of what their citizens produce (as African countries have done for decades)… it does not appear that capital mobility has been the primary factor promoting convergence of rich and poor nations. None of the Asian countries that have moved closer to the developed countries of the West in recent years have benefited from large foreign investments… all of these countries themselves financed the necessary investments in physical capital, and even more, in human capital, which the latest research holds to be the key to long-term growth."

Nonetheless, a key theme in the guiding images is "local first." The principle of subsidiarity, which keeps decision-making at the lowest feasible level, only referring to higher levels when absolutely necessary, is a common theme. It is unclear whether that translates into "just us" or whether a global camaraderie would develop. A counterargument to the local focus comes chiefly from the *Non-Workers' Paradise* image, in which the "folk politics" criticism emerged of romanticizing and being overly focused on the local.

My suspicion is that it would be challenging to have only local pockets. It makes sense that it would start that way, but if it didn't scale up quickly, it's hard to envision how a post-capitalist nation could exist next to a capitalist one without the proverbial machine guns at the border. It may be that the only way to make it work is to have almost everyone playing by the same basic rules. If so, there would likely need to be a massive effort among the affluent nations to hasten the development of the poor and emerging nations. For instance, Project 2030 argues that systems thinking dictates that the entire system needs to change, not just at the national level, as our interconnectedness means a global plan is needed (Haupt, 2017).

Nonetheless, there is currently no global movement, which makes it a moot point at present. As *After Capitalism* activities increase and scale up in the years ahead, the question will become more relevant. It would be silly to suggest that a neighborhood, city, state, region, or any community stop what they are doing to wait for a global approach. Three practical reasons stand out:

- Waiting for global may mean waiting a very, very long time. There are pockets around the world, but they are small and disparate.

- Waiting may also lead to impatience and strengthen those who might be inclined to violent revolution. As the decline of capitalism worsens and quality-of-life with it, the argument for revolution becomes more appealing.

- In my client work in implementing foresight, we are advocating for the importance of being aligned, in motion, and ready for action (Hines, 2022). It starts with the premise that if groups are aligned around a vision, in this case the three After Capitalism guiding images, then action in the present, be it pilots or experiments, starts to build a positive momentum. We learn our way into the future by trying things.

The ideal path brings the two together. Local efforts coming together and combining forces to address the bigger global picture. More work on how that could happen is a book in itself, but a worthy one.

8.5 Pathways to the guiding images

Could it be that alarmism about the disintegration of capitalism and all the associated issues — e.g. climate change, inequality, etc. — is paralyzing leaders and the public and contributing to inaction? Perhaps if the end of capitalism isn't portrayed as the end of life as we know it, it would in fact make things achievable? (Heymans, 2022). In other words, should the strategy be to make it as easy as possible?

Put another way, McBride (2022) asks: "When does a situation warrant us doing the organizational equivalent of pulling the fire alarm? I would argue that one does so sparingly. Urgency is not a sustainable trigger to pull because doing so requires a challenge that is focused and singular. Many of our issues and opportunities have solutions with many tentacles requiring alterations throughout the system. Sometimes, in preparation for the new world, what we are requesting is a transformation, the type of change that requires sustained effort, planning, and monitoring. Urgency might be sufficient to start the movement, but momentum will peter out if the understanding of the challenge hasn't simply been integrated in some way with a new mindset."

Pulling the fire alarm for something that requires a sustained long-term effort is a risky strategy. Indeed, the attention is likely to fade as the scope of the change becomes known. And we futurists also know, from experience, that reliance on "bad news" is a risky strategy that is just as likely to trigger denial as it is action.

It brings to mind a useful aphorism from 12-Step Recovery programs that people must "act their way into right thinking." The obvious temptation is the opposite: to think our way into right acting. While I certainly don't want to advocate not thinking, I respect the timing of the thinking suggested here. Indeed, this aphorism came to mind as I was studying the various ideas about pathways. I consistently came across the idea of starting small — the key idea being starting! And this also led me to another path of my work as a futurist on integrating foresight into organizations (Hines, 2012).

On the other hand, the preceding chapters suggest a sense of urgency is needed. Marx warned that class struggles are "…a fight that each time ended, either in a revolutionary reconstitution of society at large, or in the common ruin of the contending classes" (Clark, 2021).

Transformation says, no more band-aids, time for a new paradigm, new structure, new rules, and new metrics. But how to get there? How do we get to guiding images? While that's not the primary focus of this work, a few thoughts are in order. In the spirit of first things first, this work focuses on where we might want to go. If indeed we identify worthy guiding images and some degree of consensus on where we want to get to, then we can start building the pathway. Nonetheless, a few preliminary thoughts are in order to provide a sense of the task ahead. First, a reminder about the rough projected timing in Figure 25.

Next, there seem to be three main ways forward:

- Reform: the view here is that reform keeps us stuck in capitalism and that capitalism is unfixable
- Evolution: the preferred approach that builds from the existing system to a new one over time
- Revolution: the dangerous approach that says the only way is to "blow it up" and start afresh.

One common and lazy critique of alternatives to capitalism is "where's the detailed plan?" This suggests that there was a detailed plan for capitalism when it emerged, rather than it arising from a certain set of material conditions of the time. That said, the alternative guiding images to date have been less than compelling, and that is precisely what is being addressed here, albeit with a broad sense of pathways rather than a detailed plan. As we've said in many different ways, it first makes sense to identify a worthy destination before laying out the itinerary.

8.5.1 Reform delays the inevitable

Let's recap the basic case against reform. First, it is important to recognize there are far more proposals to reform capitalism than to replace it. This is the natural impulse of the power brokers and key stakeholders in any H1 Baseline. Those benefiting from the existing order will typically try to keep it going. Several celebrity capitalists have come out and called for reform. For instance:

- Fullerton's (2015) Regenerative Capitalism grapples with reform and transformation, and clearly suggests reform: "regenerative economies [are] a new stage of capitalism … reserve and build on the many strengths of our free enterprise system, while addressing its failings head on." Even though I personally have come to believe transformation is necessary, I may, of course, be wrong, and maybe there are a few iterations of capitalism left!
- US senator Elizabeth Warren's (D-Mass.) "Accountable Capitalism Act," seeks "to help eliminate skewed market incentives and return

to the era when American corporations and American workers did well together." She sought to reverse the growing inequality that has emerged over the last thirty years (Keller, 2018). She explicitly positioned herself as the more mainstream candidate in contrast to the radical Bernie Sanders.

- Many analysts and academics have also made this case. Henderson (2020) called for reimagining capitalism in a "world on fire."

In and of themselves, these are fine ideas, but as we saw in Chapter 3 in the H1 Baseline, the system cannot be saved. These reform AC Concepts simply delay the inevitable disintegration.

There is also a series of sustainability transition AC Concepts in H2 within the capitalist context in Chapter 4. Given the centrality of environmental challenges, one strategy is to keep the solution to those challenges within the capitalist context.

Chapter 3 was devoted to making the case that capitalism cannot be saved. My view is that reform AC Concepts can indeed extend its life and most probably will. Hence the view that the guiding images are 20 or 30 years away, even though they could be implemented sooner. But the key structural feature of capitalism, the inequitable distribution going mostly to the top, remains in place and is likely to be its eventual undoing.

Given that reform is deemed not viable, we are left with two options: evolution or revolution.

8.5.2 What might evolution look like

I'm reminded of a lecture from creativity guru Edward de Bono, where he talked about our tendency to keep putting band-aids as fixes on a process in order to avoid having to re-do it. This fits with New Equilibrium in the Houston Archetype Technique in which there is a challenge to the existing system, and the system does whatever is necessary to "save itself." If we anthropomorphize the system, it acts and makes the necessary compromises. Structurally speaking, it's still the same system, but with some change and adjustment. The 2008 financial crisis and Great Recession challenged and almost "broke" the existing system. In classic New Equilibrium fashion, the system compromised and bailed out the "too big to fail" organizations, put on a couple of band-aids and was back in business. There was an opportunity for Transformation, but the system was kept intact. Nonetheless, some change was made, and it may take multiple New Equilibrium challenge-and-response loops to eventually get to Transformation.

Alperovitz (2013) favors *evolutionary reconstruction*, which is a systemic step-by-step approach to nonviolent transformation that unfolds over time. It changes the basic institutions of ownership of the economy, using tools such as co-ops, land trusts, and municipal enterprises, so that the broad public, rather than a narrow band of individuals (i.e. the 1%) increase their share of productive assets. This redistribution is based on:

- democratization of wealth
- community as a guiding theme
- decentralization
- substantial democratic planning to achieve economic, democracy-building and ecological goals.

The Solidarity movement envisions a similar approach in which there is gradual transformation through an ecosystem approach. Scaling up happens through interlinking many locally controlled initiatives (Lol and Jimenez, 2017). Similarly, the wellbeing economy talks about uniting a vast array of local initiatives, such as local currencies and B-corps and many other streams of governance innovation into a coherent narrative and enabling fundamental change (Fioramonti, 2016).

The positive aspect of these approaches is that action can be taken right now, and the hopeful aspect is that they can then be scaled up. The realistic aspect is also acknowledged: the evolutionary reconstruction developmental trajectory may take several decades and may only modestly alter fundamental institutional relationships and political power balances. The era of stalemate and decay might simply continue and worsen.

Wright (2010) suggests three more confrontational approaches than Alperovitz (NOTE: where he says bourgeoisie, think of the 9.9% serving the 0.1% introduced in Section 2.3.3):

- A more *revolutionary* approach confronts the bourgeoisie. This approach is needed because traditional methods are not getting great results. Even with broad support there would likely be a temporary downturn in material quality of life. This may be more plausible and helpful on a small scale.

- A more *anarchist* approach ignores the bourgeoisie. This approach provides alternatives on the fringes of capitalism. Alternatives can show potential changes and gain support steadily for more democratic egalitarian solutions. It may require more revolutionary methods when limits are reached.

- A *social democratic* approach collaborates with the bourgeoisie. It seeks to find common ground or positive sum games with the capitalist class. It assumes that high consumer demand and minimal economic crises are in the interest of all.

Figure 8.3 *After Capitalism* headlines

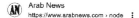

Arab News
https://www.arabnews.com › node

Capitalism requires a rethink in wake of pandemic
Oct 18, 2020 — In fact, the **pandemic** has hastened the shift toward a stakeholder model of corporate **capitalism**, following the US Business Roundtable's embrace ...

dailycampus.com
https://dailycampus.com › Opinion

The Good Fight: What is "realistic" about maintaining capitalism?
Oct 19, 2020 — The rule of capitalism is that it **must grow to survive**, hence the heavy emphasis that capitalist economists place on the growth rate of the ...

Nikkei Asia
https://asia.nikkei.com › Opinion › Myanmar-should-us...

Myanmar should use COVID crisis to end 30 years of crony ...
Oct 20, 2020 — It should also use the pandemic-**related crisis** as an opportunity to transform the economy away from the crony capitalism of the past 30 years ...

Yahoo Finance
https://finance.yahoo.com › news › big-capitalist-syste...

The Big Question: Is the Capitalist System Headed For Collapse?
(Bloomberg Opinion) -- This is one of a series of interviews by Bloomberg Opinion columnists on **how to solve today's most pressing policy challenges**.

CNBC
https://www.cnbc.com › 2020/10/17 › op-ed-heres-how...

Op-ed: Here's how Trump or Biden can help save ...
Oct 17, 2020 — U.S. President Donald **Trump** and **Democratic** presidential nominee Joe **Biden** speaking during the first 2020 presidential campaign debate. Brian ...

Green Left
https://www.greenleft.org.au › content › ecosocialism-2...

Ecosocialism 2020: From rebellion to revolution
Sep 25, 2020 — **Ecosocialism 2020** will look at capitalist globalisation, how the Global South has been robbed and the ecological crisis.

8.5.3 Revolution: Let's figure out where we want to go before we blow up the current system!

It seems that every day for the last few years there has been a story about the end of capitalism. Since I began tracking the topic in 2012, it's gone from crazy to not-so-crazy to a topic for polite conversation … to revolution. Figure 8.3 is a screen grab from a "normal" day of my daily alerts in 2023.

Is the increasing intensity of the language about the end of capitalism shifting it toward revolution? I hope not. And I really don't think so. I think most people realize that violent revolution would be disastrous. A big problem with revolution in the present is there is no vision of what to replace the current system with. And history suggests that in a vacuum, things usually end up worse. I've been reading about the 1917 Russian revolution again and one could argue that it happened much faster than expected, before they were really "ready," with obvious horrific consequences down the road. Yes, let's push for *After Capitalism*, but let's not rush it either.

There is a range of ideas on how a more revolutionary approach might come about:

- Catalytic event: Many futurists, and others, assume we'll need some sort of disaster to catalyze action. Dr. Cindy Frewen, in an email on June 30, 2018 suggested in social change terms, we might think of criticality and catastrophe theory or in more pop terms, tipping points (Gladwell, 2002). Srnicek and Williams (2016) observe that when that crisis occurs, the actions that are taken depend on the ideas that are lying around at the time. This fits with the "time bomb" idea suggested by Polak, in which the image is out there and available, and waits for the circumstances to "explode" onto the scene. But as we've noted, there is currently no time bomb image ready.

- Co-creation: Others, such as futurist Stuart Candy (2014, 88) suggest that "one of the most powerful catalysts for emergent co-creation would be to establish a participatory, plural process for public imagination." He points us to the social foresight work of Richard Slaughter. It is interesting to note that Polak, writing in the 1950s, observed that images historically came from elites, which would fit with traditional and modern values. Candy and Slaughter's more participatory ideas have a postmodern flavor that reflects the growing prevalence of postmodern values today.

- Informal overtakes the formal: Karl Schroeder (2019) describes a world in which the gamer community in effect builds an informal alternative economy alongside the "official" one that eventually overtakes it. They take advantage of the incredible potential of blockchain, DAOs, the Internet of Things, AI, and the Metaverse to build an economy far more sophisticated than the establishment is willing or capable of, and it eventually prevails.

- Walk-away: Doctorow (2017) presents an intriguing idea on how revolution comes about by people defecting from the current system. He sees the building of a post-scarcity society by those who drop out from the "default" world of massive inequality largely run by what he calls super-rich "zottas," similar to the 0.1% today. There is little pretense of fairness left in the default world. Those who don't add value are seen and treated as surplus. Those with a conscience see no way to reform the default and go into self-imposed exile and work on building a new society alongside the old. It's a more extreme version of the off-the-grid ideas that are already circulating today.

Bregman (2017) speaks to the personal level of revolutionary ideas by first noting that worldviews — values in our terminology — don't change easily. But along the lines of the catalytic event noted above, a "sudden shock" can have a significant impact. He suggests that a worldview is "a fortress that is defended tooth and nail, with all possible reinforcements, until the pressure becomes so overpowering that the walls cave in." He supports sticking to one's convictions — "a single opposing voice can make all the difference." He offers what I think is quite useful advice for suggested change agents or revolutionaries needing to cultivate a thicker skin. He notes that if we want to change the world, we need to be unrealistic, unreasonable, and impossible. If one were looking for a 10-point plan for creating utopia, it's not here. I think he would be suspicious of such a plan, but rather he looks to the power of a compelling guiding image to direct us.

8.5.4 Ways to intervene in a system

A popular futurist framework for thinking about change is Donella Meadows' masterful systems intervention framework. Table 8.3 lists Meadows' intervention points in the left-hand column and the potential actions for *After Capitalism* in the right-hand column. One of the key insights from her work is that we tend to spend most of our time on the "easy" interventions, but these fail to move the needle. The most effective interventions are the hardest to accomplish. The intervention points are characterized by a quote from the Meadow's piece. They are listed from lowest to highest, that is, leverage point #9 is the weakest (but easiest to do), and #1 is the strongest (but hardest to do).

Hopefully, this gives an idea of some of the shifts that need to take place. I hope you can also see how the shifts at the bottom are much more challenging but also have a much larger impact. And one might argue that the changes at the top, such as the move away from measuring GDP as success, ultimately is connected to the mindset or paradigm at the bottom. In a Homo Economicus context that prioritizes economics above all else, GDP makes sense as a measure. Until that mindset changes, it will be challenging to shift that measure.

Table 8.3 Meadows' systems intervention for *After Capitalism*

MEADOWS' SYSTEMS INTERVENTIONS	INTERVENTION POINT FOR *AFTER CAPITALISM*
9. Numbers (subsidies, taxes, standards) "Numbers are last on my list of leverage points. Diddling with details, arranging the deck chairs on the Titanic. Probably ninety-five percent of our attention goes to numbers, but there's not a lot of power in them."	From adjusting interest rates, tax rates, and GDP focus to GNH (Gross National Happiness) to include Triple Bottom Line/quality of life measures.
8. Material stocks and flows "There's leverage, sometimes magical, in changing the size of buffers. But buffers are usually physical entities, not easy to change."	From unfunded infrastructure to significant investment in rebuilding and expanding access to physical and digital infrastructures (e.g., along lines of Green New Deal).
7. Regulating negative feedback loops "Nature evolves negative feedback loops and humans invent them to keep system states within safe bounds," e.g., a thermostat loop.	From survival-of the-fittest to support systems to level the socioeconomic playing field.
6. Driving positive feedback loops "Positive feedback loops drive growth, explosion, erosion, and collapse in systems. A system with an unchecked positive loop ultimately will destroy itself."	From inaction to action on climate change, the circular economy, and care of the planetary commons.
5. Information flows "Delivering feedback to a place where it wasn't going before."	From "need to know" to full transparency on public and private data.

MEADOWS' SYSTEMS INTERVENTIONS	INTERVENTION POINT FOR *AFTER CAPITALISM*
4. <u>The rules of the system (incentives, punishment, constraints)</u> If you want to understand the deepest malfunctions of systems, pay attention to the rules, and to who has power over them.	From workfare to UBI.
3. <u>The power of self-organization</u> "The ability to self-organize is the strongest form of system resilience, the ability to survive change by changing."	From top-down national to bottom-up local approaches that scale up via trials, pilots, and pockets.
2. <u>The goals of the system</u> "…changing the players in a system is a low-level intervention, as long as the players fit into the same old system. The exception to that rule is…if a single player can change the system's goal.	From full employment to full unemployment.
1. <u>The mindset or paradigm out of which the goals, rules, feedback structure arise</u> "You could say paradigms are harder to change than anything else about a system… But there's nothing physical or expensive or even slow about paradigm change. In a single individual it can happen in a millisecond."	From win-lose to win-win.

Source: A Hines, based on D. Meadows, "Places to Intervene in a System," *Whole Earth*, Winter 1997.

Chapter 9 – CONCLUSION: TEN SHIFTS

> *I am a futurist. Someone who makes a living by helping other people think about the future. In my work, there is a phenomenon that occurs which I refer to as a "crisis of imagination." I use it to describe the moment when people arrive at the end of their understanding of the world and are unable to create positive-facing futures because they lack images of it. In the absence of a proper framework to conceive these possible futures, people sink to describing dystopias because, this, they understand. They know how to describe failure, destruction, and ending. They have seen the movies and they know how anarchy comes about. What is much harder to imagine is peace. What does peace look like? How do we get there? What is the picture of wellbeing for all? Images of the world in this state and the processes we use to get there are much rarer, they do not readily come to mind and so we descend into darkness once again. One could say this crisis of imagination is one reason protests turn to riots. When emotions run high, how do we channel that emotion? People need options.* — Mina McBride, Futurist

The previous chapter concluded with ways to intervene in a system and noted that the most effective, and the most difficult, way is to influence or change "the mindset or paradigm out of which the goals, rules, feedback structure arise." I'll conclude with 10 mindset shifts that are critical to *After Capitalism*. I ask readers for their indulgence if I am a bit more spirited in these suggestions than I have been in previous chapters.

1. From ONE-RIGHT-WAY to MULTIPLE WAYS or from FIRST-TIER to SECOND-TIER VALUES

If you gave me a magic wand to shift to *After Capitalism*, I would use it here. I believe our greatest hope for change is the shift away from "tier one" traditional and modern and postmodern values to "tier two" integral values. A key difference between the three guiding images is the underlying values (introduced in Section 2.3.1):

- *Non-Workers' Paradise* > traditional
- *Tech-Led Abundance* > modern
- *Circular Commons* > postmodern

> Integral

The alignment of *Tech-Led Abundance* with modern values and *Circular Commons* with postmodern values is strong. The *Non-Workers' Paradise* alignment with traditional values is less so. I admit to some concern about curve-fitting to align the guiding images to each major worldview, but I credit futurist Tim Morgan with persuading me of the connection. I see that the left is trying to reinvent itself away from what I agree is a traditional worldview — class struggle; we are right, you are wrong, noble working class, evil 1%ers, our doctrine is correct, etc. As I've dug deeper into the *Non-Workers' Paradise*, I think it is fair to interpret it as still primarily based in a social and political class struggle, and thus has its roots in traditional values. I think a lot of postmoderns are "in" on this one.

It should be noted that each of the guiding images is being "contemporized," that is evolved to fit the values of the day. The traditional class struggle is being reinterpreted through the lens of modern and postmodern supporters. I am not suggesting that only traditional values holders will support it, but that its appeal will index higher among the traditional group, but there will also be modern and postmodern supporters. Similarly, *Tech-Led Abundance* will index higher among moderns, but other types will support and try to evolve it. And *Circular Commons* will index high among postmoderns, but other types will support and try to put their imprint on it.

With this nice alignment of one guiding image for each worldview, we must next make the case for how the integrals will be needed to drive the "winner" over the top. Integral values are the earliest second-tier type to emerge. The tier concept, introduced earlier in Section 2.3.1 with the Shifting Values driver, comes from Beck and Cowan's (1996) *Spiral Dynamics*. The distinction is that holders of first-tier values believe that their value system is the best and if only everyone else would adopt their values, everything would be great. The second-tier values, of which integral is the most prominent type (though tiny at 3-5%), are flexible in their values and recognize that some values fit some situations better than others. In short, they see the value of all values, and do not believe one type is best for everyone. So, Tier 1 values holders believe their way is the right way, and Tier 2 values adopt a more practical, functional fit-to-context approach.

It is really hard to see fundamental change in first-tier mindsets that believe their values are the right values for everybody. We see tribalism in play today and the stalemate it engenders. Former Labor Secretary Robert Reich (2022) recently wrote about "Facing America's Second Civil War" in which he sees a voluntary zip code split into blue (urban) and red (rural and exurban) areas, rather than a shooting war. In short, the reds see anything they don't like as an example of blue bias, and vice versa. From a values perspective, while the overlay is not 100% accurate, it is close enough to say that the reds are mostly traditionals, and the blues are mostly postmoderns. Their percentages in the US are roughly equal, in the mid-20s (it is very difficult to pin down the precise numbers). The long-term trends favor the blues, as the postmodern cohort is growing and the traditional one is shrinking. I hope some of you are already asking, "what about the moderns in-between the traditional and postmoderns?" Indeed, that's the interesting question! You might say there is little to be done with the traditional reds and the postmodern blues — each seems to be dug deeply into their position and cannot tolerate the other. The moderns, if you will, could go either way. And if you look at US election results, they are evenly split as well! The long-term trends say they should be inching toward the postmoderns — but they ain't there yet!

Figure 9.1 The values split

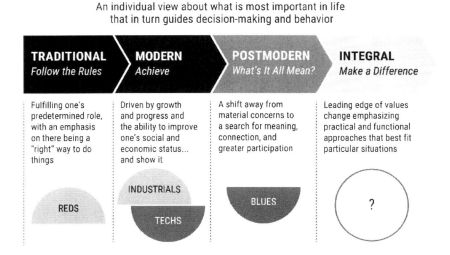

Let's recall that the moderns put a high value on competition, achievement, and growth. We actually have yet another fairly even split here: the "declining" industrial manufacturing base of the economy leans red and the "emerging" high-tech base leans blue. As an example, let's say the construction industry leans red and cloud-based tech companies lean blue.

In sum, we have a fairly even split between the "poles" of traditional red and postmodern blue. These poles sandwich a middle of moderns who in turn are split between the industrial manufacturing red and the high-tech blue. The long-term trend says momentum favors the blue, but a Tier One side winning isn't the answer. It's an evolution toward Tier 2 integral values. In Tier 2, we move off "one right way" thinking and have a chance at making the big changes needed. The hard news is that values shifts take a long time. It may seem crazy to counsel patience in the chaos of today, but that may be wise. I'm not suggesting that we sit and wait for values shifts but recognize that efforts to shift the system today are likely to be very, very difficult, so recognize that and don't despair.

We discussed that capitalism is most strongly supported by those with modern values. Today, the major "opposition" to capitalism is coming from the postmoderns. As this work has hopefully made clear, that opposition is not organized, clear, or unified, but mostly just "against." Thus the stalemate. A key strength of the postmoderns is encouraging participatory approaches and self-expression; a key weakness is their failure to act on these impulses. A postmodern meeting will often be a very boisterous and engaged gathering where everyone feels great for having been there, but then there is no follow-up.

Enter the integrals, whose motto is "make a difference." It is my view that we need the integrals to reach a critical mass for the transition to *After Capitalism* to happen in a "positive" evolutionary way (not from a disastrous collapse). They are roughly 3-5% in the US. What is critical mass — 10% 20%? 25%? I'm reminded of Margaret Meade's words: "Never doubt that a small group of thoughtful, committed citizens can change the world. Indeed, it's the only thing that ever has." Nonetheless, I'm taking a conservative view and setting the *After Capitalism* Transformation as 20-30 years away as that is probably how long the values shift takes.

2.   From ECONOMY to SOCIETY

Stop and think about our daily life. Our overriding purpose centers on economic contribution. Am I doing my duty in terms of bringing in money, and then spending that money? Practically everything is monetized. Certainly, access to the essentials of life is restricted, such as food, housing, clothing, and transportation; but also entertainment, with several hundred-dollar monthly subscriptions, romantic relationships with dating services, or even access to our attention on social media. We discussed earlier how capitalism is constantly on the lookout for new things to monetize, sinking its tentacles into every aspect of daily life.

How did we get here? That's its own book. The two-paragraph version is that the industrial revolution and the modern values it helped spawn shifted daily life from one of subsistence and getting by to one where accumulation became possible. This eventually stimulated an incredible explosion of economic growth that was unprecedented in human history. Capitalism was an excellent system for guiding this explosion. A fundamental assumption, or some might say justification, was that providing greater material goods security would make people happy. The data have later shown that this was true up to a point, but unfortunately only to a point of a very minimal level of income. After that, more money does not lead to more happiness. But we kept on and keep on trying.

At some point this economic means to social happiness or wellbeing gets confused and the economics becomes the end rather than the means to an end. We are not using our economy to build a society, but the other way around. Our society is centered around building an economy. The simplest way to look at is this is our obsession with GDP and economic growth as the measure of success. The conversations around expanding these metrics could be seen as signaling a shift away from this form of "economism" — a healthy sign. The Triple Bottom Line for instance suggests that success measures should be equal parts economic, social, and environmental. But even this approach is distorted in the sense that we have simply promoted the social to equal with the economic (and environmental). Should it not be first? Should we not put economics back in its rightful place of service to the social good?

3.   From SCARCITY to ABUNDANCE

This is related to #2 above — all are related to some degree of course — in that the need to focus on economics is because there is not enough. But there *is* enough. Number 10 will discuss distribution — here we will say there is enough, but there is a giant distribution problem. But the perception is that there is not enough, thus we need to keep "rising and grinding" and working just in case. And of course, for so many people there is not enough. Here the problem is that the capitalist system by design leads to a large percentage of the wealth going to a small percentage of the people. It's a winners and losers game with a few winners and mostly losers — this is the "perfect" system fit for modern values that prioritizes competition and achievement. The argument is that competition stimulates innovation and growth with the resulting rising tide lifting all boats. The winners feel they deserve it and fail to recognize — or don't care — that the game is not fair. Even if it was fair, it is going to produce more losers than winners.

It is in the interest of the supporters of capitalism to emphasize scarcity and the un-ending and tough battle for resources. It keeps the system afloat. But if we could just step back and look at all the wealth that is produced and run the numbers ... there is plenty. It's just so wildly unevenly distributed. The scarcity mindset keeps us playing the current economic game. If we are fortunate enough to do well, we store away money for a rainy day. And the outgrowth of the marketing and advertising apparatus, and our own stupidity, keep us buying stuff we don't need, which reinforces the scarcity idea.

The scarcity notion is not only powerful, it's subtle. We are not necessarily thinking about it on a daily basis, but it continues to indirectly influence us. Again, we see a connection to values. The long-time founder and director of the World Values Survey, Ronald Inglehart, developed the Existential Security Theory that says that the biggest enabler of values change is high levels of existential security. It provides a context where it feels safe to try something different because there is a security blanket. Conversely in times of great stress, individuals will tend to "go back" and revert to the known comfort of previous values. Scarcity in effect creates an ongoing atmosphere of fear and insecurity and makes it more difficult to change.

For example, in the scarcity paradigm, the trend toward zero marginal cost is seen as a problem. How can we make money if something is easy and practically free to reproduce? If we step back from that for a second, we might see this as a really good thing for the society, but not for the economy. Another example is that the tremendous gains in productivity and in convenience goods and services have not led to us working less, but consume more. It is a treadmill that we could choose to step off. Of course, if one does step off, one loses one's place in the economic and social pecking order, which is especially important to those with modern values.

4. From MASTERS (of nature) to PARTNERS (with nature)

It is excruciatingly difficult to rank which of these shifts is more important. I would use a hypothetical magic wand to fix our separation from nature, which is perhaps the most crippling problem facing the future. Capitalism's view of nature is that it is something to be conquered and exploited — with science and technology as the key tools. The more science and technology has advanced, the greater our sense of dominance over nature has grown ... to the point where we see ourselves above it and need to be protected from it. Nature is something to be used for the benefit of human progress and has no intrinsic value in and of itself. Our growing science and technology capabilities have encouraged a sense of hubris: the idea that we stand above all else. The needs of other species only matter in relation to us.

The irony is that this exploitation is directly responsible for the climate change and resource issues now threatening the very survival of humanity — although there are admittedly many who do not see that yet.

Again, we see the fit with modern values — winning, achieving, victory — no matter the cost.

5. From GROWTH to DEGROWTH

The growth question has been covered rather extensively and indeed earns a place among the top ten shifts for *After Capitalism*. It has been noted how difficult it will be to challenge this idea. If we use Sohail Inayatullah's (1998) CLA, growth is a foundational myth-metaphor. It is so deeply ingrained as to be effectively unquestioned. To challenge a myth-metaphor is to invite scorn, questioning looks, and whispers about one's intelligence or sanity. Ironically, here we will often get references to nature, which we just noted above is there for us to be exploited, but here it is wise and the "law of the jungle" teaches us that we grow or die. The economic argument goes something like:

Figure 9.2 The growth story

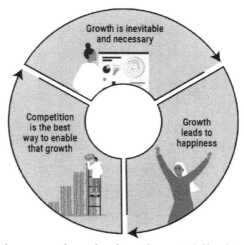

Myth-metaphors change rarely and only with great difficulty. But there is an opening here. There are examples of growth not being good, such as with cancer. Too much cell growth kills the host. The idea of humanity as a cancer upon nature is out there. Many opponents of capitalism describe the growth it encourages as cancerous.

It is thus controversial to advocate degrowth. But the analysis here suggests it is the most sensible path, at least until we stabilize and reset the current state of nature. Perhaps there is a time of healthy growth ahead. But it seems pretty clear that there is an adjustment period needed first. And, as was pointed out earlier, one can make the case that stated rates of growth are used to prop up the current system and are very likely lower than suggested. In other words, degrowth may not be as big an adjustment as we might first think.

6. From PAST to FUTURE

From a young age people are taught to look for ideas and validation by looking backward, from legal precedents to benchmarking to case histories. In looking backward, individuals, organizations or even societies are by definition borrowing used futures. Rather than create their own, they rely on what someone else has tried before (Inayatullah, 2008). Granted we ought to consider history when reviewing the future, but we don't want it to be a straitjacket that restricts the idea space.

The purpose of this book has been to identify new futures so that we don't end up recycling used futures. Granted, it is possible that a used future is a good idea — it's not inherently a bad thing. But in our *After Capitalism* case, the two used futures that have emerged are socialism and communism. The research clearly indicates that these ideologies are re-emerging as analysts and writers critiquing capitalism look for an alternative. There have been many polls suggesting that young people are more favorably disposed to socialism than capitalism. Their re-emergence makes sense, but they have little chance of succeeding, especially in the US. There are too many people negatively predisposed who will immediately shut down once these used futures are offered up. In fact, supporters of capitalism would be smart to actively promote these used futures. Indeed, one could argue that that has long been the approach. The argument is that capitalism may have problems, but it's better than the alternatives.

Thus, there is some pressure to quickly develop new futures before the debate gets framed in old capitalism versus socialism or communism terms.

7. From FULL EMPLOYMENT to FULL UNEMPLOYMENT

The post-work future is coming. Ironically, this is mostly looked at with fear and trepidation. Hopefully, the point about the need for mindset shift is sinking in. Think of how crazy it is to see everybody having to work as more desirable than everyone not having to work. Talk about setting the wrong goals! Of course, within the context of capitalism, this backwards goal makes sense. And we discussed above how jobs have become an important aspect of our identity and our daily lives. I think it is a consequence of how far we've gone in the wrong direction that something so basic is a "key insight" of this work. A clue that we've gone too far is when you start to hear arguments about how work is part of human nature and we are hard-wired to be this way. Nonsense, jobs are a social construction that we created and can be un-created.

Bringing the discussion back to a more practical level, what we see taking place is that jobs are an increasingly ineffective resource distribution mechanism. The basic bargain since the Industrial Revolution is that one gets a job in order to earn access to the goods and services of the society. Over time, some social welfare safety net protections were added, but for the last few hundred years, the job has been the primary distribution mechanism.

In my early work on the future of work with futurists Joe Coates, Jennifer Jarratt and John Mahaffie in the 1990s, we frequently reported on the long-term trend toward structural unemployment. Basically, due to automation there would be less need for human work to produce the goods and services needed by society. This has proven to be accurate, but as we've pointed out in several places, people have used increased wealth and productivity to consume more rather than work less. But we are approaching the point where there is less left to commodify. It is getting more challenging to sell scarcity. As automation and the related suite of technologies continues to improve, structural unemployment gets "worse." I say in quotes because it a case of perspective over whether not having to work is a bad thing. Perhaps for some small percentage of folks, their job is a true joy that they would work just as hard at for free. For the rest of us, I think at the very least our dedication to duty might waver a bit if we did not need the money. Even those who love their jobs would likely get rid of some percentage of it if they could. As a professor, I would gladly escape the myriad evaluation activities and reports that consume huge swaths of my time!

8. From PRIVATE PROPERTY to COMMONS

We have discussed how capitalism desperately needs to find new things to monetize to keep the engine going. The historic commons are long gone and have been incorporated into the capitalist structure. It's been going on so long that there is no institutional memory left of a commons approach. It now seems like some sort of quaint period that did not reflect the progress that has since been made. As the acquisitiveness continues, and there are fewer things to commodify, we are now selling our personal and biological data and eyeballs (what we watch). Capitalism can be viewed as a centuries-long Ponzi scheme that has to keep going by finding new dupes or face the crash and reckoning. The last great hope of the capitalists is that we'll be able to bring back resources from space. It is no accident that several wealthy entrepreneurs are funding space ventures. Earth is used up, so on to space!

A related development, which makes the shift to commons even more challenging, is the glorification of privatization. The private sector is lauded for its efficiency in comparison to the inefficient bureaucratic state. Unfortunately, there is much truth here. But probably more truth in the inefficient state than the efficient private sector. Nonetheless, this assumption has driven several decades of privatization, at least since the Reagan and Thatcher "revolutions." The results however are mixed at best. But the belief persists. In its current incarnation, there is the glorification of public-private partnerships. Our analysis of privatization is just that it is another quest for capitalism to find new commons to commodify — let's take things that were managed publicly for the common good and find a way to profit from them.

This privatization trend has been accelerated by the pandemic. In particular, the Big Four professional services firms: Deloitte, Ernst & Young, KPMG, and PricewaterhouseCoopers (PwC) — are increasingly filling the void for frozen public staffs by landing contracts for administering the reforms needed to alleviate the effects of the crisis (Ekaitz and Medina, 2021).

A reversal here would be a tremendous undertaking, especially in the US where individualism and faith in private property are so strong. A simple thought experiment might help. We can all see how Amazon is effectively taking over the retail sector. As a result, Bezos is either the richest man in the world or close to it. What if, instead of enriching Bezos and his team, that money was re-invested in the country. The immediate objection of course would be that public ownership would screw it up. But what if we put our best minds on solving that problem, instead of trying to think of new platform monopolies or complicated new financial instruments that bring no value to anyone but the financial sector?

It is hard to imagine from today's vantage point, but it's not impossible. I remember when we were introducing the ideas of the sharing economy to clients 15 or so years ago, and getting those strange "here they go again" looks. Yet here we are. The sharing economy is practically passé today. And just 15 years ago it was way out there. Yes, there is hope.

9. From GLOBAL AND LOCAL to LOCAL AND GLOBAL

It was striking how many of the AC Concepts had a more local approach and scale as part of their recommendations. The logic of capitalism is to increase efficiency and profits. As it spread globally, it brought global supply chains with it. It was very much an exploitative journey, finding new territories to "civilize", but also to exploit. The benefits were always flowing chiefly to the capitalists. Once a particular territory or country had been sufficiently "civilized", its costs of labor went up, and it was on to the next place to civilize and find cheap labor. As we've seen, capitalism is running out of places to provide cheap labor, as that labor needs to be accessible. Ongoing conflicts, for example, are not good for business.

So we begin to see the end of globalization as a source of new value to find and exploit. And thus, the value of the accompanying global supply chains begins to make less sense. It was, and still is in many cases, cheaper to make things in China and ship to the US, when the labor there is so cheap. As China develops economically, that labor will not be so cheap, and the economics of such a large percentage of US consumer goods coming from China eventually makes no economic sense. Africa is looked at as next, but if I were Africa, I might not be so eager to make this bargain.

Alongside the economic argument is the environmental one. Because the system has not accounted for "external" environmental costs, shipping things around globally looked more efficient than it really was. With the advent of automation and new manufacturing technology of additive manufacturing, the case for making things locally makes more economic sense along with the obvious environmental benefits.

Stir in the social benefit and we have a pretty solid case here that may be the least difficult of our 10 shifts. The social benefit is the preference for things local: local crafts, local brands, farmers' markets, etc. Keeping money in the community rather than seeing it accumulate in some distant corporate headquarters is an "easy" sell.

Perhaps the major caution here is to not get too romantic about local benefits. We saw this early in the folk politics that are part of the ineffective left driver. There is some thinking that local is the solution to everything and is automatically better in every case. It cannot be ignored that the world is increasingly globally interconnected and there are indeed global-scale issues that need to be addressed at the global scale. It's not as simple as every local community for itself. There does need to be global coordination.

10. From ACCUMULATION to DISTRIBUTION

I am leaving this for last, as I see it at the core of any solution. The problem and solution involve distribution ... on a gigantic scale. The three guiding images each address it:

- *Tech-Led Abundance* says technology will produce an abundance of wealth and resources so that distribution won't be an issue, although it does not specifically address the how. It just sees it as a non-issue.

- *Non-Workers' Paradise* is focused on the more equal distribution of wealth and suggests this will enable a post-work society. It acknowledges the role of technology in creating abundance, although it is very concerned about the transition in which workers are likely to lose jobs to automation.

- *Circular Commons* focuses more on the distribution of resources and says we should use and share rather than consume and accumulate.

This point reminds us that the structure of capitalism by design creates a warped, unequal distribution system of a small number of winners getting the largest share of the resources. All else aside, that is what the system produces. As we learned from Meadows in the last chapter, and in this chapter on the 10 shifts, we need to change the metrics, rules, and mindset of this system if we are to successfully get to *After Capitalism*. It won't be easy, but hopefully this work has made clear that the alternative of failure to change is likely to be much worse.

9.2   In closing

<u>How close to the edge?</u>

One wonders how close we will get to the edge of disaster before we pull back. It seems we are heading right to the edge, leaning over, and maybe starting to fall, before we will pull back. It is rather puzzling, ironic, or sad in that very few people seem to be happy about the Neoliberal Capitalist system we are saving. It would be one thing if we were living in this wonderful utopia of lavish consumption and we were all happy, and we were forced to change to curb those excesses. This may be true for a tiny minority of the population, but hardly true for the vast majority. Most polls suggest people think we are going in the wrong direction, and they are worried and afraid about the future. The understandable impulse is to stick with what is known and familiar in a time of uncertainty … especially since there are not clear alternatives. Thus, we can hope that we have at least started the conversation about alternatives with our three guiding images.

<u>It's a combination of the three guiding images!</u>

I suspect many readers at this point will join me in thinking that the best case combines aspects of the three guiding images together. The connections are evident:

- *Circular Commons* flourishes with a *Non-Workers' Paradise* society in which the role of work and economics has been reconfigured — which could be aligned with the commons idea; and *Tech-Led Abundance* provides the technology to achieve circular and manage and finance a commons.

- *Non-Workers' Paradise* still has "work" to be done, and *Circular Commons* provides a focus to working to address climate and go circular, and the commons approach fits with the more egalitarian social approach of *Non-Workers' Paradise*; *Tech-Led Abundance* provides the means to fund UBI or whatever scheme enables the shift away from job/work/economics.

- *Tech-Led Abundance* will continue to be pressured to address social and environmental problems and what better focus than using technology to address the issues of *Circular Commons* and to enable *Non-Workers' Paradise* and create a society that finds new ways to use its time.

The "separate" treatment suggests where the emphasis will be. The environmental focus of *Circular Commons* does not mean that work/economics or technology are ignored or neglected — they are secondary. Different people will be drawn to the different topical foci. Some will be drawn to the environmental focus of *Circular Commons*; some will be drawn to the work focus of *Non-Workers' Paradise*; and some drawn to the technological focus of *Tech-Led Abundance*. Similarly, some people will be turned off by different aspects of the three guiding images. *Circular Commons* will be seen by some as another environmental tree hugger scheme. Some will see *Tech-Led Abundance* as a gadget freak's wet dream. Some will see *Non-Workers' Paradise* as a communist plot. So, perhaps the menu opens up the possibility that more people will see a positive guiding image of the future that appeals to them. And that is our first step!

My goal here has been to suggest that there are positive guiding images of the future *After Capitalism*. It has been to inform rather than enlist. I hope you have better information upon which to base your views and decisions about the future. Perhaps, you will spread the word to others. Maybe the guiding images coalesce and there is consensus. Then we do the movement and start enlisting!

Glossary

Foresight terms

AC Concept	After Capitalism Concept; for this work, one of the books or reports reviewed as a potential component of a guiding image.
Archetype	A common pattern of change in a domain.
Baseline	Archetype scenario in which the domain continues along its current trajectory without any major disruptions or surprises.
Collapse	Archetype scenario in which the domain breaks or falls into a state of dysfunction.
Domain	Synonymous with topic, it is the sphere of inquiry for a futures exploration that sets the boundary conditions.
Domain map	A visual map of categories and sub-categories for organizing the exploration of a domain.
Driver	A thematic cluster of trends, scan hits, or other research information that describes an influential change in a domain and serves as a building block of scenarios.
Focal issue	A key framing issue typically in the form of a question that guides an exploration of a domain.
Framework Foresight	The University of Houston's six step method for exploring a domain: Framing, Scanning & Researching, Futuring, Visioning, Designing, and Adapting.
Framing	Identifying and bounding the domain to be explored.
Futuring	Crafting the Baseline and alternative scenarios.
Guiding Images	A positive aspirational view of the future that serves as a North Star for guiding people into the future.
HAT (Houston Archetype Technique)	Scenario development technique using archetypes plotted across the Three Horizons.
Horizon scanning (scanning)	A process for finding, collecting, and analyzing signals of change.
Implications analysis (Visioning)	Identifying the impacts or consequences of scenarios.
New Equilibrium	Archetype scenario in which a domain is confronted with a major challenge and is forced to adapt and compromise in order to "save itself."
Predetermined	A driver that is relatively certain to occur, e.g. aging population.
Three Horizons	A framework describing how domains evolve over time. H1= current system; H2=zone of transition away from current system and toward a new one; and H3=transformation to a new system.

Scan hit	An article, blog post, video or other piece of information describing a signal of potential change.
STEEP	Acronym (Social, Technology, Economic, Environmental, Political) used to organize the broad external context outside of a domain.
TIPPs	Acronym (Trends, Issues, Plans, Projections) that groups together specific types of information that can be used to develop drivers and/or scenarios.
Transformation	Archetype scenario of fundamental change that entails new rules for how the domain operates.
Uncertainty	A driver with a wide range of potential outcomes.
Weak signals	Early indications of change that typically come from the fringe.

After Capitalism terms

Apartness	Signifies the growing separation between nature and humanity.
Automation	Use of various technologies for performing tasks, physical or digital, with minimal or reduced human intervention.
Additive manufacturing	3D, 4D, and nano-scale "bottom-up" manufacturing approaches that allow for decentralized on-demand fabrication.
Anarcho-capitalism	A radical ideology of an absolutely free market and the abolition of the state.
Autonomous zones	Temporary protest camps that have a degree of autonomy from external authority.
Barter	The exchange of goods or services without using money.
B-corp	A designation that a business meets high standards of performance, accountability, and transparency on factors, such as employee benefits and contributions to the local community.
Bioregional	Regions that are defined environmentally rather than politically.
Blockchain	A secure, shared, distributed ledger that facilitates recording transactions and tracking assets in a network.
Bretton Woods	A post WW2 agreement in which the US dollar was designated the world's reserve currency on the basis of a gold standard.
Capitalism	An economic system based on private property and ownership, free markets, limited regulation, and the prioritization of efficiency and profitmaking.
Carrying capacity	The number of people, other living organisms, or crops that a region can support without environmental degradation.

Class consciousness	Marxian notion of awareness of one's socioeconomic status.
Circular Commons	Expands the concept of sustainability to embrace circular principles as part of a social, political, and economic commons.
Class struggle	Marxist notion of inherent conflicting interest between bourgeoisie and proletariat.
Class War	Collapse image in which class tensions boil over into violence.
Collaborative Sharing Platforms	A New Equilibrium image in which digital platforms enable collaboration and sharing.
Commons	Resources that are organized and managed on the basis of public ownership, cooperation, and sharing.
Commodification	Process by which resources once publicly owned and managed are assigned market value to be used in capitalist exchange.
Conscious communities	Communities that aim to create a mutually supportive environment for the growth and development of their members in an environmentally sustainable way.
Convivial Conservation	A more democratic form of resource management in which humans and nature coexist.
Co-ops	Businesses managed collectively by workers for their benefit.
CRISPR	A new gene editing technology.
Crypto	Decentralized digital currency.
Cyberpunk	A dystopian future based in capitalist corruption, technological authoritarianism, and the deification of fossil fuels.
Dataism	A philosophical — almost religious — embrace of the promise of big data.
Dependency ratio	The ratio of those not in the labor force (ages 0-14 and 65+) to those in the labor force (ages 15-64).
Direct democracy	A consensus decision-making approach without intermediaries that encourages deliberation and direction action.
Durables	Goods designed for re-use and obtained primarily by using leasing rather than purchasing/consumption models.
Earth Overshoot Day	The day of the year on which humanity's demand for ecological resources and services exceeds what Earth can regenerate in that year.
Ecommony	Emphasizes common space production centered on ideals of sharing and mutual aide.
Ecotats	Local networks of autonomous settlements contained within environmental regions that are able to fulfill the particular needs of their inhabiting community.
Exchange value	Value assigned through pricing mechanisms on the free market.

Exterminism	A world of scarcity except for a small elite within an "Elysian" bubble.
Ecofascism	Embraces a racialized view of nature that blames immigrants for population growth that is damaging the planet.
Ecological footprint	A measure of the human impact on the environment that suggests carrying capacity is being exceeded.
(ESOP) Employee Stock Ownership Plan	A benefit plan that grants workers a stake in a company.
Enclosure	The process by which public lands were privatized via eminent domain of government.
Enoughness	A term for the growing distaste with consumerism and materialism.
Extinction Rebellion (XR)	A protest group that stages "rebellions" to highlight the escalating climate and ecological emergency.
Evolutionary reconstruction	A systemic institutional step-by-step non-violent transformation of the political economy that unfolds over time.
Feudalism	The precursor to capitalism in medieval Europe in which land was divided into large manors owned by lords who employed vassals to use for labor.
Fiat money	Currency that derives its value from government decree.
Financialization	An increase in influence of the finance sector within the economy.
Folk Politics	A critique of the contemporary left's approach to politics in which the transient, small-scale, unmediated and particular are the primary focus of the movement as opposed to larger structural issues.
Geoengineering	Counteracting climate change via large-scale technical intervention into the earth's natural systems.
GPI (Genuine progress indicators)	A more holistic measurement system that takes into account dozens of factors that GDP ignores.
Great Resignation	A large-scale withdrawal from the labor-force that began post-pandemic during which a record 47 million people left their jobs in 2021.
Green New Deal	Legislative plan introduced in the US by Reps. Alexandria Ocasio-Cortez and Ed Markey for a transition to a green, renewable economy.
Growth imperative	The implicit drive for capitalism to expand to maintain rate of profit that require new things to enclose, commoditize, and sell.
Homo economicus	The prevailing economic model of humanity as rational actors that promote individual wellbeing above all.

Imagining After Capitalism | 307

Humanism	The focus on humanity above all else.
Income topping	Pledging never to earn more than a certain amount of money in a year.
Internalized capitalism	A term that has emerged to highlight the idea that our self-worth is directly linked to our productivity, not our value as human beings.
Land-trusts	Used for conservation that enable groups to purchase, protect, and manage land that typically has natural resources, is a historical site, or a public recreational area.
Left vs Liberal	Leftism, in the US, we use to refer to politics which include a critique of capitalism and its superstructure.
LETS System (Local Exchange Trade Network)	A system for organizing and rationalizing reciprocal labor.
Machine learning	A type of artificial intelligence (AI) that allows software applications to become more accurate at predicting outcomes without being explicitly programmed to do so.
Municipal enterprise	A business organization owned by local governments that work for the benefit of the community.
Negative interest	A credit system based on depreciating currency that allows zero-interest loans to discourage accumulation.
Neofeudalism	A form of mass serfdom in which a property-less underclass must survive by servicing the needs of high earners as personal assistants, trainers, child-minders, cooks, cleaners, etc.
Neoliberalism	The current capitalist Baseline which is defined by privatization, deregulation, free trade, commodification of public goods, and managed by international institutions, and using other decentralized institutions like NGOs and think tanks to influence public opinion.
NFTs (Non-fungible tokens)	Unique digitalized versions of various digital products contained on a blockchain that are bought and sold on crypto markets.
Non-Workers' Paradise	A play on the attributed-to-Marxism idea of a worker's paradise, but in the After-Capitalism world we are not working in paid jobs as a means of sustenance.
Not-for-profits	100% of any profits these businesses make must be reinvested into the business or community; basically not-for-private-profit.
NRx	A neo-reactionary movement broadly defined for its anti-liberal attitudes that often embraces autocratic, monarchic, hierarchal, fascistic forms of governance.
Oligopoly	Market monopoly shared by a small number of cooperative firms.

Overshoot	A Collapse image which depicts failure to address growth imperative and leads to ecosystem failure.
Populism	A form of politics that centers on appeals to ordinary people with anti-establishment sentiments.
Pluralistic relativism	The philosophy that everybody's view is equally true and legitimate.
Precariat	A class of people living through insecure jobs interspersed with periods of unemployment or labor-force withdrawal.
Predatory/ Vulture Capitalism	A popular concept to capture how capitalism has been structured for corporate survival and success for shareholders at the expense of workers, managers, communities, and country.
Privatization	Something that was publicly managed (held in common) is turned over to the private sector.
Production-for-Use	A system prioritizes use-value and produces goods and services in direct relation to fulfilling human needs.
Proletariat	Marxist term designating the working class that exchange their labor in return for wages.
Real value	Promotes use value, and more holistic measures related to pro-social and pro-ecological outcomes.
Rentier Capitalism	Having and owning, thereby controlling access, is enormously more profitable than making or serving.
Rogue AI	A Collapse image in which algorithms nudge us for their purposes and humans lose control to intelligent or even superintelligent AI.
Scarcity	The basis for an economic system in which the need for resources exceeds the supply.
Sharing economy	Takes underutilized assets and makes them available, often via digital platforms, to reduce the need for owning those assets.
Social capital	Relationships and skills, the "services" that people once provided for themselves and each other in a gift economy, such as cooking, childcare, healthcare, hospitality, entertainment, advice, etc.
Social democratic approach	Seeks to find common ground or positive sum games with the capitalist owner class.
Socialism	A transitional phase preceding communism in which control over the means of production shifts from private to public.
Solarpunk	Blends aesthetics and politics to explore the kind of world that will emerge when we finally transition to renewables.
Sovereign wealth fund	A state-owned pool of money that is invested in various financial assets.
Stakeholder Capitalism	A system in which corporations are oriented to serve the interests of all their stakeholders, not just the shareholders.

Steady-state economy	A green economy that aims for stable population and stable consumption of energy and materials at sustainable levels.
Structural unemployment	Unemployment that arises due to a mismatch in skills between workers and the jobs available.
Subsidiarity	Keeping decision-making at the lowest feasible level, and only referring to higher levels when absolutely necessary.
Stagnation	A decreased rate of economic growth.
Sustainability Transition	A transition image that emphasizes sustainability within the framework of capitalism.
Tech-Led Abundance	Technological progress drives and leads to an abundance of wealth that fixes the core distribution problem of capitalism.
Techno-feudalism	The big platforms essentially extract rents while the economy is buoyed by central bank money.
Time banks	Involve using and spending time credit, in which one spends an hour helping and later receives an hour of help.
Tribalism	An umbrella term to capture strong group loyalties that have been making it difficult for the sides to get along or agree.
UBI (Universal Basic Income)	A periodic cash payment unconditionally delivered to all on an individual basis, without a means-test or work requirement.
UBS (Universal Basic Services)	Publicly funded and provided access to programs that ensure the basic needs of citizens are met (access to food, housing, healthcare, etc.)
Utopia	A visionary system of political or social perfection.
Value	An individual view about what is most important in life that guides decision-making and behavior; traditional values are about following the rules; modern values are about achievement, postmodern values are about the search for meaning, and integral values are about making a difference.
Vision	A vivid, imaginative conception of the future.
Walk-away	A post-scarcity society that emerges by dropping out from the "default" world of massive inequality.
Woke Capitalism	Involves social pressure on firms to conform to a "progressive" version of social justice.
Workism	The idea that humans are being wired to work.
Zebras	Startup companies seeking to balance profit and purpose to help create a more just and responsible society.

REFERENCES (put tinyurl links into your browser – preceded by https:// if necessary)

Abraham, Roshan. 2023. "Hedge Funds Have Invaded the Housing Market. A New Bill Would Ban Them." *Vice*, Dec 7, 2023, tinyurl.com/aftercap001

Aguilar-Millan, Stephen, Jason Swanson, Kate Burgess-MacIntosh & Laura Schlehuber. 2014. "An Age of Stagnation?" *World Futures Review* 6(2), 120-129.

Ahmed, Nafeez. 2018. "Scientists Warn the UN of Capitalism's Imminent Demise." *Motherboard*, Aug 27 2018, tinyurl.com/aftercap002

Ahmed, Nafeez. 2021. "MIT Predicted in 1972 That Society Will Collapse This Century. New Research Shows We're on Schedule." *Vice*, July 14, 2021, tinyurl.com/aftercap003

Akbuluta, Bengi and Fikret Adaman. 2020. "The Ecological Economics of Economic Democracy." *Ecological Economics* 176(20), 1-9.

Alexander, Samuel. 2012. *The Sufficiency Economy: Envisioning a Prosperous Way Down*, Simplicity Institute Report 12s.

Allen, Cameron. 2012. *A Guidebook to the Green Economy: Issue 2: Exploring Green Economy Principles*. UN Division for Sustainable Development (UNDESA).

Alperovitz, Gar. 2013. "The Possibility of a Pluralist Commonwealth and a Community Sustaining Political-Economic System." *The Pluralist Commonwealth*, tinyurl.com/aftercap004

Alvaredo, Facundo, Lucas Chancel, Thomas Piketty, Emmanuel Saez & Gabriel Zucman. 2017. *World Inequality Report 2018*. World Inequality Lab.

Andersen, Kurt. 2020. "College-Educated Professionals Are Capitalism's Useful Idiots." *The Atlantic*, August 7, 2020, tinyurl.com/aftercap005

Anderson, William. 2019. "The Rise of Woke Capitalism." *Mises Wire*, July 25, 2019, tinyurl.com/aftercap006

Anzilotti, Eillie. 2017. "Young People Are Really Over Capitalism." *Fast Company*, December 8, 2017, tinyurl.com/aftercap007

Arthur, W. Brian. 2011. "The Second Economy." *McKinsey Quarterly*, October.

Aspin, Gordon, George Collins, Pavel Krumkachev, Marlin Metzger, Scott Radeztsky & Srivats Srinivasan. 2017. "Everything as a Service: Modernizing the Core through a Service Lens." *Tech Trends 2017: The Kinetic Enterprise*. Deloitte University Press.

Ayres, Robert. 2020. "How Universal Basic Income Could Save Capitalism." *Insead Knowledge*, August 12, 2020, tinyurl.com/aftercap008

Aziz, Afdhel. 2022. "How the World's Largest B Corp Natura (Owner of Body Shop, Avon and Aesop) Uses Purpose to Drive Performance and Well-Being." *Forbes*, May 11, 2022, tinyurl.com/aftercap009

Balle. ND. "Local Economy Framework." *Balle*, tinyurl.com/aftercap010

Barker, Joel. 1996. "The Mondragon Model: A New Pathway for the Twenty-First Century." In Hesselbein, Frances, Marshall Goldsmith, and Richard Beckhard, (Eds) *The Organization of the Future*, The Peter F. Drucker Foundation. Jossey Bass.

Barnes, Peter. 2019. "How to Save the Middle Class When Jobs Don't Pay." *The Good Men Project*, August 4, 2019, tinyurl.com/aftercap011

Barry, Glen. 2014. "Terrestrial Ecosystem Loss and Biosphere Collapse." *Management of Environmental Quality* 25(5), 542-563.

Bastani, Aaron. 2019. *Fully Automated Luxury Communism*. Verso.

Beck, Don and Christopher Cowan. 1996. *Spiral Dynamics: Mastering Values, Leadership and Change*. Wiley-Blackwell.

Beckett, Andy. 2018. "Post-Work: The Radical Idea of a World without Jobs." *The Guardian*, January 19, 2018, tinyurl.com/aftercap012

Beganski, André. 2023. "ApeCoin Crashes to All-Time Low as Bored Ape Yacht Club NFT Prices Sink." *Decrypt*, July 10, 2023, tinyurl.com/aftercap013

Benanav, Aaron. 2023. "We're All Stagnationists Now." Jacobin.com, September 29, 2023, tinyurl.com/aftercap014

Benioff, Marc. 2019. "Marc Benioff: We Need a New Capitalism." *New York Times*, October 24, 2019.

Benyus, Janine. 2009. *Biomimicry: Innovation Inspired by Nature*. HarperCollins.

Bergquist, Magnus, Andreas Nilsson, and P. Wesley Schultz. 2019. "Experiencing a Severe Weather Event Increases Concern about Climate Change." *Frontiers in Psychology* 10, 220.

Bergstein, Brian. 2018. "Basic Income Could Work — If You Do it Canada-Style." *MIT Technology Review*, June 20, 2018, tinyurl.com/aftercap015

Bernstein, William. 2010. *The Birth of Plenty*. McGraw Hill.

Berthin, Gerardo. 2023. "Why Are Youth Dissatisfied with Democracy?" *Freedom House*, September 14, 2023, tinyurl.com/aftercap016

Bevan, Stephen. 2014. "A Bad Job Is Harder on your Mental Health than Unemployment for the Conversation." *Mashable*, Dec 17, tinyurl.com/aftercap017

Bishop, Matthew and Michael Green. 2008. *Philanthrocapitalism: How the Rich Can Save the World*. Bloomsbury Press.

Blasi, Joseph and Douglas Kruse. 2018. "Today's Young Adults Want to Redesign Capitalism. But into What?" *Yes! Magazine*, April 5, 2018, tinyurl.com/aftercap018

Blauwhof, Frederik Berend. 2012. "Overcoming Accumulation: Is a Capitalist Steady-State Economy Possible?" *Ecological Economics* 84: 254-261.

Bollier, David. 2014. *Think Like a Commoner: A Short Introduction to the Life of the Commons*. New Society Publishers. Kindle Edition.

Bond, Shannon. 2020. "Uber and Lyft to Continue Treating Drivers as Independent Contractors." *NPR All Things Considered*, November 4, 2020, tinyurl.com/aftercap020

Bortun, Vladimir. 2023. "The Radical Left Today Is Not Radical, and Why that Matters." *The Good Men Project*, August 13, 2023, tinyurl.com/aftercap021

Bostrom, Nick. 2014. *Superintelligence: Paths, Dangers, Strategies*. Oxford University Press.

Bowles, Nellie. 2018. "Dorm Living for Professionals Comes to San Francisco." *New York Times*, March 4, 2018.

Bowles, Samuel. 2016. *The Moral Economy: Why Good Incentives Are No Substitute for Good Citizens*. Yale University Press.

Boyle, Peter. 2020. "Why the Alternative to Capitalism has to be Ecosocialist." *Green Left*, October 23, 2020, tinyurl.com/aftercap022

Brandel, Jennifer, Mara Zepeda, and Astrid Scholz. 2017. "Zebras Fix What Unicorns Break." *Medium.com*, March 8, 2017, tinyurl.com/aftercap023

Braudel, Fernand. 1981. *The Structures of Everyday Life*. Vol. 1 of *Civilization and Capitalism, 15th-18th Century*. Harper & Row.

Bregman, Rutger. 2017. *Utopia for Realists: How We Can Build the Ideal World*. Little, Brown and Company.

Brin, Dinah Wisenberg. 2021. "Countries Experiment with Four-Day Workweek." SHRM, May 11, 2021, tinyurl.com/aftercap024

Brown, Ellen. 2018. "Universal Basic Income Is Easier than it Looks." *Truthdig*, December 27, 2018, tinyurl.com/aftercap025

_____ 2021. "Mom-and-Pop Capitalism to Techno-Feudalism." *LA Progressive*, May 22, 2021, tinyurl.com/aftercap026

Brundtland Commission. 1987. *Our Common Future*. Oxford University Press.

Brynjolfsson, Erik and Andrew McAfee. 2016. *The Second Machine Age: Work, Progress, and Prosperity in a Time of Brilliant Technologies*. W.W. Norton. Kindle Edition.

Bullock, D.A. 2021. "The Actions of the (Well-Funded) Capitol Police Show Why We Need to Defund the Police." *In These Times*, January 12, 2021, tinyurl.com/aftercap027

Bureau of Labor Statistics. 2018. "Contingent and Alternative Employment Arrangements Summary." *Bureau of Labor Statistics*, June 7, 2018, tinyurl.com/aftercap019

_____ 2021. "Employment by Major Industry Sector." *Employment Projections*, September 21, 2021, tinyurl.com/aftercap028

_____ 2022. *American Time Use Survey*, tinyurl.com/aftercap029

_____ 2023. Tellers. *Occupational Outlook Handbook*, September 6, 2023, tinyurl.com/aftercap030

Burns, Katelyn. 2020. "The Violent End of the Capitol Hill Organized Protest, Explained." *Vox*, July 2, 2020, tinyurl.com/aftercap031

Burns, Rebecca. 2019. "What's at Stake in Chicago Teachers' Strike." *In These Times*, October 14, 2019, tinyurl.com/aftercap032

Buscher, Bram and Robert Fletcher. 2020. *The Conservation Revolution: Radical Ideas for Saving Nature Beyond the Anthropocene*. Verso.

Byleckie, Ashlar. 2020. "You Don't Have to Turn your Passions into Profit." *The Signal*, October 20, 2020, tinyurl.com/aftercap033

Cancela, Ekaitz and Stuart Medina. 2021. "Consultancy Capitalism Is Allowing Private Firms to Control Public Funds." *Jacobin*, August 11, 2021, tinyurl.com/aftercap034

Candy, Stuart. 2014. "Why Christchurch Should Not Plan for the Future." In Barnaby Bennett et al. (Eds.). *Once in a Lifetime: City-building after Disaster in Christchurch*. Freerange, 84-89.

Canon, Gabrielle. 2021. "Los Angeles Could Become Largest US City to Trial Universal Basic Income." *The Guardian*, April 21, 2021, tinyurl.com/aftercap035

Carlson, Neil, Harold Miller, Donald Heth, John Donahoe, and G. Neil Martin. 2009. *Psychology: The Science of Behavior*, 7th Ed. Pearson Education.

Carnegie, Megan. 2022. "After the Great Resignation, Tech Firms Are Getting Desperate." *Wired*. February 11, 2022, tinyurl.com/aftercap036

Castro, Nazaret. 2022. "The Dispute over Sustainability: False Solutions Versus Real Alternatives." *Equal Times*, April 28, 2022, tinyurl.com/aftercap037

Cellan-Jones, Rory. 2019. "Robots 'to Replace up to 20 Million Factory Jobs by 2030." *BBC News*, June 26, 2019, tinyurl.com/aftercap038

Chace, Calum. 2023. "Pioneering Transhumanism: A Conversation with Natasha Vita-More." *Forbes*, February 1, 2023, tinyurl.com/aftercap039

Chandrasekhar, C.P. and Jayati Ghosh. 2018. "How Unequal Are World Incomes?" *Real World Economics Review Blog*, April 4, 2018, tinyurl.com/aftercap040

Chang, Clio. 2023. "There's a War Going on in Your Local Buy Nothing Group." *Curbed*, February 23, 2023, tinyurl.com/aftercap041

Chapin, Simeon. 2021. "What Does Economy Mean? The Difference of Real vs. Financial Economics." *VSECU*, August 12, 2021, tinyurl.com/aftercap042

Chappell, Bill. 2019. "4-Day Workweek Boosted Workers' Productivity By 40%, Microsoft Japan Says." *NPR*. November 4, 2019, tinyurl.com/aftercap043

Chen, Katherine and Victor Tan Chen. 2021. "Cooperatives Can Make Economies More Resilient to Crises like COVID-19." *Fortune*, May 19, 2021.

Christophers, Brett. 2020. *Rentier Capitalism: Who Owns the Economy, and Who Pays for it?* Verso.
Chua, Amy. 2018. "How America's Identity Politics Went from Inclusion to Division." *The Guardian*, March 1, 2018.
Clark, John. 2020. "What Is Eco-anarchism?" *The Ecological Citizen* 3 (Supp C), 9-14.
Claughton, David and Michael Condon. 2021. "Robots and Artificial Intelligence to Guide Australia's First Fully Automated Farm." *ABC News*, May 27, 2021, tinyurl.com/aftercap044
Clifford, Catherine. 2019. "Billionaire Marc Benioff: Capitalism has 'Led to Horrifying Inequality' and Must Be Fixed." *CNBC.com*, October 14, 2019, tinyurl.com/aftercap045
Coates, Joseph, John Mahaffie, and Andy Hines. 1996. *2025: Scenarios of US and Global Society Reshaped by Science and Technology*. Oakhill Press.
Cobbing, Madeleine, Edie Miller, and Yewande Omotoso. (2023). "Chapter One." *Growing the Alternatives: Societies for a Future Beyond GDP*. Greenpeace.
Collins, Jim. 2001. *Good to Great: Why Some Companies Make the Leap… and Others Don't*. HarperCollins.
Colombo, Jesse. 2019. "Why Has the US CEO-To-Worker Pay Ratio Increased So Much?" *Forbes*, August 31, 2019, tinyurl.com/aftercap046
Cortright, Joe. 2019. "Dr. King: Socialism for the Rich and Rugged Free Enterprise Capitalism for the Poor," *City Observatory*, January 21, 2019, tinyurl.com/aftercap047
Cowen, Tyler. 2011. *The Great Stagnation*. Dutton Adult.
Crawford, J. 2018. "GM's Vulture Capitalism." *Irontown Tribune*, Nov 30, 2018.
Curry, Andrew and Anthony Hodgson. 2008. "Seeing in Multiple Horizons: Connecting Futures to Strategy." *Journal of Futures Studies* 13(1), 1-20.
Dalio, Ray. 2020. "We Must Reform Capitalism, Not Abandon It." *CNN Business Perspectives*, May 15, 2020, tinyurl.com/aftercap048
Daly, Herman. 2010. "The Operative Word Here Is 'Somehow'." *Real-World Economics Review* 54, 103, tinyurl.com/aftercap049
D'Angelo, Chris. 2021. "Climate Change Could Shut Down a Vital Ocean Current, Study Finds." *Huffington Post*, August 5, 2021, tinyurl.com/aftercap050
Dao, David. 2017. "AI Smart Contracts: The Age of A.I. Powered Incentives." *Medium.com*, November 23, 2017, tinyurl.com/aftercap051
Dator, Jim. 2009a. "The Unholy Trinity, Plus One." *Journal of Futures Studies* 13(3), 33-48.
_____ 2009b. "Alternative Futures at the Manoa School." *Journal of Futures Studies* 14(2), 1-18.
_____ 2014. "New Beginnings with a New Normal for the Four Futures." *Foresight* 16(6), 496-511.
_____ 2017. Posting to Association or Professional Futurists (APF) listserv, February 14, 2017.
Davenport, Coral. 2018. "Major Climate Report Describes a Strong Risk of Crisis as Early as 2040." *New York Times*, October 7, 2018.
Davenport, Thomas and John Beck. 2000. "Getting the Attention You Need." *Harvard Business Review*, September/October, 118-126.
Dean, Jodi. 2020. "Neofeudalism: The End of Capitalism?" *Los Angeles Review of Books*, May 12, 2020, tinyurl.com/aftercap052
De Angelis, Massimo. 2017. *Omnia Sunt Communia: On the Commons and the Transformation to Postcapitalism*. Zed Books.
DeCosta-Klipa, Nik. 2021. "Chelsea Launched a Guaranteed Income Experiment to Give Money Directly to Residents. Here's how they Spent it." *Boston.com*, May 10, 2021, tinyurl.com/aftercap053
Delaney, Jack. 2021. "On The Green New Deal, Nationalization, & Class Politics," *Counterpunch*, January 31, 2021, tinyurl.com/aftercap054

Denning, Steve. 2017. "From a Casino Economy to a New Golden Age: Carlota Pérez at Drucker Forum." *Forbes*, Nov 25, tinyurl.com/aftercap055

Diamandis, Peter. 2009. "Founding of the Singularity University." *Huffington Post*, Aug 6, 2009, tinyurl.com/aftercap056

_____ 2012. *Abundance: The Future Is Better Than You Think*. Simon & Schuster.

Dickson, EJ. 2020. "TFW No GF' Is a Deeply Uncomfortable Portrayal of Incel Culture." *Rolling Stone*, May 4, 2020, tinyurl.com/aftercap057

DiGirolamo, Mike. 2021. "We've Crossed Four of Nine Planetary Boundaries. What Does this Mean?" *Mongabay*, September 8, 2021.

DiNatale, Natale, and Kayla West. 2022. "Union Representation Petitions are up 57 Percent, but That's Not All!" *The National Law Review*, May 16, 2022, tinyurl.com/aftercap058

Dixon, Jim. 2019. "Here's How We Solve the Global Crisis of Tribalism and Democratic Decay." *World Economic Forum*, January 9, 2019, tinyurl.com/aftercap059

Doctorow, Cory. 2017. *Walkaway: A Novel*. Tor Books.

_____ 2018. "Private Equity Bosses Took $200m Out of Toys R Us and Crashed the Company, Lifetime Employees Got $0 in Severance." *Boingboing*, June 3, 2018, tinyurl.com/aftercap060

_____ 2019. "Wework, Uber, Lyft, Netflix, Bird, Amazon: Late-Stage Capitalism Is all about Money-Losing Predatory Pricing Aimed at Creating Monopolies." *Boingboing*, Sept 26, 2019, tinyurl.com/aftercap061

Downen, Robert. 2023. "What to Know about Nick Fuentes?" *Texas Tribune*, October 10, 2023, tinyurl.com/aftercap062

Downey, Lucas. 2021. "Local Exchange Trading Systems." *Investopedia*, August 31, 2021, tinyurl.com/aftercap063

Dunlop, Tim. 2017. "Is a Universal Basic Income "Challenging but Possible"? *Inside Story*, November 10, 2017, tinyurl.com/aftercap064

Eaton, George. 2023. "Yanis Varoufakis: The Democrats Are Helping to Elect Trump." The New Statesman, October 7, 2023, tinyurl.com/aftercap065

Eberstadt, Nicholas. 2016. *Men without Work: America's Invisible Crisis*. Templeton Press.

Economy Team. 2020. "TikTok Teens Are Fighting Capitalism with Shoplifting." *Our Economy*, November 20, 2020, tinyurl.com/aftercap066

Eisenstein, Charles. 2011. *Sacred Economics: Money, Gift, and Society in the Age of Transition*. Berkeley, CA: North Atlantic Books.

Eisler, Riane and Douglas Fry. 2019. *Nurturing Our Humanity: How Domination and Partnership Shape Our Brains, Lives, and Future*. Oxford University Press.

Ellen MacArthur Foundation. 2013. *Towards the Circular Economy: Economic and Business Rationale for an Accelerated Transition, Volume 1*, tinyurl.com/aftercap067

_____ 2020, June. *The EU's Circular Economy Action Plan*. Ellen MacArthur Foundation and the European Commission, tinyurl.com/aftercap068

Ellickson, Robert. 1998. "New Institutions for Old Neighborhoods." *Duke Law Journal* 48, 75-110.

Ernst and Young. (2023). "EU Commission and Council Take Steps as Part of the Circular Economy Action Plan." *Tax News Update*. July 21, 2023, tinyurl.com/aftercap069

European Commission. 2021. *Circular Economy Action Plan*, tinyurl.com/aftercap070

European Council. 2023. "Rights for Platform Workers: Council Agrees its Position." *Council of the EU*, June 12 2023, tinyurl.com/aftercap071

Ellsmoor, James. 2019. "New Zealand Ditches GDP For Happiness and Wellbeing" *Forbes*, July 11, 2019

Eversberg, Dennis. 2019. "A Dangerous Courtship: The Authoritarian Nationalist Right and the Post-Growth Debate." *Degrowth*, April 29, 2019, tinyurl.com/aftercap072

Fennell, Lee Anne. 2011. Ostrom's Law: Property rights in the commons. *International Journal of the Commons* 5(1), 9-27.

Feola, Giuseppe and Olga Koretskaya. 2020. "Degrowth and the Unmaking of Capitalism." *Resilience*, December 7, 2020, tinyurl.com/aftercap073

Fioramonti, Lorenzo. 2016. "Well-Being Economy: A Scenario for a Post-Growth Horizontal Governance System." *The Next System Project*, November 3, 2016, tinyurl.com/aftercap074

Flyer, Richard. (2022). "Sri Lanka's Untold Story of Resilience: Sarvodaya's Pathway Can Work Anywhere." *Shareable*, Oct 6, 2022, tinyurl.com/aftercap075

Folke, Carl, Jamila Haider, Steven Lade, Albert Norström, & Juan Rocha. 2021. "Commentary: Resilience and Social-Ecological Systems: A Handful of Frontiers." *Global Environmental Change* 71, 102400.

Forget, Evelyn. 2011. *The Town with No Poverty: Using Health Administration Data to Revisit Outcomes of a Canadian Guaranteed Annual Income Field Experiment.* University of Manitoba.

Forman, Laura. 2021. "At Uber and Lyft, Ride-Price Inflation Is Here to Stay." *Wall Street Journal*, October 4, 2021, tinyurl.com/aftercap076

Frase, Peter. 2016. *Four Futures: Life after Capitalism.* Verso Brooks.

Frey, Ulrich. 2019. "Long-Term Evidence on Cooperation and Cultural Differences in Public Goods Dilemmas." *Biology Letters* 15, 20190143.

Friedman, Gerald. 2014. "Workers without Employers: Shadow Corporations and the Rise of the Gig Economy." *Review of Keynesian Economics* 2(2), 171-188.

Friedman, Milton. 1970. "A Friedman Doctrine." *New York Times*, Sept 13, 1970.

Fullerton, John. 2015. *Regenerative Capitalism: How Universal Principles and Patterns Will Shape Our New Economy.* Capital Institute.

Gabriel, Elliott. 2017. "Capitalism, Exterminism and the Long Ecological Revolution (Interview of John Bellamy Foster)." *Telesur*, December 22, 2017, tinyurl.com/aftercap077

GAO. 2015. *Contingent Workforce*, GAO-15-168R. Washington, DC: GAO.

Galeon, Dom. 2017. "New Report Claims UBI Would Grow the US Economy by $2.5 Trillion." Futurism.com, Sept 1, 2017, tinyurl.com/aftercap078

Galeon, Dom and Kristin Houser. 2017. "This Google AI Created a 'Child' AI to Help it Solve Problems." *World Economic Forum*, Dec 12, 2017, tinyurl.com/aftercap079

Gardiner, Ariel. 2019. "Modern Capitalism: Is It Any Different Than a Ponzi Scheme?" Medium.com, October 1, 2019, tinyurl.com/aftercap080

Gaspar, Vitor, Marcos Poplawski-Ribeiro, and Jiae Yoo. 2023. "Global Debt Is Returning to its Rising Trend." IMF Blog, Sept 13, 2023, tinyurl.com/aftercap081

Ghosh, Jayati. 2018. "After Capitalism, What? Giacomo Corneo Tackles the Beast." *The Telegraph*, September 21, 2018, tinyurl.com/aftercap082

Gladwell, Malcolm. 2002. *The Tipping Point: How Little Things Can Make a Big Difference.* Back Bay Books

Global Footprint Network. 2021a. *Earth Overshoot Day*, tinyurl.com/aftercao083

_____ 2021b. "Media Background: Earth Overshoot Day." *Earth Overshoot Day*, tinyurl.com/aftercap084

Gore, Al. 1993. *From Red Tape to Results: Creating a Government that Works Better & Costs Less*, Report of the National Performance Review. (Monograph). US Government Printing Office.

Graeber, David. 2018. *Bullshit Jobs: A Theory.* Simon & Schuster.

Gray, Rosie. 2017. "Behind the Internet's Anti-Democracy Movement." *The Atlantic*, February 10, 2017, tinyurl.com/aftercap085

_____ 2023. "How Bronze Age Pervert Built an Online Following and Injected Anti-Democracy, Pro-Men Ideas Into the GOP." *Politico*, July 16, 2023, tinyurl.com/aftercap086

Gruss, Bertrand and Natalija Novta. 2018. "The Decline in Manufacturing Jobs: Not Necessarily a Cause for Concern." IMF Blog, April 9, 2018, tinyurl.com/aftercap087

Gutierrez-García, Raul, Corina Benjet, Guilherme Borges, Enrique Méndez Ríos, and María Elena Medina-Mora. 2018. "Emerging Adults not in Education, Employment or Training (NEET): Socio-Demographic Characteristics, Mental Health and Reasons for Being NEET." *BMC Public Health*, Oct 25, 2018, tinyurl.com/aftercap088

Habermann, Friederike. 2016. *Ecommony umCARE Zum Miteinander*. Ulrike Helmer.

Hackl, Thomas. 2020. "Mondragón: One of Spain´s Largest Corporations Belongs to its Workers." Scoop.me, March 8, 2020, tinyurl.com/aftercap089

Hahnel, Robin. 2022. *A Participatory Economy*. AK Press.

Hancock, Tom. 2022. "China Wants Young Workers to Love Capitalism Again." *Bloomberg*, July 22, 2023, tinyurl.com/aftercap090

Hannah, Simon. 2019. "The Fight against Climate Change Is a Fight against Capitalism." *Open Democracy*, August 13, tinyurl.com/aftercap091

Hanes, Stephanie. 2022. "How Climate Change 'Doomerism' Fuels Violent Extremism." *The Christian Science Monitor*, May 26, 2022, tinyurl.com/aftercap092

Haque, Umair. 2011. *Betterness: Economics for Humans*. Harvard Business Review Press.

_____ 2020, "Can the Dems Really Defeat Donald Trump and His Army of Idiots?" Medium.com, August 18, 2020.

Harari, Yuval Noah. 2017a. *Homo Deus: A Brief History of Tomorrow*. Kindle Edition. NY: Harper.

_____ 2017b. "The Meaning of Life in a World without Work." *The Guardian*, May 8, 2017, tinyurl.com/aftercap093

Haridy, Rich. 2021. "Iceland's Short Work Week Trial Declared an 'Overwhelming Success'." *New Atlas*, July 6, 2021, tinyurl.com/aftercap094

Harris, Katelynn. 2020. "Forty Years of Falling Manufacturing Employment." *Beyond the Numbers: Employment & Unemployment* 9(16), tinyurl.com/aftercap095

Haskel, Jonathan and Stan Westlake. 2017. *Capitalism without Capital: The Rise of the Intangible Economy*, Kindle Edition. Princeton University Press

Haupt, Michael. 2017. "Project 2030: A Radical Plan to Solve Global Challenges." *Project2030*, August 3, 2017, tinyurl.com/aftercap096

Hawkins, Andrew. 2020. "Uber's Fraught and Deadly Pursuit of Self-Driving Cars Is Over." *The Verge*, Dec 7, 2020, tinyurl.com/aftercap097

Hawksworth, John, Richard Berriman, and Saloni Goel. 2018. *Will Robots Really Steal our Jobs?* Price Waterhouse

Heilbroner, Robert. 1996. *Visions of the Future*. Oxford University Press.

Henderson, Hazel. 2021. "Valuing Love Economies." *Ethical Markets*, June 4, 2021, tinyurl.com/aftercap098

Henderson, Rebecca. 2020, *Reimagining Capitalism in a World on Fire*. Public Affairs.

Heritage Foundation. 2023. Index of Economic Freedom, tinyurl.com/aftercap099

Hermann, Christoph. 2021. *The Critique of Commodification: Contours of a Post-Capitalist Society*. Oxford University Press

Herring, Stephanie, Nikolaos Christidis, Andrew Hoell, James Kossin, Carl Schreck, and Peter Stott, Eds. 2018. *Explaining Extreme Events of 2016 from a Climate Perspective*, Special Supplement to the *Bulletin of the American Meteorological Society* 99(1), January.

Heymans, Amy. 2022. Personal communication, March 22, 2022.

Hickel, Jason. 2019. "Bill Gates Says Poverty Is Decreasing. He Couldn't Be More Wrong." *The Guardian*, January 29, 2019, tinyurl.com/aftercap100

_____ 2021. *Less is More: How Degrowth Will Save the World*. Random House

Hines, Andy. 2005. "Limits to Growth: The 30-Year Update." *Foresight* 7(4), 51-53.

_____ 2011. *ConsumerShift: How Changing Values Are Reshaping the Consumer Landscape*. No Limit Publishing.

_____ 2012. *The Role of an Organizational Futurist in Integrating Foresight into Organizations* (Unpublished doctoral dissertation). Leeds Metropolitan University.

_____ 2013. "Shifting Values: Hope and Concern for 'Waking Up.'" *On the Horizon* 21(3), 187-196.

_____ 2014, September/October. "A Training Ground for Professional Futurists." *The Futurist* 43.

_____ 2015. "The End of Work as We Know It." *Career Planning and Adult Development Journal*, Summer, 10-19.

_____ 2016, Fall. "Preparing for the Unknown: Anticipating the Future Economy." *MISC*, 118-119.

_____ 2017a. "Emerging Student Needs Disrupting Higher Education." *On the Horizon* 25(3), 197-208

_____ 2017b, June. *The Future of Work*. NASA Langley Research Center.

_____ 2019. "Ten Things we could do if we did not have to Work." *Hinesight*, April 17, 2019, tinyurl.com/aftercap101

_____ 2020a. "The Evolution of Framework Foresight" *Foresight* 22, 643-651. tinyurl.com/aftercap102

_____ 2020b. "Change Is Slower than We Think." *Hinesight*, Sept 1, 2020,

_____ 2022. "Aligned and in Motion." *Hinesight*, June 22, 2022, tinyurl.com/aftercap103

_____ 2023. "Profit or Purpose? Open AI & After Capitalism." *Hinesight*, November 23, 2023, tinyurl.com/aftercap104

Hines, Andy and Peter Bishop. 2013. "Framework Foresight: Exploring Futures the Houston Way." *Futures* 51, 31-49.

Hines, Andy and Peter Bishop. 2015. *Thinking about the Future: Guidelines for Strategic Foresight*, 2nd edition. Hinesight.

Hines, Andy, Jay Gary, Cornelia Daheim, and Luke van der Laan. 2017. "Building Foresight Capacity: Toward a Foresight Competency Model." *World Futures Review* 9(3), 123-141.

Hines, Andy, Adam Cowart, Denise Worrell, Lavonne Leong, Heather Benoit, and Laura Schlehuber. 2024. "Mapping Archetype Scenarios across the Three Horizons." *Futures*, Accepted for publication, June 16, 2024.

Hoffman, Nick. 2018. "The Gatekeepers Must Go: How Disintermediation Is Changing Business Models." Medium.com, Jan 8, 2018, tinyurl.com/aftercap105

Hollo, Tim. 2018. "Tim Hollo on an Ecological Democracy where "Everything Is Connected" and Embedded in Nature." *The Fifth Estate*, March 1, 2018, tinyurl.com/aftercap106

Homer-Dixon, Thomas. 2006. *The Upside of Down: Catastrophe, Creativity, and the Renewal of Civilization*. Island Press

Hudson, Michael. 2016. "Fix our Debt Addiction to Fix our Economy." Michael-Hudson.com, April 20, 2016, tinyurl.com/aftercap107

Human Rights Watch. 2021. "Brazil: Bolsonaro Threatens Democratic Rule," Sept 15, 2021, tinyurl.com/aftercap108

Hurst, Aaron. 2016. *The Purpose Economy, Expanded and Updated: How Your Desire for Impact, Personal Growth and Community Is Changing the World*. Elevate Publishing

Hussain, Murtaza. 2022. "The Importance of Bronze Age Pervert." *UnHerd*, January 25, 2022, tinyurl.com/aftercap109

Hyatt, Diccon. 2023. "Think Inflation Is Bad in the US?" *Investopedia*, March 22, 2023, tinyurl.com/aftercap110

Irwin, Neil. 2016. "With 'Gigs' Instead of Jobs, Workers Bear New Burdens." *New York Times*, March 31, 2016.

Illing, Sean. 2019. "Why Are Millennials Burned Out? Capitalism." *Vox*, March 16, 2019.

Inayatullah, Sohail. 1998. "Causal layered analysis: Poststructuralism as Method" *Futures* 30(8) 815-829

_____ 2008. "Six Pillars: Futures Thinking for Transforming." *Foresight* 10(1), 4-21.

Inglehart, Ronald. 2000. "Globalization and Postmodern Values." *The Washington Quarterly*, 23(1), 215-228.

_____ 2018. *Cultural Evolution: People's Motivations are Changing, and Reshaping the World.* Cambridge University Press.

International Labour Organization. 2019. "A Human-Centred Agenda Needed for a Decent Future of Work." *ILO*, January 22, 2019, tinyurl.com/aftercap111

_____ 2023. "How Are Trade Unions Adapting to Changes in the World of Work?"

Istvan, Zoltan. 2016. "Forget Trump, Zoltan Istvan Wants to Be the 'Anti-Death' President." *Wired*, Nov 8, 2016, tinyurl.com/aftercap112

Jackson, Tim. 2015. *Prosperity without Growth? The Transition to a Sustainable Economy.* Np: Sustainable Development Commission.

_____ 2021. *Post-Growth: Life after Capitalism.* Polity.

Jamaluddin, Mushfiqa. 2021. Email communication, Dec 2, 2021.

Jie, Soo Sze. 2020 "Platform Capitalism: A Data Revolution." *The Boar*, July 31, 2020, tinyurl.com/aftercap113

Johnson, Khari. 2017. "Pew Study Experts: Artificial intelligence Threatens the Future of Capitalism." *VB (Venture Beat)*, May 5, 2017, tinyurl.com/aftercap114

Jones, Owen. 2021. "Eat the Rich! Why Millennials and Generation Z Have Turned their Backs on Capitalism." *The Guardian*, Sept 20, 2021, tinyurl.com/aftercap115

Joyce, Kathryn. 2022. "Who is Nick Fuentes? A Young White Nationalist Who Hopes to Pull the GOP all the way to Hitler." Salon.com, March 2, 2022, tinyurl.com/aftercap116

Kallis, Giorgos, Federico Demaria & Giacomo D'Alisa. 2015. "Introduction: Degrowth." In Giacomo D'Alisa, Federico Demaria & Giorgos Kallis, Eds. *Degrowth: A Vocabulary for a New Era*, Routledge

Katz, Lawrence. 2014. "The Coming Artisan Economy." *Making Sen$e, PBS Newshour*, July 15, 2014, tinyurl.com/aftercap117

Katz, Bruce, and Jeremy Nowak. 2018. *The New Localism*. Brookings Inst. Press.

Kauffman, Draper and Morgan Kauffman. 2021. *Systems 1: An Introduction to Systems Thinking,* 4th Edition. Center for Systems and Public Policy.

Keller, Megan. 2018. "Warren Introduces Accountable Capitalism Act." *The Hill*, Aug 15, 2018, tinyurl.com/aftercap118

Khan, Razib. 2021. "Why the West Lost India's Culture Wars," UnHerd, April 14, 2021, tinyurl.com/aftercap119

Kim, Daniel. 2018. "Success to the Successful: Self-Fulfilling Prophecies." *Systems Thinker*, tinyurl.com/aftercap120

Kim, Whizy. 2022. "The Young, Rich, Anti-Capitalists." *Vox*, May 31, 2022, tinyurl.com/aftercap121

Kimmerer, Robin Wall. 2020, December. "The Serviceberry: An Economy of Abundance." *Emergence Magazine*, tinyurl.com/aftercap122

Knights, Sam. 2021. "Saving the World from Capitalism by Taking Power." *Jacobin*, April 29, 2021, tinyurl.com/aftercap123

Kottasova, Ivana. 2020. "The Sixth Mass Extinction Is Happening Faster than Expected. Scientists Say it's our Fault." CNN.com, June 1, 2020, tinyurl.com/aftercap124

Koty, Alexander Chipman. 2021. "China's Circular Economy: Understanding the New Five Year Plan." *China Briefing*, July 16, 2021, tinyurl.com/aftercap125

Kurzweil, Ray. 2005. *The Singularity Is Near: When Humans Transcend Biology.* The Viking Press.

Lamb, Jeffrey. 2020. "B Corporations: A Potential Path to a Better Form of Capitalism?" *Real Clear Markets*, Dec 28, 2020, tinyurl.com/aftercap126

Lanier, Jaron. 2013. *Who Owns the Future?* Simon & Schuster.
Le Blanc, David. 2012. *Back to Our Common Future: Sustainable Development in the 21st Century,* (SD21) Project (Summary for policymakers). United Nations.
Leguichard, Stephanie. 2021. "Here's Why Bill Gates' "Solutions" to Climate Change are Utterly Foolish." Medium.com, Oct 4, 2021, tinyurl.com/aftercap127
Lepore, Jill. 2017. "No, We Cannot." *The New Yorker* 93(16), 102.
Lessig, Lawrence. 2008. *Remix: Making Art and Commerce Thrive in the Hybrid Economy.* Penguin.
Levitz, Eric. 2019. "The One Percent Have Gotten $21 Trillion Richer Since 1989. The Bottom 50% Have Gotten Poorer." *Inequality,* June 16, 2019.
_____ 2022. "Modern Capitalism Is Weirder Than You Think. *New York Magazine*, March 15, 2022, tinyurl.com/aftercap128
Lewis, Matt. 2022. "Why Right-Wing Traditionalism Is So Appealing to So Many." *Daily Beast*, Oct 1, 2022, tinyurl.com/aftercap129
Linke, Rebecca. 2018. "Negative Income Tax, Explained." *MIT Management Sloan School*, Feb 7, 2018, tinyurl.com/aftercap130
Livingston, Eve. 2022. "Why We Need to Let Go of the Side Hustle." *Vice*, April 8, 2022, tinyurl.com/aftercap131
Llach, Laura. 2023. "Spain Isn't Bowing to the Rise of the Far-Right in the EU. Why?" *Euronews*, July 27, 2023, tinyurl.com/aftercap132
Loh, Penn and Sarah Jimenez. 2017. *Solidarity Rising in Massachusetts: How Solidarity Economy Movement Is Emerging in Lower-Income Communities of Color,* Solidarity Economy Initiative, tinyurl.com/aftercap133
Lomas, Natasha. 2021. "Europe Lays Out a Plan to Flip the Odds on Gig Economy Exploitation". TechCrunch, Dec 9, 2021, tinyurl.com/aftercap134
Lu, Marcus. 2020. "Is the American Dream Over? Here's What the Data Says." *World Economic Forum*, September 2, 2020, tinyurl.com/aftercap135
Lubell, Sam. 2020. "How Milan's Bosco Verticale Has Changed the Way Designers Think About Sustainable Design." *Architectural Digest*, Nov 3, 2020, tinyurl.com/aftercap136
Lyman, Eric. 2021. "The IPCC Climate Report Offers Dire Warnings — And a Last, Best Chance to Minimize the Damage." *Fortune*, August 9, 2021.
Lyotard, Jean-François. 1984. *The Postmodern Condition: A Report on Knowledge.* University of Minnesota Press.
MacAskill, William. 2022. *What We Owe the Future.* Basic Books.
Mackey, John and Raj Sisodia. 2013. *Conscious Capitalism: Liberating the Heroic Spirit of Business.* Harvard Business Review Press.
Maclurcan, Donnie. 2016. "How on Earth: The Future is Not for Profit." *Post Growth Institute*, November 30, 2016, tinyurl.com/aftercap137
Magnuson, Joel. 2013. *Approaching the Great Transformation: Toward a Livable Post Carbon Economy.* Seven Stories Press
Marcus, Ezra. 2020. "In the Autonomous Zones." *New York Times,* July 1, 2020.
Martinko, Katherine. 2021. "The 'Buy Nothing Project' Began as a Social Experiment. Now It's a Global Movement." *Treehugger*, March 31, 2021, tinyurl.com/aftercap139
Marx, Karl, and Friedrich Engels. 2011 (1848). *The Communist Manifesto.* Penguin. Cited in Clark, Taylor. 2021. "Capitalism Will Die, It's Up to Us to Choose How." *Daily Nexus* (University of California, Santa Barbara), June 8, 2021, tinyurl.com/aftercap140
Marx de Salcedo, Anastacia. 2019. "How Men and Women Spend Their Time." *The Atlantic*, June 26, 2019, tinyurl.com/aftercap141

Masini, Eleonora Barbieri and Bart Van Steenbergen. 1983. "Introduction." In Elanora Barbieri Masini and Van Bart Steenbergen (Eds.). *Visions of Desirable Societies*. Pergamon Press, 3-8.

Masini, Eleonora Barbieri. 1993. *Why Futures Studies*. London: Grey Seal Books.

Mason, Paul. 2015. *Postcapitalism: A Guide to Our Future*. Farrar, Straus & Giroux.

Mastini, Riccardo. 2017. "Degrowth: The Case for a New Economic Paradigm." *Resilience*, June 12, 2017, tinyurl.com/aftercap142

Matthews, Lipton. 2021. "Understanding Inequality Requires Much More Than Calling Everything Racist." *Eurasia Review*, January 18, 2021, https://tinyurl.com/aftercap143

Mayer-Schonberger, Viktor and Thomas Ramge. 2018. *Reinventing Capitalism in the Age of Big Data*. Basic Books. Kindle Edition.

McBride, Mina. 2022. "An Open Letter to Futurists and Change Agents," LinkedIn, March 12, 2022, tinyurl.com/aftercap144

McBrien, Justin. 2019. "This Is Not the Sixth Extinction. It's the First Extermination Event." *Truthout*, September 14, 2019, tinyurl.com/aftercap145

McDonough, William and Michael Braungart. 2010. *Cradle to Cradle: Remaking the Way We Make Things*. North Point Press.

_____ 2013. *The Upcycle: Beyond Sustainability: Designing for Abundance*. North Point Press.

McGuire, Robert. 2018. "Ultimate Guide to Gig Economy Data: A Summary of Every Freelance Survey We Can Find." *Nation1099*, May 11, 2018, tinyurl.com/aftercap146

McKeever, Chuck. 2021. "You're Not Lazy — But Your Boss Wants You to Think You Are." *Jacobin*, February 4, 2021, tinyurl.com/aftercap147

McKibben, Bill. 2008. *Deep Economy: The Wealth of Communities and the Durable Future*. St. Martin's Griffin.

McKinsey Global Institute. 2016. *Poorer Than Their Parents? Flat or Falling Incomes in Advanced Economies* (July). McKinsey.

Meadows, Donella, 1997. "Places to Intervene in a System." *Whole Earth*, Winter.

Meadows, Donella, Dennis Meadows, Jorgen Randers, and William Behrens. 1972. *The Limits to Growth*. Potomac Associates - Universe Books.

Meadows, Donella, Dennis Meadows, and Jorgen Randers. 1993. *Beyond the Limits: Confronting Global Collapse, Envisioning a Sustainable Future*. Chelsea Green Publishing Co.

Meadows, Donella, Jorgen Randers, and Dennis Meadows. 2004. *The Limits to Growth: The 30-Year Update*. Chelsea Green Publishing Co.

Medina Vasquez, Javier. 2003. *Vision Compartida de Futuro*. Univ del Valle.

Menezes, Murilo Johas. 2019. "Can We Create an Empathic Alternative to the Capitalist System?" *Big Think*, October, 9, 2019, tinyurl.com/aftercap148

Merchant, Brian. 2020. "Coronavirus Is Speeding Up the Amazonification of the Planet." *OneZero*, March 19, 2020, tinyurl.com/aftercap149

Meza, Summer. 2017. "Black Lives Matter Wants to Bring Down White Capitalism With 'Black Christmas'. *Newsweek*, Nov 28, 2017, tinyurl.com/aftercap150

Michaels, Jon. 2015. "Running Government Like a Business . . . Then and Now." (Book Review). *Harvard Law Review* 128(4), 1152-1182.

Michalski, Jerry. n.d. "What Is the Relationship Economy?" *Rex*, tinyurl.com/aftercap151

Mikulka, Justin. 2018. "How Wall Street Enabled the Fracking 'Revolution' That's Losing Billions." *Ecowatch*, May 7, 2018, tinyurl.com/aftercap152

Ministry of the Environment of Japan. 2010. *Satoyama Initiative*, October, tinyurl.com/aftercap153

Miller, Riel. 2006. "Equity in a twenty-first century learning intensive society: Is schooling part of the solution?" *Foresight* 8(4), 13-22.

Molitor, Graham. 1999. "The Next 1,000 Years: The 'Big Five' Engines of Economic Growth." *The Futurist*, December, 13-18.

Monbiot, George. 2016. "Neoliberalism: The Ideology at the Root of all our Problems". *The Guardian*, April 16, 2016.

Monetta.org. N.d. "LETS and Time Banks." *Monetta.org: Network for Monetary Diversity*, tinyurl.com/aftercap154

Moore, Geoffrey. 1991. *Crossing the Chasm*. Harper Business Essentials.

Moore, Noah. 2021. "GameStop Stock Manipulation Exemplifies Disillusionment with Capitalism." *Indiana Daily Student*, Jan 31, 2021, tinyurl.com/aftercap155

More, Max. 2013. "The Philosophy of Transhumanism." In Max More and Natasha Vita-More, Eds. *Transhumanist Reader: Classical and Contemporary Essays on the Science, Technology, and Philosophy of the Human Future*. Wiley-Blackwell, 1-17.

Morgan, Tim. 2017. "Values-Driven STEEP Entities." *Houston Foresight*, June 22, 2017, tinyurl.com/aftercap156

Morris, David. 2016. "Ray Kurzweil: Here's Why Solar Will Dominate Energy within 12 Years." *Fortune*, April 27, 2016.

Morrison, Rose. 2023. "The Global Housing Crisis: Facts, Figures, and Solutions." *Unsustainable*, July 11, 2023, tinyurl.com/aftercap157

Motani, Kosuke. 2017. "Satoyama Offers a Chance to Narrow Economic Gaps." *Japan Times*, Dec 31.

National Academy of Sciences, Committee on Extreme Weather Events and Climate Change Attribution Board on Atmospheric Sciences and Climate. 2016. *Attribution of Extreme Weather Events in the Context of Climate Change*. National Academies Press.

Nelson, Anitra. 2022. *Beyond Money: A Postcapitalist Strategy*. Pluto Press.

Network Capitalism. 2018. Manifesto, tinyurl.com/aftercap158

Newport, Frank. 2018. "Democrats More Positive about Socialism than Capitalism." *Gallup*, August 13, 2018, tinyurl.com/aftercap159

Noor, Saleha. 2020. "Why We Need to Change Capitalism for Climate Action." *Earth.org*, July 30, 2020, tinyurl.com/aftercap160

Nugent, Ciara. 2021. "Amsterdam Is Embracing a Radical New Economic Theory to Help Save the Environment. Could It Also Replace Capitalism?" *Time*, January 22, 2021, tinyurl.com/aftercap161

Oberhaus, Daniel. 2017. "A World Bank Report Found that Two-Thirds of all Jobs in the Developing World Face Being Automated Out of Existence." *The Outline*, March 29, 2017, tinyurl.com/aftercap162

O'Connell, Mark. 2018. "Review of A History of the World in Seven Cheap Things — How Capitalism Works." *The Guardian*, June 14, 2018, tinyurl.com/aftercap163

O'Hehir, Andrew. 2018. "Is the Global Economy Just a Giant Debt Scam? What the Financial Elite Doesn't Want You to Know." Salon.com, June 9, 2018.

O'Keefe, Derrick. 2020. "Imagining the End of Capitalism with Kim Stanley Robinson." *Jacobin*, October 22, 2020, tinyurl.com/aftercap164

Ongweso, Edward. (2022). "Plastic Recycling Is a Disaster and a 'Myth,' Report Says." *Vice*, October 24, 2022, tinyurl.com/aftercap165

Ostrom, Elinor. 1990. *Governing the Commons: The Evolution of Institutions for Collective Action*. Cambridge University Press

_____ 1999. "Private and Common Property Rights." In Boudewijn Bouckaert and Gerrit De Geest, Eds. *Encyclopedia of Law and Economics*, 332-379.

_____ 2000. "Collective Action and the Evolution of Social Norms." *Journal of Economic Perspectives* 14(3), 137-158.

_____ 2009. "Design Principles of Robust Property Rights Institutions: What Have We Learned?" In: Gregory Ingram and Yu-Hung Hong, Eds. *Property Rights and Land Policies*. Lincoln Institute of Land Policy, 25-51.

Our Changing Climate, 2021. "Why Solarpunk Gives Me Hope for the Future." *EcoWatch*, September 28, 2021, tinyurl.com/aftercap166

Owyang, Jeremiah and Alexandra Samuel. 2015. *The New Rules of the Collaborative Economy*. Vision Critical.

Pabst, Adrian. 2023. "Capitalism Is Driving the Culture Wars." *The New Statesman*, September 5, 2023, tinyurl.com/aftercap167

Painter, Anthony. 2017. "Universal Basic Services or Universal Basic Income?" RSA, Oct 17, 2017, tinyurl.com/aftercap168

Palmer, Liz. 2021. "Stop Monetizing your Happiness." *The Torch* (Valparaiso Univ), April 18, 2021.

Parkins, Keith. 2017. "Universal Dividend." *Medium*, February 11, 2017, tinyurl.com/aftercap169

Patel, Raj and Jason Moore. 2017. "Unearthing the Capitalocene: Towards a Reparations Ecology." *Roar*, Issue #7, Autumn

Patten, Terry. 2018. *A New Republic of the Heart: An Ethos for Revolutionaries*. North Atlantic Books

Pauli, Gunter. 2010. *The Blue Economy. A Report to the Club of Rome*

Perez, Carlota, 2002. *Technological Revolutions and Financial Capital: The Dynamics of Bubbles and Golden Ages*. Edward Elgar

Peters, Adele. 2018. "Why Panera's Experiment with Pay-What-You-Want Dining Failed." *Fast Company*, June 8, 2018, tinyurl.com/aftercap170

_____ 2020. "Public Transport Will Now Be Free in Luxembourg." *Fast Company*, Feb 27, 2020, tinyurl.com/aftercap171

Piketty, Thomas. 2014. *Capital in the Twenty-First Century*. Belknap Press.

Pine, Joe and James Gilmore. 1998. "Welcome to the Experience Economy." *Harvard Business Review*, July/August, 97-105.

Pogue, James. 2022. "Inside the New Right, Where Peter Thiel is Placing His Biggest Bets." *Vanity Fair*, April 20, 2022, tinyurl.com/aftercap172

Polak, Fred. 1973. *The Image of the Future*. Elsevier

Polychroniou, C. J. 2021. "Is Saving the Planet Under Capitalism Really Possible?" *Global Policy*, April 20, 2021, tinyurl.com/aftercap173

Posner, Richard. 1974, May. *Theories of Economic Regulation*. NBER Working Paper No. w0041, tinyurl.com/aftercap174

Quinn, Megan. 2021. "California Governor Signs Full Slate of Circular Economy Bills." WasteDive, Oct 6, 2021, tinyurl.com/aftercap175

Radjou, Navi and Jaideep Prabhu. 2015. "The Rise of the Frugal Economy." *Project Syndicate*, Feb 6, 2015, tinyurl.com/aftercap176

Ramirez, Vanessa Bates, 2023. "The World's Biggest Guaranteed Income Trial Will Launch in India This Year." *Singularity Hub*, March 29, 2023, tinyurl.com/aftercap177

Rand, Ayn. 2007. *Atlas Shrugged*. Penguin Classics.

Randers, Jorgen. 2012. *2052: A Global Forecast for the Next Forty Years*. Chelsea Green.

Raworth, Kate. 2017. *Doughnut Economics: Seven Ways to Think like a 21st Century Economist*. Chelsea Green Publishing

Reedy, Christianna. 2017. "Kurzweil Claims That the Singularity Will Happen by 2045," *Futurism*, October 5, 2017, tinyurl.com/aftercap178

Reese, Byron. 2019. "AI Will Create Millions More Jobs Than It Will Destroy. Here's How." *Singularity Hub*, January 1, 2019, tinyurl.com/aftercap179

Reetz, Allan. 2019. "The Next Economy Will Be a Cooperative Economy." *Co-Op News*, October 24, 2019, tinyurl.com/aftercap180

Reich, Robert. 2013. *Aftershock: The Next Economy and America's Future*. Vintage.

_____ 2022. "Facing America's Second Civil War." *LA Progressive*, May 6, 2022, tinyurl.com/aftercap181

Reno, Kaleigh. 2020. "Legislation's Role in Creating a Resilient Circular Economy." *Sustainable Packaging Coalition*, November 1, 2020.

Rifkin, Jeremy. 1994. *The End of Work*. Tarcher/Penguin.

_____ 2014. *The Zero Marginal Cost Society: The Internet of Things, the Collaborative Commons, and the Eclipse of Capitalism*. St. Martin's Press.

Roberts, Michael. 2021. "The US Rate of Profit in 2020." *Michael Roberts Blog*, Dec 5, 2021, tinyurl.com/aftercap182

Robinson, William. 2020. "A Global Police State Is Emerging as World Capitalism Descends Into Crisis." *Truthout*, Nov 28, 2020, tinyurl.com/aftercap183

_____ 2022. "Mass Protest Is Rising — Can It Confront Global Capitalism? *Truthout*, May 14, 2022, tinyurl.com/aftercap184

Rock, Julia. 2022. "Biden Is Aiming to Destroy a Historic Climate Change Lawsuit." *Jacobin*, May 26, 2022, tinyurl.com/aftercap185

Rogers, E. (1976). "New Product Adoption and Diffusion." *Journal of Consumer Research* 2(4), 290-301.

Rothbard, Murray. 2021. "Should the Police Be Privatized?" *The Punching Bag Post*, July 9, 2021, tinyurl.com/aftercap186

Rottenberg, Catherine. 2018. *The Rise of Neoliberal Feminism*. Oxford Scholarship Online.

Ruiz, Jorge. 2021. "Reinventing Capitalism: Why We Need to Move Toward Guaranteed Income." *Harvard Political Review*, April 16, 2021.

Rushkoff, Douglas. n.d. "Commodified vs. Commoditized." *Rushkoff*, tinyurl.com/aftercap187

Saed, Null. 2021. "Anti-Communism and the Hundreds of Millions of Victims of Capitalism, *Capitalism Nature Socialism* 32(1), 1-17.

Samuel, Sigal. 2020. "Everywhere Basic Income Has Been Tried, in One Map." *Vox*, Oct 20, 2020, tinyurl.com/aftercap188

Samuelson, Robert. 2017. "Economic Cannibalism." *Investor's Business Daily*, Oct 8, 2017.

Santens, Scott. 2015. "Everything You Think You Know About the History and Future of Jobs Is Likely Wrong." *Huffington Post*, Aug 20, 2015, tinyurl.com/aftercap189

Sato, Mia. 2022. "Buy Nothing Exploded on Facebook — Now It Wants a Platform of Its Own." *The Verge*, January 12, 2022, tinyurl.com/aftercap190

Satter, Raphael and Diane Bartz. 2023. "US, Britain, other Countries Ink Agreement to Make AI 'Secure by Design'," *Reuters*, November 27, 2023, tinyurl.com/aftercap191

Savage, Maddy. 2018. "Thousands of Swedes Are Inserting Microchips under their Skin." *NPR*, Oct 22

Scharmer, Otto. 2013. *Leading from the Emerging Future: From Ego-System to Eco-System Economies*. Berrett-Koehler

Schiener, Dominik. 2015. "Liquid Democracy: True Democracy for the 21st Century." Medium.com, Nov 23, 2015, tinyurl.com/aftercap192

Schmelzer, Matthias, Aaron Vansintjan, and Andrea Vetter. 2022. *The Future Is Degrowth: A Guide to a World beyond Capitalism*. Verso.

Schofield, Daisy. 2022. "How Capitalism Is Destroying your Friendships." *Vice*, Feb 2, 2022, tinyurl.com/aftercap193

Schor, Juliet. 2014. "Debating the Sharing Economy." *Great Transition Initiative*, October. tinyurl.com/aftercap194

Schroeder, Karl. 2019. *Stealing Worlds.* Tor Books

Schultz, Wendy. 2016. "Images of the Future." Lecture Series, University of Houston, Summer 2016.

Schwab, Klaus. 2016. *The Fourth Industrial Revolution: What it Means, how to Respond.* World Economic Forum

Schweickart, David. 2011. *After Capitalism*, 2nd Ed., Rowman & Littlefield.

Scott, Brett. 2017. "Reversing the Lies of the Sharing Economy." *How We Get to Next*, April 6, 2017, tinyurl.com/aftercap195

Semuels, Alana. 2020. "Millions of Americans Have Lost Jobs in the Pandemic -- And Robots and AI Are Replacing Them Faster Than Ever." *Time*, August 6, 2020, tinyurl.com/aftercap196

Shareable. 2017. "How Food Assembly Created a Sustainable, Community-driven Food Sharing System in Europe." *P2P Foundation*, Sept 16, 2017, tinyurl.com/aftercap197

Sharpe, Bill. 2013 (2020). *Three Horizons: The Patterning of Hope.* (Second Ed.) Triarchy Press.

Shaw, Ian and Marv Waterstone. 2020. *Wageless Life: A Manifesto for a Future beyond Capitalism.* University of Minnesota Press.

Shead, Sam. 2021. "Silicon Valley Leaders Think A.I. Will One Day Fund Free Cash Handouts. But Experts Aren't Convinced." *CNBC*, March 31, 2021, tinyurl.com/aftercap247

Shipley, Robert. 2002. "Visioning in Planning: Is the Practice Based on Sound Theory?" *Environment and Planning* 34(1), 7-22

Siegel, Eric. 2013. *Predictive Analytics: The Power to Predict Who Will Click, Buy, Lie, or Die.* Wiley.

Simms, Andrew. 2019. "History of the Green New Deal." *The Green New Deal Group*, tinyurl.com/aftercap198

Simon, Julian. 1981. *The Ultimate Resource.* Princeton University Press.

Singularity Group. 2022. Our Mission, tinyurl.com/aftercap199

Sivaramakrishnan Arvind. 2021. "Welcome to Planet Rentier." *The Hindu Business Line*, April 4.

Slaughter, Anne-Marie, Roy Bahat, and Kristin Sharp. 2016. *Shift: The Commission on Work, Workers, and Technology.* New America & Bloomberg.

Slaughter, Richard. 2020. "Farewell Alternative Futures?" *Futures* 121, 102496.

Sledge, Collin. 2020. "Introduction to Capital & Ideology by Thomas Piketty." *Medium*, March 28, 2020, tinyurl.com/aftercap200

Sledge, Collin. 2020. "Capital & Ideology Part Four." *Medium*, July 26, 2020, tinyurl.com/aftercap201

Smart, John M. 2015. *The Foresight Guide: Predicting, Creating, and Leading in the 21st Century.* Foresight University

Spinney, Laura. 2020. "'Humans Weren't Always Here. We could Disappear:' Meet the Collapsologists." *The Guardian*, Oct 11, 2020, tinyurl.com/aftercap202

Srinivasan, Bhu. 2017. "Capitalism Isn't an Ideology, it's an Operating System." *TEDNYC*, tinyurl.com/aftercap203

Srnicek, Nick and Alex Williams. 2016. *Inventing the Future: Postcapitalism and a World without Work.* Brooklyn, Verso Books. Kindle Edition

Stahel, Walter. 2019. *The Circular Economy: A User's Guide.* Routledge

Standing, Guy. 2014. *A Precariat Charter: From Denizens to Citizens.* Bloomsbury Publishing.

Standing, Guy. 2018. "Why the World Should Adopt a Basic Income." *The Economist*, July 4, 2018, tinyurl.com/aftercap204

Stanford Basic Income Lab. ND. Map of Universal Basic Income Experiments and Related Programs. tinyurl.com/aftercap301

Stephenson, Neal. 2000. *The Diamond Age: Or, a Young Lady's Illustrated Primer.* Bantam.

Sterelny, Kim. 2021. "How Equality Slipped Away." *Aeon*, June 10, 2021, tinyurl.com/aftercap205

Sterling, Bruce. 1995. *Heavy Weather*. Bantam

Steverman, Ben. 2019. "The Wealth Detective Who Finds the Hidden Money of the Super Rich." *Bloomberg Businessweek*, May 23, 2019, tinyurl.com/aftercap206

Stewart, Matthew. 2018. "The Birth of the New American Aristocracy." *The Atlantic* 322(2), 8-12.

Streeck, Wolfgang. 2014. "How Will Capitalism End?" *New Left Review* 87, May-June, 35-64.

Streeck, Wolfgang and John Pilger. 2016. *How Will Capitalism End? Essays on a Failing System*. Verso.

Sullivan, Kate. 2019. "Here are the 4 Congresswomen Known as 'The Squad' Targeted by Trump's Racist Tweets." *CNN.com*, July 16, 2019, tinyurl.com/aftercap207

Sundararajan, Arun. 2016. *The Sharing Economy: The End of Employment and the Rise of Crowd-Based Capitalism*. MIT Press, Kindle Edition.

Swenson, Rob. 2020. "Employee Ownership: The Growing Trend of ESOPs." *TeamTSP*, April 6, 2020, tinyurl.com/aftercap208

Swift, Trisha and Susan Hannon. 2010. "Critical Thresholds Associated with Habitat Loss: A Review of the Concepts, Evidence, and Applications." *Biological Reviews* 85(1), 35-53.

Tangermann, Victor. 2023. "CEO Fires 90 Percent of Support Staff, Saying AI Outperforms Them." *The Byte*, July 12, 2023, tinyurl.com/aftercap209

Taylor, Daniel. 2020. "David Graeber's Anarchism and the Occupy Movement." *Red Flag*, September 5, 2020, tinyurl.com/aftercap210

Tegmark, Max. 2018. *Life 3.0: Being Human in the Age of Artificial Intelligence*. Vintage.

Tepper, Jonathan and Denise Hearn. 2018. *The Myth of Capitalism: Monopolies and the Death of Competition*. Wiley.

The Economist. 2018. "After Decades of Triumph, Democracy Is Losing Ground." June 14, 2018, tinyurl.com/aftercap211

The Future Hunters. 2015. *The Metaspace Economy*. Weiner, Edrich, Brown.

The News Scroll. 2018. "Yunus Says Capitalism Can't Create Sustainable Nations." July 2, 2018, tinyurl.com/aftercap212

The World Counts. 2022. "Number of Planet Earths We Need," tinyurl.com/aftercap213

Thomas, Leigh and Myriam Rivet. 2019. "Inequality Could Crush Capitalism, French Finance Minister Warns." *Reuters*, Jan 22, 2019, tinyurl.com/aftercap214

Tong, Goh Chiew. 2022. "'I Accept Being Ordinary': China's Youth Are Turning their Backs on Hustle Culture." *CNBC*, Oct 9, 2022, tinyurl.com/aftercap215

Travel Earth. 2010. "What is an Ecovillage? Here Are Some of the Best International Ecovillages." Medium, March 10, 2020, tinyurl.com/aftercap216

UBI Works. 2021. "How to Pay for Recovery UBI." *UBI Works*, Feb 2, 2021, tinyurl.com/aftercap217

UNDESA. 2013. *A Guidebook to the Green Economy Issue 2: Exploring Green Economy Principles*. UN Division for Sustainable Development (UNDESA).

UNIDOHappiness. 2019. "United Nations New Economic Paradigm Calls on all People & all Nations to Adopt 'Happytalism' over Capitalism." *GlobeNewsWire*, April 22, 2019

United Nations. 2015. *Transforming our World: The 2030 Agenda for Sustainable Development*, A/RES/70/. United Nations.

Upwork and Freelancers Union. "Freelancing in America in 2020." Lili, Feb 14, 2020, tinyurl.com/aftercap218

Urie, Rob. 2019. "Toward an Eco-Socialist Revolution." *Counterpunch*, July 12, 2019, tinyurl.com/aftercap219

_____ 2020. "Capitalism and the Green New Deal." *Counterpunch*, Dec 11, tinyurl.com/aftercap220

Ustek-Spilda, Funda, Fabian Ferrari, Matt Cole, Pablo Reneses Aguera & Mark Graham. 2020. "The Infrastructural Power of Platform Capitalism." *Social Europe*, Dec 16, tinyurl.com/aftercap221

Van Alstyne, Marshall, Geoffrey Parker and Sangeet Choudary. 2016. "Pipelines, Platforms, and the New Rules of Strategy." *Harvard Business Review*, April, 54-62.

Van der Duin, Patrick (Ed.). 2009. *Knowing Tomorrow? How Science Deals with the Future*, 2nd edition. Eburon Publishers.

Various. 2002. "The Transhumanist Declaration." *Humanity Plus*, tinyurl.com/aftercap222

Vaughan, Gareth. 2021. "RIP Capitalism & the Free Market as We Knew Them." *Interest.co.nz*, Dec 5, 2021, tinyurl.com/aftercap223

Vibes, John. 2017. "Does Hydraulic Fracking Trigger Earthquakes? Officials Caught Forcing Scientist to Alter Findings." *Global Research*, Nov 22, tinyurl.com/aftercap224

Victor, Peter. 2008. *Managing Without Growth: Slower by Design, Not Disaster*. Edward Elgar Pub.

Vita-More, Natasha. 2018. *Transhumanism: What Is It?* Bowker.

Wichmann, Jonathan. 2018. "Regenerative Capitalism Is Coming: A Conversation with … John Fullerton." *Jonathanwichmann.com*, October 31, 2018, tinyurl.com/aftercap225

Wilber, Ken. 2000. *A Theory of Everything: An Integral Vision for Business, Politics, Science, and Spirituality*. Shambhala.

_____ 2003. *Boomeritis: A Novel that Will Set you Free*. Shambhala.

Wilkinson, Richard and Kate Pickett. 2009. *The Spirit Level: Why More Equal Societies Almost Always Do Better*. Allen Lane.

Williams, Terri. 2022. "Can B Corporations Save Capitalism?" *Economist Education*, tinyurl.com/aftercap226

Wilson, Richard. 2022. "An Introduction to Sovereign Wealth Funds." *Investopedia*, Jan 31, 2022, tinyurl.com/aftercap227

Wolff, Richard. 2020. "Why Capitalism Is in Constant Conflict with Democracy." *Alternet*, Aug 7, 2020, tinyurl.com/aftercap228

Wolff, Richard. 2021. "How Capitalism's Dogged Defenders and Propagandists Defend it." *New Age*, Jan 26

Wood, Robert. 2020. "Uber & Lyft Ordered to Treat Drivers as Employees, Are Any Contractors Independent Now?" *Forbes*, August 11, 2020, tinyurl.com/aftercap229

Woods, Keith. 2022. "Factions of the Dissident Right." YouTube. May 18, 2022. Educational Video, 33:32, tinyurl.com/aftercap230

World Bank. 2024. "World Labor Force Participation Rate 1990-2024" *Macrotrends*, tinyurl.com/aftercap231

World Commission on Env. and Development. 1987. *Our Common Future*. Oxford University Press.

World Population Review. 2023a, "Countries with Universal Basic Income 2023," tinyurl.com/aftercap232

World Population Review. 2023b. "Countries with Universal Healthcare 2023," tinyurl.com/aftercap233

Wray, Ben. 2020. "Platform Capitalism: How Digital Platforms Took Over the World and What to Do about it." *Source*, July 22, 2019, tinyurl.com/aftercap234

Wright, Erik Olin. 2010. *Envisioning Real Utopias*. Verso.

Xiang, Feng. 2018. "AI Will Spell the End of Capitalism." *Washington Post*, May 3, 2018, tinyurl.com/aftercap235

Zaitchik, Alexander. 2020. "The Urgent Case for Shrinking the Economy." *The New Republic*, Dec 28, 2020, tinyurl.com/aftercap236

Zahoor, Adil, 2021. "The Pathology of 'Motivational' Speakers." *The News International*, September 13, 2021, tinyurl.com/aftercap237

Ziehan, Peter. 2022. *The End of the World is Just Beginning: Mapping the Collapse of Global Civilization*. HarperBusiness.

Zuboff, Shoshana. 2019. "'Surveillance Capitalism' has Gone Rogue. We Must Curb its Excesses." *Washington Post*, Jan 24, 2019.

About the Author

Dr. Andy Hines is Associate Professor and Program Coordinator at the University of Houston's Graduate Program in Foresight, bringing together the experience he earned as an organizational, consulting, and academic futurist.

Previously, he was Managing Director of Social Technologies/Innovaro and served as an Adjunct Professor with the university since 2004. Andy enjoyed earlier careers as a consulting and organizational futurist. He was a partner with Coates & Jarratt, Inc., a think tank and consulting firm that specialized in the study of the future. He was also Futurist & Senior Ideation Leader at Dow Chemical with a mission of using futures tools and knowledge to turn ideas into new business opportunities. Before that, Hines established and ran the Global Trends Program for the Kellogg Company.

Andy has written six other books about futures and foresight as well as dozens of articles and speeches, including the 2003 Emerald Literati Awards' Outstanding Paper accolade for best article published in Foresight for "An Audit for Organizational Futurists" and the 2008 award for "Scenarios: The State of the Art."

Andy co-founded and is former Chair of the Association of Professional Futurists and speaks and consults through his firm Hinesight.

ahines@uh.edu
www.andyhinesight.com

About the Publisher

Triarchy Press is an independent publisher of alternative thinking about possible futures for government, organisations and society at large – as well as the creative lives of the people who participate in them.

Other related titles include:

Dancing at the Edge: Competence, Culture and Organization in the 21st Century (Maureen O'Hara and Graham Leicester)
Designing Regenerative Cultures (Daniel Christian Wahl)
Growing Wings on the Way: Systems Thinking for Messy Situations (Rosalind Armson)
Humanising Healthcare: Patterns of Hope for a System Under Strain (Margaret Hannah)
Managing the Future: A Guide to Forecasting and Strategic Planning in the 21st Century (Stephen M. Millett)
Ready for Anything: Designing Resilience for a Transforming World (Tony Hodgson)
Strategic Foresight (Patricia Lustig)
The Decision Loom: A Design for Interactive Decision-Making in Organizations (Vince Barabba)
The Possibility Wheel: Making better choices in a fractured world (Patricia Lustig and Gill Ringland)
Three Horizons: The Patterning of Hope (Bill Sharpe)
Thrivability: Breaking Through to a World that Works (Jean Russell)
Transformative Innovation: A Guide to Practice and Policy for System Transition (Graham Leicester)

For details of all these titles, visit
www.triarchypress.net/possiblefutures